THE
PRIDE
OF THE LIONESSES

THE
PRIDE
OF THE LIONESSES

The Changing Face of Women's Football in England

FOREWORD BY RACHEL BROWN-FINNIS
Carrie Dunn

First published by Pitch Publishing, 2019

Pitch Publishing
A2 Yeoman Gate
Yeoman Way
Worthing
Sussex
BN13 3QZ
www.pitchpublishing.co.uk
info@pitchpublishing.co.uk

A CIP catalogue record is available for this book
from the British Library.

ISBN 978-1-78531-541-1

Typesetting and origination by Pitch Publishing

Printed and bound by TJ International, UK

Contents

DEDICATION

To Julian. Thank you for tiptoeing around the house when I'm doing a phone interview, thank you for all the cups of coffee you make me when I'm working, thank you for chauffeuring me round the country and accompanying me round the world in the name of research. You make everything wonderful.

Foreword

By Rachel Brown-Finnis
Former England goalkeeper (82 caps)
London 2012 Olympian for Team GB

IT HAS been great to see women's football in England move towards professionalisation – and when football clubs and other businesses are fully embracing the commercial potential of the game, the results can be spectacular, with the very best in the world now coming to our league and shining. With the England Lionesses now long established as one of the top international teams, this is a landmark time for our sport.

It's also important to remember those clubs and players further down the pyramid – who keep the sport running with nothing but sheer determination and love for the game fuelling them. I began my career with the help of many volunteers, including former international Sylvia Gore, whose story of a life in football featured in Carrie's previous book *The Roar of the Lionesses*. They deserve to have their stories told too.

Acknowledgements

THANK YOU so much to everyone who has spoken to me for this book, particularly those players, managers, coaches, officials and administrators who have allowed me to follow them over the course of a year; being welcomed into a changing room for a pre-match team talk is a huge honour and I do not take it lightly. Thank you especially to those who featured in *The Roar of the Lionesses* and were prepared to be part of another book, and a shout-out to Rebecca James, Arsenal communications manager and a former student of mine – endlessly helpful, and I couldn't be more proud of her. A shout-out too to Josh Chapman, press officer at Barnsley, for the photo that forms the back cover art.

Thank you to Julie Welch for the lovely quote on the front cover and to Kait Borsay for the endorsement on the back cover.

Thank you to Ruth Deller for letting me sleep on her sofa during those weekend trips to Yorkshire – always appreciated.

And thank you to everyone who has worked and continues to work to make women's football a success.

PROLOGUE

1

A growing roar

ONE FRIDAY in September 2016, I was woken up by the ping of an email. I had slept in later than usual; I had been out late the night before at an event to promote my recently released book *The Roar of the Lionesses*.

The email was from an editor I knew, asking me to write the obituary for Sylvia Gore.

It was not the way anyone would wish to learn about the death of someone they knew. I had been fortunate enough to speak to Sylvia when I was writing that book; she was assured of her place in history as the first official goalscorer for England once the FA had lifted the ban on women's football, but her career before and after that was just as fascinating. She loved to tell the tales of playing on terrible pitches not fit for purpose, and the lengths they would go to just to have a wash after a game – splashing on icy water from buckets, or jumping in a duck pond if they were playing in a park. She was generous with her time, and generous with the stories she was passing on as an oral tradition to the next generation; so few tangible documents of her playing career survived.

Or so I thought. Her next-of-kin spoke to me shortly after the funeral; Sylvia had kept plenty of mementoes of her life in football, and they were in a series of hefty boxes. There might not have been the years of match reports in newspapers that she deserved, but there were videos, there were trophies, and, yes, there were some press clippings. A local university now has all the items carefully catalogued and stored in an archive bearing Sylvia's name, there for the use of any historian of the women's game.

I had known that Sylvia was ill; when we had last spoken on the telephone, she had complained about the sciatica that continued to limit her mobility. By the time that she received the diagnosis that it was not sciatica that was causing her so much pain, it was too late; the next I heard from a mutual friend was that she was in a hospice. I am grateful that I was quick to write to her then, to thank her for talking to me, but also for being such a trailblazer for all future generations of footballers.

Her death made me realise once again how quickly we were losing so many decades of women's football history. The thousands of women who played football during the half-century-long ban in England got so little chance to tell their stories; and even after that, there were decades during which women and a small number of male allies were running their own game, with little help (or indeed money) from the governing bodies. As the nation's attention turned to France, where England would go into the 2019 Women's World Cup as one of the favourites to lift the trophy, I wanted to revisit the state of play in England – from the very top back down to grassroots, from modern day to the invisible histories.

Like *The Roar of the Lionesses*, *The Pride of the Lionesses* is not a comprehensive account of everything that happened in English women's football during the 2018/19 season; indeed, so much is happening so quickly it would be impossible to do. (The week after *Roar* was released, the FA announced a major change to their women's football fixture calendar. I was asked by a football writer if I regretted having such an early deadline, and I said that I did not – the game remains in so much flux that there is a significant piece of news almost every week and no deadline could ever include them all.) Rather, this book provides a series of snapshots of the people and clubs at all levels of the game, showing the challenges they face, the targets for which they aim, and their ultimate achievements. Some of the players, coaches, officials and teams featured in 'Roar' also feature here; there are also always new stories to tell.

2

2017 and all that

ENGLAND'S QUEST for a major title continued. They had gone into 2017's European Championships with high expectations; after all, of all the European teams in the 2015 World Cup, they had progressed the furthest. When former winners Norway crashed out in the group stages – without a single point or a goal – followed quickly by reigning champions Germany in the quarter-finals, the path looked almost clear. More than that, the Lionesses had enjoyed a comfortable cruise to the top of Group D, thrashing Scotland 6-0, beating Spain 2-0, and then defeating Portugal 2-1. A Jodie Taylor goal on the hour was enough to beat France in the quarter-final, setting up a clash with hosts Netherlands in the semi-final.

Going in as overwhelming favourites, it may have crossed a few minds that the result was a formality. Yet it was the Netherlands who produced a wonderful display leading to a crushing result – 3-0, with goals from Arsenal duo Vivianne Miedema and Danielle van de Donk, topped off with a Millie Bright own goal. It was another semi-final defeat at a major tournament, but this one stung more because of the heightened hopes.

Two months later, the qualification campaign for the 2019 Women's World Cup began. Once more England began in fine style, notching up six goals against Russia at Tranmere's Prenton Park, courtesy of Nikita Parris, Jodie Taylor, Jordan Nobbs, Lucy Bronze and a brace from Toni Duggan. The day after that victory, the news broke that Mark Sampson had left his position as England coach after a protracted and messy situation in which striker Eniola Aluko accused him of racism, although this was not enough to force him out of the hot seat; only the revelation that he had been subject to a disciplinary recommendation at his former club for an inappropriate relationship with a player ended his tenure.

Yet, despite the senior team's comparative success in recent years, there was no line of candidates beating the FA's door down to take on the vacant role. The most likely successors indicated that they had no interest in the position, not keen to assume a job where they had little control over the top-to-bottom talent pathway, nor where their personal lives would become a matter of more public interest. Indeed, the FA themselves indicated that the acting manager Mo Marley had long decided she was not interested in taking the job on permanently. A former England international and Everton legend, Marley had had success with Everton domestically and with the under-19s in junior competition, and was the obvious choice as interim coach after Sampson's departure, known to be reliable and a safe pair of hands.

After the turn of the year, the whispers grew louder that the new England coach would be another man, and this one would have no track record in women's football at all. Former England men's international Phil Neville was appointed at the end of January 2018, with the FA announcing that the former Manchester United, Valencia and England men's under-21s coach had impressed them 'with his coaching expertise, his vision for the future and his determination to build on the

Lionesses' rapid rise to be ranked third in the world after successive semi-final appearances at the 2015 World Cup and the 2017 European Championship'.

Neville himself was quoted as saying: 'I am honoured to be given the chance to lead England. With the new coaching team we are putting in place, we can help the players build on their great progress in recent years. This squad is on the verge of something special and I believe I can lead them to the next level.

'I can't wait to get out on the training pitch and down to work with an elite group of players at the top of their game. I am also passionate about working within the wider set-up at St George's Park, with influential people such as Mo Marley and Casey Stoney, and with the support of Baroness Sue Campbell and the wider women's game. There is a commitment to excellence that has paid dividends in recent years and I know we can continue the great growth of women's football inspired by the Lionesses.

'There is no greater honour than representing your country and it will be a privilege to do it again.'

He began his tenure by leading his team into the SheBelieves Cup, the annual four-team round-robin invitational, and reaching the final, where the Lionesses were defeated only by an own goal from goalkeeper Karen Bardsley. The competitive fixtures started with a nail-bitingly close goalless draw against Wales in the World Cup qualification tournament, followed by comprehensive wins over Bosnia and Herzegovina, then Russia. They guaranteed their place at France 2019 with a 3-0 away win against Wales, and concluded with a thumping 6-0 victory over Kazakhstan at the start of September.

Neville was more than satisfied with his first months in management, saying after qualification: 'When I took the job, I said I wanted to win the World Cup … I'm proud and I'm looking forward to the next 12 months.'

* * *

Scotland had also qualified for the Women's World Cup, but Wales had narrowly missed out, eventually finishing second in a group that also included Russia, Bosnia and Herzegovina, and Kazakhstan. Their crucial match against England at the end of August 2018 had been scheduled to be played at Newport, a more intimate ground, with louder and more fervent home support, and less room for the visiting fans. They hoped to generate an atmosphere that would urge the team on even more.

It was not to be. Veteran striker Helen Ward, at the age of 32, was wondering whether that might have been her final chance to play at a major tournament.

'It's obviously a really tough one to take,' she said a few days later. 'We weren't expected to qualify when the group was drawn, and then when it went on, within ourselves we always had an inner belief that if we had a good start and we got the points away from home in the tough places then we'd give ourselves a chance with three home games at the end of the group. But I think from outside perhaps it was always still a case of, "Well, they'll come up against England in April and that'll end it."

'We got the draw there [against England at St Mary's Stadium in Southampton in April 2018], which was obviously an amazing result and the girls that played that day were absolutely fantastic, they did their jobs perfectly, and then you start thinking, "We've done that away from home, maybe it could be our time," but it wasn't to be in Newport. We had a fantastic crowd behind us. Although it's not the biggest crowd I've played in front of it's definitely the best, the most packed crowd, as a player, so that was amazing. It really hurt, but not straight away.'

After the match, Ward headed back to her home in north-west London, and to her husband and two small children, and even took herself off to watch a football match the next day.

'Then it got to Monday and reality hit,' she said. 'I was like, "Actually, we haven't done it."'

She focused on family life, visiting the zoo with her family, and then remembered that Tuesday evening was when the final games in all the other groups were happening; if an unlikely combination of results transpired, Wales had a chance of a place in the play-offs for a last-chance qualification spot.

'Then, again, reality hit me that it definitely wasn't happening – although we didn't think the play-offs were going to happen because we needed too many things to go our way that weren't likely at that point,' she said. 'I went to training on Tuesday night and I could have been anywhere else, I might as well have not been there.'

With a few more days of perspective, Ward hoped that Wales had taken the first steps in a journey that would eventually secure their place at the top of the international game, creating a legacy for the next generation of players.

'I think it's something we will look back on with a lot of pride,' she said. 'Also the experiences we've had, now we've had that little taste … we don't want that [missing out] again, we want to go to the next step and qualify. We're hoping that everybody [in the squad] stays involved for the Euros, and it's obviously a slightly easier route to a major tournament because more teams qualify in Europe. We've got a year to prepare now for those qualifiers. We're confident that it wasn't a one-off – it's the start of something, regularly competing to get to those major tournaments.'

Of course, the population of Wales is much smaller than that of England, meaning that there are fewer players available. National team manager Jayne Ludlow had been working with the FA of Wales to set up a system to support potential talent, and was already bringing in younger women to senior camps to gain experience.

'There's a college set up with eyes on developing the next Jess Fishlock and Tash Harding, and that sort of thing can only stand them in good stead,' said Ward. 'The only thing I hope is that they don't think it's too easy – they've got it all laid on a plate for them, doesn't mean they don't have to work hard. The players who are my sort of age and three or four years younger, we've always had to work hard and go and find opportunities for ourselves, and that perhaps gives you a different mindset when it comes to achieving things. But I think as long as these young players appreciate what they've got, and use it to their advantage rather than take it for granted, hopefully the future is really bright for Wales.'

* * *

Domestically, the Women's Super League had changed its shape once again. In the summer of 2016, the FA had announced plans to revert to the usual winter season, mirroring the FA Cup competition, and moving away from the summer league that had been part of the innovation at the league's launch. The FA had then announced plans at the end of 2017 to make its top tier fully professional in the coming year, leaving the second tier part-time, and invited applications from clubs who wished to be part of this newly-named Championship. The third tier was renamed the National League, and retained its northern and southern divisions, with the winners securing promotion into the Championship – and thus moving to semi-professional status.

The new requirements left some clubs wondering what the point of their season to come would be. They knew they would not be able to find the money to create a squad of full-time professionals; and with the announcement that the part-time players would need to train with their club for an increased number of hours, they suspected they would not be able to compete there either. Watford confirmed shortly afterwards that they would not be applying to be part of the revamped Super League structure; and before the start of the new season Sheffield and Doncaster Belles joined them in dropping down the pyramid.

Plenty of players had to consider their position. If they had been playing part-time previously, did they want to step up to full-time, which would mean quitting their job, or abandoning their studies? Or would they stay semi-professional, and look for a new club? It was a difficult decision.

Ward was one of the players who had had to think about her options. She decided to stay at Watford, whose application for the top two tiers was unsuccessful. With a settled home and family life, moving to another club was ultimately unworkable.

'My options were limited,' she said. 'The clubs locally are the likes of Arsenal and Chelsea, which are on a different level – I'm fortunate enough to have played for them in the past, but that's not an option right now. I did have a couple of offers from teams in the Championship but they didn't quite fit with my personal situation.

'The majority of players, fair play to them, they give up a lot of time and a lot of effort and work and long hours at their own jobs to be able to play football. They do it for a very small amount of money, and of course nobody plays for money, but it does come into consideration the older you get and the more responsibilities you have. So I hold my hands up to the girls who are doing it, they're putting in a lot of time for it and I think it's fantastic, it's what women's football is about, it's about playing because you love it.'

With a fully professional top tier and a second division moving towards that, football is becoming a realistic career for younger players on their way up, and money is an inevitable part of that. One coach in England suggested that the new generation of players, offered comparatively big salaries at a young age, are very different to their predecessors, and have less of a team ethic along with a greater degree of self-interest.

While not so critical, Ward pointed to the number of her younger squadmates who opted to leave Watford when the club initially made it known they were not intending to bid for a top-tier playing licence from 2018 onwards.

'It's hard,' she said, 'because we've never been in this position before, and if someone does come in and says, "Look, we've got this amount to offer you," it's going to be hard to turn down because the chances are you've never been offered money to do something you love every day, so I fully understand that. I just hope the players that do it are doing it with open eyes, and that they still have something for afterwards, because football is a short career.'

When faced with the choice, former Sunderland captain Steph Bannon decided to retire altogether at the age of 28.

'It wasn't a decision that was taken lightly,' she said. 'It just felt like it was the right time for me. I'm one of these people who if I'm going to play, I'm going to play, and I'm going to do it properly, I'm going to train every time that training's on and I'll be at every game, and I couldn't commit to that.'

Bannon had been working full-time as a teacher while also playing in the WSL for Sunderland. For her last seasons with the club she was a part-time player while her team-mates were full-time professionals, and she found that her fitness was suffering by comparison.

'I had two jobs,' she said. 'I had a football job, and I had a teaching job, and the sole reason I retired – regardless of money, regardless of Sunderland Football Club, regardless of anything else – was I could no longer do two jobs. I was doing two jobs poorly, and something had to give for me to be able to do a better job at one of the two. I couldn't keep going the way I was going. I was running myself into the ground. I didn't have a life outside of football and work. I didn't see my friends, I didn't see my family, I didn't see my boyfriend, and I couldn't continue that, it wasn't a lifestyle for me. I was getting up, going to work, going straight from work to training, coming home, going to bed, and it really was that for five days solid, then at the weekend I was training, then I was travelling to a game. My life just became one big circle, there was never any rest time, and at some point I needed to stop and think, "I can't do this any more, this isn't for me now."'

Bannon never considered going to another club further down the pyramid where the time commitment would be less.

'In my heart of hearts, maybe retiring wasn't the right thing – maybe it was going to a club where I didn't have to do as much,' she admitted. 'However, Sunderland Football Club is my life, and has been my life, and to go somewhere else, it's never really crossed my mind.'

Clubs who applied for tier-one status from 2018 onwards had to outline a commitment to have full-time professional playing staff with a minimum of 16 hours of daytime contact per week, increasing to 20 hours by the 2021/22 season; while those wanting to compete in tier two – the new Championship – needed to have semi-professional players, with eight hours of contact every week.

Another former WSL captain dropped down a couple of leagues. Ellie Curson joined Keynsham Town – that means training once a week and playing at the weekend. For a 24-year-old with rent and bills to pay, it was more straightforward to combine with her full-time job as a primary school teacher.

'I finished my degree and thought, "I'm in the big wide world now, I need to think about what I want to do,"' she recalled. Curson moved to Taunton in 2014 to train as a teacher and play part-time with Yeovil, who she captained to promotion to WSL1 two years later.

'When I realised the salary options and living options of being a full-time footballer with Yeovil, that made my mind up for me. It just wasn't affordable to live. I did consider it, but it was a no-brainer for me if I wanted to have my own place. They do provide accommodation if you're playing full-time, but it was based in student halls, which I'd lived in at uni for three years. It wasn't an option for me.'

Helen Ward completely understood Curson's feelings. Although the job title 'footballer' sounded glamorous, the reality of professionalism in the women's game was somewhat less so. House-sharing, she thought, was necessary; it was something the players were willing to do in order to pursue their dream, but it was not ideal – and for many experienced competitors it was simply not practical.

'There are a lot of people who just aren't at that stage in their lives and they're not in a position where they want to do that – or they can bear doing that,' she said. 'People are in relationships, and even if you're not, if you've got used to living on your own, you don't want to go and share a bathroom with another two or three people. It's just not the kind of thing – even if I didn't have my family, I don't think I could do it. I like having my own space. People say, "If you're playing football maybe you could get on with it," and yes, perhaps you could, but if you're not happy and comfortable in a home situation, are you going to produce your best on the pitch anyway?

'This is a conversation I have with quite a few of my team-mates with Wales, and I say to them, "How do you do it?" And a lot of them say it is a struggle – it is difficult to come home from training and be with the people you've just been training with. I've always said I could never do the same job as my husband because what would you talk about when you go home? You've seen each other all day, what is there to talk about? I think for me personally I'd really struggle with that, and if I wasn't able to find my own accommodation that would be a big sticking point.

'Yeah, I think when you hear the words 'professional footballer' you think 'massive house and lovely car' – it's not quite at that stage at the moment – not for the majority of players anyway. If they're happy with it and they're enjoying it, then good luck to them, and hopefully they'll progress to a point where they can go and buy their own house and live the dream.'

Ward was thrilled that women were able to play football every day for a living, and focus on what they were doing on the pitch rather than worry about going to work all day and needing to save some energy for training or a midweek match, or to fret about juggling their time off to get to a fixture. After Fulham's women's team turned professional in the year 2000, and reverted to semi-pro status just three years later, she never thought she would see another pro team in England during her career – let alone a whole league. Now she was hoping that financial investment would improve to enable more teams to pay their players, and for it to become an option for more women.

'It's a real tricky balance because you can't make everybody full-time in the top two, three divisions, it's impossible at the moment, the funding and the support's not quite there in that many teams, but I don't know. I'd like to think there'll be a time when at least two divisions will be professional, but I don't think it's going to be too soon.'

Ward was happy with her choice to stay at Watford, compete in the National League, live in London, and spend time at home with her children.

'I know there are other girls who have got children in football – Sophie Bradley-Auckland who's now at Liverpool has obviously found a way to manage having her daughter as well as playing full-time football, and that's fantastic,' she said, 'but for me, I'm based here, and the travelling I can do is pretty limited. My husband has got a good job and we're not in a position where we're going to move just for the sake of a year or two's contract in football.'

There were plenty of other clubs around the Wards' home in London, but none which would have suited Helen's plans; the family were not prepared to move, having spent time and money creating their home, and the location was in ideal proximity to both sets of the children's grandparents. Despite being confident in her own abilities, she did not think she was in a position to play full-time football with a team like Arsenal or Chelsea; and the London teams competing in the Championship were less flexible than Watford.

'I had a bit of time away with the family – so many conversations back and forth,' she remembered. 'I made one decision, then I thought, "No, that's not for me," then I made another decision. Everything was back and forth. The amount of times I thought, "Right, I've left Watford. Actually, no, I haven't" – it was bizarre, and it was quite a stressful time, because I didn't know what the right thing to do was. I knew it wasn't time to stop playing, so it was just a case of finding the right home for me. It's early days, but I think I made the right decision, hopefully that will be proved on the pitch as well and we can have a good season as a club as well, and hopefully get ourselves back up to where we want to be.

'Watford have always been really good to me,' she added. 'They've understood my situation, and it is a club that I've got a lot of heart for and a lot of love for, and I don't think any other club would have persuaded me to drop down into the National League. That's not me being arrogant, it's just the way I feel – I like to think I've still got enough about me to play in a higher league. But it IS Watford.'

It was also the team Ward supported; on the wall of her living room hung a replica street sign for Vicarage Road, the club's home ground. She hoped that when she did decide to retire she would be able to stay there in some capacity, possibly in the media team; she had already gained a degree in sports writing and broadcasting, and was racking up experience as an analyst and co-commentator.

The previous season had been difficult for Watford as they had opted not to apply for a place in the WSL or the Championship very early on, meaning that essentially most of the year had been spent competing in a league knowing that the results were meaningless; they would be in the third tier for 2018/19 regardless. She thought that most of the WSL2 teams had felt similarly, whether they were going to be aiming for a licence or not, because there was no real promotion or relegation to play for.

'It was a real odd sort of feeling, going into games knowing that both teams kind of knew their fate at the end of the season whatever happened,' she said. 'Every game teams try and win, but it was just a bit of a nothing season from start to finish. It's not like one I've been involved in before.'

Ward used that season for personal development. She was only a few months back from giving birth to her son, so she set her own targets – beginning with getting back on the pitch in the first place, and then increasing her game time.

'Because I had other focuses, I was able to keep positive and keep thinking, "Right, this is why I'm doing it – for next season, and internationals, and stuff like that." Yeah, I can't speak for the other girls, but I think most found it quite a tricky situation to be in.

'We've signed quite a few new players who don't have the burden, if you like, of last season, and those of us who are still here, I think, have got quite good mental strength,' she said. 'We're happy to be going into games and expecting to win them. It's a different sort of pressure, of course it is, but it's a nice pressure. I'm very competitive, I play to win, so last season I found really tough, but the group is doing OK. I think we're starting to see the style of play that we're trying to achieve this season and we create a lot of chances, which as a forward is always nice – not so nice when you don't put them away! But we've had some good results, performances have been up and down, but I think you get that with a new team – you have some really good moments and some really interesting moments within games, but yeah, we're pleased.'

Ward had achieved most of her career aims – except for qualifying for a major international tournament. That absence on her CV meant she was not ready to retire.

'I think I made it quite clear if we did qualify for the World Cup then I probably would have achieved everything I wanted to, and I probably could have called it a day quite happily next summer,' she said. 'Because we didn't make it, I promised myself that I'd give it one more shot, which means probably another two or three years playing, depending on how our campaign goes. If it doesn't happen, it obviously wasn't meant to be. But in terms of club football, I've won I think most domestic trophies and I've played in the Champions League or the UEFA Cup, the equivalent of the Champions League. Yeah, I'm quite happy.

'People quite often say does it make you sad or angry that you're coming to the end of your career when everything is taking off. Not really. I'm quite pleased with how my career has gone. I've achieved everything that I probably set out to do, without the stress of worrying about how long my next contract is going to be. I've earned what I've got, and I'm happy with it, and good luck to those coming through now, I think it's great for them, but it's not for me, and that's fine, I'm OK with that, it's not a problem. I've potentially missed out on becoming a professional footballer – well, technically I'm not a professional footballer but I think the way I've handled myself from a young age, I've been as professional as I could have been in terms of how I train and play and look after myself away from the pitch, so I don't necessarily think I would have done anything differently had I been a pro, other than had a bit more chance to train – and probably got a bit more sleep!'

Ward's daughter was at an age when she was just starting to understand the rules of football, and was old enough to concentrate on watching a match and enjoying it. In ten years' time, would she be encouraging her daughter to become a professional footballer?

'I'd never tell her not to do it,' she said, 'but at the same time I wouldn't push her towards it. I'd like both my children to be into sport. I think sport, whether it's grassroots level or elite level, there's so many benefits, not only for your physical health but your mental health and your social skills. I've learnt so much from being in a sporting environment from a young age. Both my parents played sport, my mum still plays netball – she retired from work last summer and she plays netball two or three times a week, she plays tennis two or three times a week, she plays badminton, and growing up with that sort of family around me I was always going to be into sport. If she says to me, 'I want to play football,' then great, I'd be more than happy to support her, but I'd never try and tell her one way or the other. I'd like her to decide for herself if it's something that she wants to do.'

* * *

Some clubs stepped up their provision, and increased the opportunities for women to play professional football. Manchester United, pressured for years to introduce a women's team, finally did so, under the managership of England legend Casey Stoney, moving away from her role with the national team, and captaincy of Lioness Alex Greenwood. Their squad full of internationals was full-time and fully professional, but given a licence to compete in the Women's Championship.

Across the Pennines, Sheffield United joined them in the league. Carla Ward, the long-serving Sheffield player, had hung up her boots to concentrate on coaching, and was now managing the Blades.

'I never thought that I could walk away from Sheffield,' she admitted before the season began. She made that decision with no intent to switch to a new club any time soon, but when the call from United came, it was an offer she could not refuse, giving her the chance to progress her coaching career.

She already had her B licence, and was planning to start her A licence in the near future.

She was impressed with the way United were going about building their women's side, and it was that which made her mind up for her.

'It was very much, "we've got the backing, we've got the facilities, we've got the model, we've got the drive, we've got everything, but we haven't got anyone from within the women's game with knowledge and expertise of how to get us there,"' she explained. 'They'd never run a women's football club, so what they do is run it like the men. They've stuck to every single word they said they'd stick to – it's been fascinating, to be honest. It's quite funny actually, when you look at the squad they've put together, a lot of people immediately think, "Well, they've got money." No. It's the complete opposite. They run it like a business.'

With only part-time contracts on offer, Ward was honest with the players she wanted to recruit from the start. She admitted the financial deal for them was essentially 'pocket money', but pointed out that this was really attractive for the younger ones who were still at university; the older players who balanced football with their day jobs were also completely focused on what they needed to do on the pitch without thought of the remuneration. Those with other commitments also benefitted from the flexibility that went with being part of the Sheffield United set-up, giving them access to the pitch and gym facilities, so that if a player had to miss a squad training session, they could make it up in their own free time.

'We're essentially saying to the players, "Come and be an elite footballer and work hard, and you'll get the development side of it – you'll get to be an elite athlete, you'll get to play at nice grounds, you'll get to train here, you'll get to eat here, you'll get to use the gym here, physio here, all under one roof." So when signing players, you show them around and tell them everything and they're astounded by it, and then you get to, "Here's the downfall, the money," and they don't care. Well,' she quickly corrected herself, 'I say they don't care. The squad I've got in don't care.'

As part of the Sheffield squad that moved up to the old WSL2, Ward knows how the lure of money on offer can change a player's attitude.

'I made it quite clear from day dot that it had to be, for me, person before player, and I've been quite strict with that to the point that we've turned down two exceptionally good players because they just wouldn't fit the ethos I want,' she revealed. 'I'm very old school, I want hardworking players with a good attitude, who will run through walls for each other, and there are a lot of players now who are very self-centred – I've seen that a lot in WSL in the last few years.'

* * *

One of Sheffield United's first matches in the new Championship was against fellow new girls Manchester United, who had begun their league campaign with a 12-0 demolition of Aston Villa. Although to the outsider that might appear an abysmal result for the Villa, in reality it would be fair to say that a team of amateurs competing against full-time pros did well to contain them to just the dozen. Ward was very well aware that Manchester United and their fans were expecting to trounce every opponent they faced.

'I think it's one of those where we say to the girls, "We've got nothing to lose, the expectation is on Manchester United,"' she said. 'Everybody I speak to thinks we're going to get absolutely hammered, so I'll say to the girls, "Go and prove a point, go and give all you've got, and that's all we can ask for."'

Ward's opposite number in the dugout did not have the same kind of problems to deal with. The Blades squad was reduced on matchday because of the 7pm kick-off time, meaning that some of the players with day jobs would not be able to get to the ground for the warm-up. She was still confident that the players who did start would be able to put in a good performance.

'We've had three defeats – obviously we've had a tough start, Bristol, Durham and Birmingham – and they're still positive,' she said. 'You want your tough games early, because you learn a lot more from your tough games, and it'll set you up brilliantly when you go into the other games you think you can get something from.'

AUTUMN

3

New beginnings

THE HEATWAVE was over. The Yorkshire skies were grey and full of pregnant cloud. Groups of young women made their way on foot towards Oakwell and its neighbouring academy buildings, complete with 3G pitches.

Barnsley were about to play their final home friendly of their pre-season preparations. It had been a big change from the previous season, when they had avoided relegation by a single goal. Now under new administration and new management, they were making big plans. Natalie Jackson, a former lawyer and now founder of a company working to get girls into sport, had been asked to coach one of the junior age groups – and since then had been co-opted on to the board of directors.

'I'd done some coaching about ten years ago at uni,' she revealed, drinking coffee in a chain café near the station. 'I hadn't really done much – I'd coached boys, not a girls' team, so I was excited about coaching a girls' team, especially when it was a case of "we don't know who else is going to coach them, there's not necessarily going to be a team for them". So I said, "Yes, OK, I'll do it."

'Then the new guys came in. They said, "Look, here's our vision for the club." It would have been easy at that point to be threatened by the situation, not knowing what's going on, but it actually sounded so brilliant.'

Jackson had moved to Yorkshire after growing up in the Isle of Man and studying in Durham. Although she did not live in Barnsley, her company's offices were based there, and she was travelling there to coach her team; she was excited to join the board and be part of their wide-ranging plans for the future, including encouraging local girls to take up sport and to represent their town's team.

'What I was bothered about them getting right was the messages for girls,' she explained. 'I had a couple of chats with them about how important the language was, and I loved the way they were thinking – it was super-positive. It was about empowering girls in Barnsley to not look elsewhere or give up, and so that any girl in Barnsley would have somewhere to go. It resonated with me because I was a massive football fan as a kid. I had posters of Manchester United on my walls, I subscribed to *Match* magazine as far back as I can remember, but it never crossed my mind that I could play, because I was a girl.'

Jackson took up football when she was at university, and discovered that her team-mates there had spent their younger years playing in boys' teams. She thought that girls having a pathway of their own would be much more beneficial than having to battle to be permitted to play – and the offer of a directorship, a position where she could actively help that, was irresistible.

'I thought, "I'd love that. I'd love to change the world for girls growing up who like football – for it not to be weird,"' she said.

The paperwork was all processed in May 2018 – the week in which Jackson was expecting her first child – and she joined a six-person board as the only woman.

'I think it's a massive gap if they don't have the voice of somebody who grew up without that structure, knows what it's like to grow up as a girl, all of that,' she reflected. 'There's a massive opportunity for me to slot in there and make a difference.'

Chris Hamilton and Andrew Glossop joined her at the table. Both were newly appointed in their roles at the club, manager and assistant manager respectively.

'It's lucky we both have the same views on football and style of play,' said Hamilton. 'If we'd come in and we'd clashed, it would be poor, but it's been good so far. There's a good feel about the club.'

'Very good,' agreed Glossop.

CEO Steve Maddock had taken over the club at the end of the previous season, when the first team had avoided relegation by a single goal.

'The old management had been there for a long, long time,' he said, adding that he had seen plenty of disharmony among the squad in the last few matches of the campaign; he had also seen that some of the players were not interested in progressing their careers or improving their fitness and skill any further. He also reported that he never heard a single laugh in the dressing room or in training before the new coaches came in, and he had felt uneasy when he had overheard the way the previous regime had spoken to players. 'It was time for a complete and utter change.'

'When we turned up, that was the first thing we said, wasn't it?' asked Hamilton, and Glossop concurred. 'We need to get them fit, because if they were fit, the last team we put out last season would have won the league.'

'The girls have bought into it really well,' added Glossop.

'They seem to be enjoying it,' said Hamilton. 'They're good listeners. Because they had last season, staying up by a goal, they want to succeed.'

That target of success was shared by local companies, who – like Jackson, Hamilton and Glossop – had bought into Maddock's plans for the club, and were showing their support with sponsorship, both financial and in kind, including gym membership in the town centre for each squad member and away travel with a local coach firm.

'They're really behind this idea of Barnsley Women getting to the top,' he said. 'I'm a salesman anyway, but it doesn't take much of a conversation before I've convinced them. It's unbelievable.'

* * *

As the team began their warm-ups, there was one particularly interested observer. Balanced on crutches at the back of the stand, trainee teacher Dani Lowe watched her friends and wished she was out there. She had torn her cruciate ligaments earlier in the year, on an astroturf pitch while she was warming up for a friendly match, and was in the middle of arduous, gruelling rehabilitation.

Initially she had been told that it was just a soft tissue injury, so after resting for six weeks she tried to play again, but her knee simply wouldn't hold up. She returned to the hospital for an MRI scan, and after the more serious diagnosis was confirmed, she underwent an operation, putting her into a protective brace.

'I've had this on for four weeks,' she said. 'I can't bend my knee, only to 90 degrees, it's all locked in.

'But,' she added, brightening, 'I get it off tomorrow.'

That did not mean her return was imminent. She knew there would be at least nine months of recovery after the brace's removal, meaning she would miss the entire season.

'Since the age of five, I've played every year,' she said. 'Fifteen, 16 years I've played football and this is the only season I've not played. It's my first ever injury and it's a big one.'

She looked out on to the pitch, and pointed out one of her squadmates.

'That number eight, it should be me. That's my shirt. I'll let her have it this season,' she grinned.

Having spent four years at Barnsley, Lowe was well placed to assess the changes at the club. She was particularly happy with the addition of a physio to the support staff, and the access to gym facilities the team now had; a new focus on football-based fitness was vital, she thought.

'We would have done a lot of road-running [before],' she explained. 'We'd have been hill-sprinting up a road, whereas with these new managers it's hidden fitness what he's doing – like play little football games and there's fitness included in it, so you wouldn't know that there's fitness. I think the girls are getting more out of that. Just watching that, I know I would have done, because I hated just running.'

She was impressed with the way things had changed in a matter of weeks, praising the appointment of a specialist goalkeeping coach.

'It's a lot more professional. We're even training twice a week now whereas last season it was just once a week because we couldn't afford the premises to train on – it's just little stuff that needed improving that has now been improved.'

The new professional attitude was something to which she kept returning, contrasting it with the previous season.

'The atmosphere is so much better now,' she said. 'You can tell what [the coaches] want and their vision for the season. They know what they're doing. You go to training and everything is set up. I'm not saying it wasn't last season, not saying it wasn't organised, but they know what they're doing more – you do one thing and you'll be on to another thing, like it's no messing about. Last season you'd mess about in between, kick a ball about – and you can't get away with that this season.'

* * *

Hull City were expected to be tough opponents. League champions last season, they were a strong, hard-working team.

Barnsley's coaches reminded their squad that after their narrow dodge of relegation, all their rivals would be expecting a straightforward six points from them in the coming season.

'But they don't know the work you've put in,' Hamilton reminded them.

After even opening exchanges, the Lady Tigers began to look slightly frustrated; Hamilton had evidently been right, they had been anticipating an easier encounter.

Barnsley won 4-0, and it was a fair reflection of the match.

The Barnsley under-12s cheered on the senior team for the entire 90 minutes, and piled on to the pitch afterwards to pose for photos with them. They were joined by a special guest, baseball cap pulled over her head. Amy Turner, of Manchester United and England, was there to cheer on her younger sister Lucy, the Barnsley captain, and she was just as happy to take selfies with the little girls.

The under-12s went away thrilled at having met a professional footballer – but they were just as excited to have been able to talk to the Reds.

'That's the first time we've had chanting from the sidelines, and it does help, when you're in the last five, ten minutes of the game and your legs are tired and you're thinking, "Right, we need to get to that final whistle,"' said Lucy Turner. 'The chanting, it just gives you that little bit of a lift.'

Turner and her team were beginning to realise just how important they were to the younger girls watching them.

'We do try and carry ourselves professionally,' she said. 'Everyone gets frustrated on the pitch, but we always try and just remember who's watching. There's young girls there. Don't lose your head. Keep on the ball, make sure they look up to you and they want to be you on that pitch. The role models are a bit closer to home – a bit more realistic than thinking I want to be Steph Houghton, playing for Man City. Yeah, that's a massive aspiration to have, but if they see you every Tuesday at training and get to know you as a friend, I think that helps and it keeps them involved with the club.'

She had only worn the armband for a year, but worked hard at leading the team (Steve Maddock had earlier praised her as 'leading from the front'), and, like Lowe, she had observed a difference since the new management had taken over.

'It's just so positive!' she said. 'Everyone is looking forward to the games, whereas last year it was a bit depressing, people used to hate coming to training, and it was hard to motivate yourself when you were getting beat every week. This season, Chris has come in with such a positive attitude, which has rubbed off on all this lot.'

Turner referred to the squad as her 'little sisters', adding, 'There's quite a few young ones – I feel like I mother them a bit, but I think they need that – gaining experience in the game, that's what they need.'

Her heart went out to Lowe, whose support she and the first eleven really appreciated.

'She's like us team mascot! I don't know whether she'll like me saying that,' she smiled. 'But people that are out injured still like to be involved, which I think shows a lot about the training that's going on, and the results on game day.'

* * *

Chris Hamilton was driving. He spent plenty of his free time in his car and on the road, living in Lincolnshire and travelling up to Yorkshire for training and for matches – a three-hour round trip.

'I haven't really told the girls that,' he admitted. 'I don't mind putting that time in. An hour and a half drive goes a lot faster when you're thinking about your session, about the Sunday match, the injuries that you've got.'

He had played professionally himself before retiring at the age of 27, joining the RAF police, and signing for a series of local teams in Lincolnshire. The clash of commitments became too much, and he opted to concentrate on coaching, something he had always seen himself doing eventually.

'I thought to myself, "If I start early enough I think I can go quite far with it,"' he remembered.

His first job was at Nettleham Ladies, where he led the team to the league title as well as the County Cup in his first year in management. That was his first exposure to women's football.

'I was going in blind,' he said, thinking back to his first training session there. 'I didn't know what to expect or what levels to expect, and I just went, "Oh, I'm so happy I made the decision!" I just went in and they surprised me with their ability, their technique, and it was clear they were there to work hard and they wanted to achieve something, which is great.'

His pre-season emphasis on Barnsley's fitness came from experience the year before. He knew that insisting on so much physical work had not made him popular with the Nettleham players in the early days; equally he knew that the success that had followed had proved him entirely correct, and that his popularity inevitably soared when the team lifted trophies.

'It should have been an easy decision to stay there,' he said. 'Expectations probably wouldn't have been as high, probably staying up would have been what they were happy with, but I felt like I needed another challenge, a step forward. I knew I wanted to be in football, and Barnsley is another good challenge for me to take on.'

Although he'd only been in post for a few weeks, he was pleased with the start that he had made, and how the squad were performing; he was also bringing in little pushes towards a more professional attitude, including a small-scale fines list for misdemeanours such as lack of punctuality or having dirty boots at a session.

'I've just tried to bring what I enjoyed as a player and what worked last season!' he explained. 'That's included a couple of players from my old team, and it's also included new signings that have come on trial and impressed. We've got a style of play together that we want to try and achieve, and straight away we've said that to do that we need to be fit. That was a big thing that kept coming back when I was asking questions and doing a bit of digging into last season – this was not very good.

'But,' he went on, 'that's a good thing – it wasn't ability that was getting mentioned, it was the fitness. So we got in straight away, worked on fitness, made the sessions enjoyable for them, and they seem to have bought in to what we were trying to do and want to play.'

Hamilton had been appointed in July following a lengthy interview process, and found himself working alongside Andrew Glossop, who had also initially applied for the managerial role but was offered the assistant job instead. The pair clicked right away.

'He's been absolutely brilliant for me,' said Hamilton. 'He's more local to the area than I am, and his knowledge of the game and the way he is as a person has been brilliant. He's a great person to bounce ideas off, and we'll challenge each other on thoughts as well, so if I've got an idea on who should play right of a midfield or whoever, he'll say, "Have you thought about this?" It's good because we challenge each other the way people on the outside looking in will be challenging us, but we can challenge each other and come up with a game plan. I'm just really happy with how he's fitted in with what I want to do, and how he's been supportive. He's great with the players as well. I think the players seem really happy with what's going on at the moment, and that's all we can ask.'

He was hopeful that his ambitions would match Barnsley's, and they would progress together in the coming years. Fans, he thought, were drawn to winning teams, and he hoped that the men's team would rise as well as the women, promoting the profile of the entire club.

'Now I'm 30 and should pass my UEFA B in February, hopefully – that's another step,' he said. 'I just thought, "Get in there, start early, have the achievements that you didn't quite get as a footballer in management." Making the career I wanted as a player in management is my target. It's given me drive – the feelings that I had in football as a player to make sure I don't have them as a manager and just help players to get as far as they can go as well.'

Hamilton knew that pre-season friendlies were not an accurate indicator of how the rest of the campaign would go, but he thought the squad's confidence was increasing along with their fitness, and that had been reflected in the atmosphere around the club; and he had been impressed by their willingness to work hard.

Glossop was looking forward to the season ahead too. He had seen the advert for the Barnsley head coach position, and when he was invited for interview, he was immediately sold on the club's plans for the future, intensely impressed by chairman Steve.

'It just seemed that the position they were in last year wasn't great and they were looking for a turnaround this year, they wanted things changing,' he recalled. 'I then went back to have a coaching session where I was watched, and I spoke to Steve then, and he said they were going to give Chris the head coach position because he had a bit more experience with a women's team. Then he said, "Would you rather be in charge of the development squad, or be his assistant?"'

He opted to gain more first-team experience by working alongside Hamilton – who he had not met before a pre-season trials day.

'I speak to Chris so much in the week, it's unbelievable,' he said. 'When I was away in Cornwall for two weeks, my full-time manager tried to ring me, and I didn't answer it. Two minutes later Chris tried to ring me and I was like, "Yeah, hello?" He's been spot on. We get on really well and our coaching sessions work really well. I try and bounce a lot of ideas off Chris. Of course we have slight differences in some things, but Chris has got the final decision, I'll support whatever he does, but he's more than happy for me to take sessions or step in and change things or tweak things, and likewise. It works really well. It feels like we've known each other for years.'

A secondary school PE teacher by training, he had changed career to become a football coach, and was collecting as many qualifications as possible, from futsal to goalkeeping.

'I decided that I loved coaching – I didn't want to do teaching, really, because I liked teaching people who want to be there,' he said wryly. 'So from that I went to China for five months and coached football out there, came back in March, and when I came back I decided football is definitely what I want to do.'

* * *

When the season proper started, the Reds did not continue their excellent pre-season form, losing their first league match to Chester-le-Street Town 3-1. Glossop thought afterwards, though, that an early loss would ultimately serve the team well in the long run, giving them more realistic expectations for the year ahead.

'We were 2-0 down after 28 minutes and I don't think we got three passes in a row,' he reflected. 'From the half-hour point we turned it around, second half we were a lot better, and scored a goal, they nicked one again late on so it was 3-1. At half-time we said to them that the first 38 minutes wasn't anything to do with the tactics, they just looked as if they were a bit all over the place, the energy wasn't there, which we've had all pre-season.

'On the coach journey home we called every player that had played to the front of the bus individually, and just asked them, "What do you think about your own performance and the team performance?" and we got some really good feedback. Three, four, five girls mentioned the fact that they were nervous and they felt pressure. Pre-season it's something you don't notice day to day, but when they line up to kick-off, I think all of a sudden the kit we've got, the good pre-season, the talks about winning the league and stuff like that – they suddenly realised, "What happens if we don't win?" They get nervous, they don't want to make a mistake.

'It's brought us back down to earth a little bit off the high of the really good pre-season, and we can just build again from there. At training last night, we had a bit of a warm-up and then we sat them down and spoke to them and we said we want them to enjoy their football and play how we want them to play and enjoy that as well. We said, "If you make a mistake trying to do what and how we want to play, then so be it, that's going to happen in football, but what we don't want is to be nervous and just kick it." We played a lot of route-one balls, we kept punting it forward, which we've not done all pre-season, so we just said, "We want you to go out and express yourselves and play, and if you make a mistake because you're trying to do what we've asked you to do, then fine, if anything that's our fault, it's not your fault." We had a chat, got everything in the open, and then last night was an unbelievable session. Two of the girls messaged Chris afterwards and said, "I just want to let you know that I thought training tonight was absolutely spot on." We're back on track, so I think the result has probably helped us in the long run, if anything.'

4

A full-time job

MILLWALL LIONESSES' place in the history books has long been assured. With an honour roll including names such as former England coach Hope Powell and Team GB Olympian Katie Chapman, their track record of developing top players over three decades has been impressive. Part of the men's club's community programme, they have never had access to huge budgets, and have in effect operated independently. At the start of 2018, they were forced to launch a crowdfunding campaign to raise enough cash to get them to the end of the season after a series of bills required immediate payment.

The club's official statement referred to 'significant financial discrepancies' and the requirement for 'a substantial influx of money' if they were to complete the season.

The squad themselves were kept in the dark about the problems until close to the kick-off of an important fixture – at that time they were still on an excellent run in the league and had aspirations to challenge for one of the top slots in WSL2.

'It was so bizarre, the whole thing – we still continued to play for the entirety of the rest of the season, not really knowing if we were going to fold before the end of it,' says a player who was part of that squad. She says that they were expecting a winding-up order any minute.

'Had that have happened, we would have had no option but to fold.'

She says the players knew that they would need cash in as soon as possible to settle the club's debts, and then that they would need to find sponsors, both for themselves and for matches and the club itself, to enable them to continue competing. The squad also agreed to a delay in the payments they themselves were owed – but there was never a question they would not play.

'At that point, we were doing really well,' she says. 'We were unbeaten, we were going to push for the title. As players, stopping playing wasn't a solution. Where would that leave us? We would struggle to get other clubs, we were more than halfway through the season. Leaving wasn't an option.'

The club set up an online donation page, reaching their initial target very quickly with donors including former players from the men's team, but even then their general manager admitted to the media, 'Sponsorship is crucial to securing the club's long-term future.'

Over the summer, Millwall had also lost their first-team coach, Lee Burch. He had finished the year as WSL2's manager of the year, but then had taken up the reins in June at top-tier side Yeovil as they moved from part-time to full-time, as per the rules about professionalisation in the Women's Super League.

'I was happy at Millwall,' he emphasised during the close season. 'I was happy at the club and also did feel that the changes they put in place there ensured they would be in a good place going forward, and I'm sure they will be, but I think on the other hand the opportunity to go full-time in WSL1 is something I've always wanted to do, and having the opportunity to do that with Yeovil … once I started speaking to them, the opportunity started to become too good to turn down. It's an exciting opportunity, not just for me but for the players.'

Burch and the Glovers as an entirety were faced with a tough prospect, converting the set-up to a fully professional one over the course of a summer. Although they had good support from their men's club, enabling them to play some games at Huish Park, they needed to sort out a squad of players who could compete at the highest level, and, obviously, were willing and able to play football for a living, giving up their previous careers.

And a squad of professional players also necessitates a substantial wage bill, which triggered a smart, social media-led crowdfunding campaign before the start of the new season.

'The work [the club staff have] done in the background has been brilliant, and it's given me and my players the opportunity to play full-time, so that side of things was really impressive,' said Burch. 'Now we've had to start to make that transition on the field as well, which has been huge because there were no full-time players at the club. We're not signing one or two players – we've had to sign a whole squad. Even the players that were at Yeovil already were not on full-time contracts, so everyone was signing from scratch.'

With Burch taking over in the midst of the close season, he was already at a disadvantage, with other managers stealing a march on him as they chased free agents and those looking for a move. Still, he was happy with the squad he had assembled, and was confident they would compete well in the Women's Super League; Yeovil had won promotion in 2016 but had not managed a single win in the league since then. One of his biggest challenges during pre-season was to ensure that those players turning professional for the first time were supported and settling in to their new jobs – as well as their new homes if they were moving into the area.

'The first few weeks are very much about individuals getting settled and moved into new housing, adjusting to life as a full-time footballer, giving them opportunities to get away from their jobs, and the human side of things, making sure that the person is happy before the footballer,' he explained. 'Now we think we can start to look at the footballer now the person is happy. It's all been around that. I think it's gone well. At this moment we haven't announced any of our players that we've signed because we've just taken our time and used every sort of inch of the off-season to make sure we're getting it right.'

He did, however, wonder if the swift push towards a fully professional WSL meant that some of the best players had been forced out of the game too soon; and, in turn, if that would affect the quality of the competition.

'It won't just be us,' he said, adding, 'We know that the league won't have the best players in it, because some of the best players will choose to not play at that level. They will have careers outside of football that they may be doing very well in, or they see beyond football – once they get a little bit older they maybe get a little bit wiser. A few players have been in tears, turning down opportunities because they had such good opportunities elsewhere, away from football: they're stuck between a rock and a hard place. That was always going to be one of those things. We are going to be a young side because of that.

'It's a young person's game at the moment; young players who are coming through, it does suit them a little bit more, but you also need that blend of youth and experience, which we think we've got right as well, so yeah, recruitment has been really tough, but we've also had a lot of interest in the club, which is great. I've spoken to a lot of very good players, and we've been able to get some over the line, we haven't been able to get others over the line for different reasons, but it's certainly not been because people aren't interested in the opportunities that we can give them, which is a great first footing, I think.'

* * *

At Sheffield United, Carla Ward felt similarly.

'I think there's no secret that we've probably got the lowest budget in the league, but the squad doesn't reflect that, which tells you a lot about the club drawing people in – the facilities and the ambition,' she said. 'It's a time where people do want to be involved, which is good. We'll use that again, and I think the girls that are here know how lucky they are. Our girls get more than the under-23s [men] get – everything, they get the hotels, they get the nice flash fancy hotels, they get their own room, they get to use the whole facility at the academy, at the ground, so they're treated well and I don't think a single player could say otherwise.'

The team's results were up and down, though, as they struggled to hit the back of the net despite creating dozens of chances.

'I genuinely think that when we're on it, we're as good as anyone,' she said. 'You look on paper and we've probably got one of the strongest squads in the league, but we've had players in, players out, we've got no centre-forward, so we've got quality all over but we've got no number nine. That's killed us, really.'

Ward was convinced that the fully professional Manchester United already had the title sewn up, but wondered whether they should have been slotted into the primarily part-time Championship at all. Indeed, as clubs worked hard to sort out contracts for those who were prepared to turn semi-professional and bade farewell to those who could not give up their day jobs, she wondered (much like Burch) whether, even though the results indicated a more competitive competition, the quality on the pitch had actually lessened. She also feared that with the new regulations requiring Championship teams to give their players eight hours of contact time, their minutes on the training pitch had actually shrunk. Her hope was that there would be no more restructures in the near future, and that the league would be allowed to settle.

But she knew there would be plenty of changes at her own club. Working full-time as a coach on the men's side, she had limited time with her team during the week, but spent most of the weekend with them if they had an away game.

'It's been an interesting first season because we've had to get whoever we could together as quickly as we could,' she said, 'but in the summer I think there might be big changes again, because we'll be established and we'll have a bit more time to recruit instead of just a few weeks.'

Even so, her team would still be part-time, and faced with problems that the professionals did not even have to think about – including those early midweek kick-off times that depleted Ward's squad.

'That's still a problem,' she said. 'When we play Man City [in the Continental Tyres Cup] it's seven o'clock and we're actually discussing whether we should send half the development squad just because we know they can make it, because we can't do what we did at Man United last time – two players turning up five minutes before kick-off and we had to change the team around last minute. It's not ideal: it's Man City, you want your best players available. Already that night we're without our captain, our vice-captain, our only centre-forward, and a couple of others, so it's going to be tough. It could be an interesting night.'

A few days later, Manchester City, the 2016 Women's Super League champions, twice Continental Cup winners, FA Cup winners in 2017, beat Ward's Sheffield United 6-0.

5

Belles are ringing

THE CASUAL attendee would not have looked twice. The stall selling programmes and raffle tickets by the turnstile was staffed by a lady in her senior years, clad in club logo-emblazoned sportswear.

She could have been anybody. But she was one of the most important figures in English women's football history.

Sheila Edmunds had been there at the foundation of Doncaster Rovers Belles half a century previously. Then Sheila Stocks prior to her marriage to the team's future manager Paul Edmunds, she and some friends set up their own team, the Belle Vue Belles; the group had met when they all sold Golden Goal tickets at the men's matches. For a quarter of a century, Edmunds was an integral part of the successful Belles team that dominated the game in England, winning the FA Cup six times and the Premier League National Division twice (and in both those championship years, they completed the league and cup double too). Edmunds's playing career, balanced with her vocation as a teacher, mirrored the Belles' meteoric rise as a club, and her contributions to the game have been rewarded with prizes from the FA as well as honorary academic awards, hence her formal title of 'Doctor'.

Now the club president, she thought she would continue to be involved for the rest of her life.

'When the chips are down, I question myself, do I still want to do this?' she confessed. 'Is it not time to pass the baton on to someone else and let them run with it? And then I get to a game and I'm on the gate and doing various things, or I go down to training and there's a nice buzz, and I'm thinking this is why I'm still here, because it still motivates me.'

Julie Chipchase had a similarly lengthy association with the club, as player, manager, and now director of football.

'I tweeted something around all the special stories that fans, players, staff can tell within those 50 years,' she said. 'We've got thousands of stories that we could tell. So I guess you look back on those 50 years with pride – and the fact that we're still here when we could quite easily have gone under. Would that be fair to say, Sheila?'

Her friend concurred. The pair sat together in the clubhouse prior to the team's match against Nottingham Forest Ladies. The Belles were playing their home fixtures at Rossington Main FC, about five miles outside the town centre – a few minutes in the car, but slightly tricky for anyone planning to get there on public transport with no train station nearby; Rossington station had closed many years before. It was a ground firmly situated in its local community, next to a school, and placed within a sizeable residential area, an old mining village with a population of almost 14,000; there was a small area by the side of the pitch with some mini goalposts, marked out as a children's play zone, and of course spectators were welcome to bring their dogs into the stands, in the best tradition of amateur football.

Belles had briefly been semi-professional, and they had played their first-team matches at the men's Keepmoat Stadium. Proud of their independence and equally proud of their good relationship with Rovers after a short-lived merger at the turn of the millennium, Belles had competed in the initial Women's Super League, that closed league of eight top teams, helping to move the sport towards professionalism in England.

When the league expanded to two divisions three years later, Belles were shunted down to the second tier; many observers viewed it as an unfashionable club being brushed aside to allow the more glamorous Manchester City to take their place among the elite. Another reshuffle took place four years later, with the intent being for all the top-tier clubs to employ full-time professionals, and for all the second-tier clubs to be semi-professional. Belles were aiming for a place in the revamped Women's Championship, knowing they did not have the resources to compete in the Super League against City, Arsenal and Chelsea; and they were awarded a licence in May 2018 after the FA's deliberations.

Two months later, Belles announced that they would not be playing in the Championship after all. Instead, they would step down a level, and play once more in the National League. It was all due to finance; after losing a major sponsor, they simply would not have the funds to complete a season in a semi-professional competition.

It was not just the sponsor they lost; they also lost their first-team coach, and almost all of their first-team squad. This was hardly a surprise; moving from semi-professional football, where at the minimum they would have their expenses covered, to amateur would be a major change, and there were no shortage of teams in the area more than eager to take on experienced players.

But just a few weeks before the start of the 2018/19 season, this left Belles with a dearth of players. Without money, they knew they would not be able to attract big names, who would not be interested in amateur football anyway. Instead, they made the brave decision to promote their development squad – mostly teenagers, who leapt at the chance to represent the historic Belles.

'We've just had to respond to the situation we've found ourselves in – in a nutshell we've totally had to restructure and rebuild, set the foundations again, and we've got this young team that are now competing in the third tier of women's football,' said Edmunds. 'Bit of a kick in the teeth, I would go so far as to say, at the time when it was all happening. It wasn't our fault in any shape or form, it was all to do with sponsorship, we'd already got the licence to be in that second tier and then lost our main sponsor, so we had to react to that.'

'We were quite successful on the pitch, obviously – we won the league by ten clear points, and were looking to plan forward from that,' Chipchase went on. 'We were looking at how we could go forward from that season, after winning the league, how we could build and then as Sheila says our major sponsor pulled out and left us in the situation we found ourselves in.'

'That was only, like, four weeks before the season started,' added Edmunds.

'So we didn't really have a chance to respond in trying to find another major sponsor,' said Chipchase. 'We just really had to go with the situation that we were in and withdraw from the Championship because we didn't meet the criteria because of the funding element of it and decided that we would continue in tier three.'

They were not surprised that they lost players and staff who wanted to make a career in football.

'What Doncaster Belles are about and have always been about is developing players,' explained Chipchase. 'What we want to do is develop them for our first team, but we're always aware of other teams wanting to come and take the players, I guess, in a way. In one way it's good for us because we're doing our job in developing players, but then in another way it's really hard because we're also trying to develop a team that can operate at the highest level.'

'But it's not just developing players, is it, the reason why they go?' asked Edmunds rhetorically. 'It's all to do with finance now, because people can make a living out of playing football, and even if they're only getting expenses, that's contributing towards them, and we just can't afford to do that now. We've got a real shortfall of what we would have had, so it was inevitable that we would lose players, lose the manager and have to restart. Fortunately we've got a development team that we've had to fall back on, and work with that group of players.'

Chipchase was quick to interject: 'I would say not necessarily fall back on, because we've always done succession planning. When our first team and everything that went with it went, we did have Zoey [Shaw] who was the development manager who we could then put into the head coach position, and we had the players we were developing in the development squad that could come into the first team. Our succession planning really had to come to the fore when all this happened.'

'It was a bit of a baptism of fire for them, but they've survived. They've battled through it and started off with probably the most difficult game they could have got – our first game was Blackburn [the previous year's league champions],' said Edmunds. 'But they're still here, they're still smiling, they're still enjoying. I was at training this week and I looked round and I think they've come so far in such a short time. We must be doing something right.'

There was an overwhelming air of optimism about the duo, along with an undercurrent of wry realism.

'We try and be as positive as we can, but I'll be perfectly honest, it does get to you at times, and you think I've had enough now – but I can't give it up,' said Edmunds. 'I couldn't give it up when I was pregnant!'

She laughed as she reflected on the memory.

'When I was pregnant and couldn't be as involved as I wanted to, I found that so, so difficult. I took up photography, and even that annoyed me because I couldn't sit down with the bump, and I thought, oh, please, just hurry up!'

'It's in your blood,' murmured Chipchase.

They exchanged memories of past players and favourite matches, and it was completely understandable that Edmunds felt such an inextricable pull to the club she helped create.

'If you've got a passion for football, and you're involved in football, it's got to be something major to stop you being involved,' she explained. 'It's not something you just say, "Oh, I'm not doing that any more," because if you've got that passion, it's so difficult to give up. For me, I've only ever been at this club, I've not been anywhere else, never wanted to go anywhere else, so I feel like it's my family as much as my own real family.'

'You can't imagine your life without Doncaster Belles,' added Chipchase.

The two were already thinking about the club's future, and returning to a higher level of football. Chipchase, as director of football, had plans to strengthen the talent pathway at the club, for players and coaches – especially female coaches. Between them, they agreed that playing at Rossington was the best option for the young first team rather than making a home at Doncaster Rovers's Keepmoat Stadium – much bigger, and creating more of a spotlight. Not only that, but it gave them a chance to build links with a new local community, beginning with the school across the road, and potentially creating a new generation of Belles fans.

Edmunds was thoughtful.

'In some ways, because we moved here, and the whole way of running things is different to what it was, it's a little bit like going back in time to some of the – I won't say the good times, but when times were hard. We've come from there to where we were at the end of last season, and I don't think there's anything wrong with going back that little bit. It's all about moving forward. Sometimes you do need to take a step back to step forward. The people that are here, they've totally embraced what we're trying to do, they're very supportive, and it just takes me back to the 90s when we were in a similar mining village community, and what they did for us then. It's nice that people like that are still here and want to support Doncaster Belles.'

She thought it was still possible for a club like Belles to reach the top of the game, but it would require an entirely new level of investment, the likes of which they had not seen before.

'The benchmark has just gone so high financially,' agreed Chipchase. 'It's not about what happens out there on the pitch, it's all about your bank balance and whether you can afford to be in there. It's got to be sustainable as well. A million and a half [pounds] might get you through one season, but then what's going to happen the season after, and the season after?'

She was very concerned about the sustainability of the Women's Super League project, fearing that more clubs might be forced to a lower tier of competition, or even fold, like Notts County Ladies had done two years previously, and suggested that women's teams remaining independent from men's clubs should be encouraged, with community stadia built primarily for the women's game.

'There are a few [clubs] out there that have got the money [for facilities] from the men's clubs, and good luck to them, it's fantastic for the game, but what about everybody else?' she pointed out, adding that there were a lack of training facilities on the Doncaster side of the country, while there were plenty nearer to Leeds and Sheffield.

'You get frustrated with things like that,' said Edmunds.

'Yeah, you do,' agreed Chipchase.

'You're trying to develop, but there's so many barriers that are in your way, and they're the things that make you think, "How am I going to do it, then?"' reflected Edmunds. 'You do need new blood, new ideas coming in all the time, because otherwise you get a bit stale in your thoughts and where you're going.'

Belles, for all their immediate struggles, did not have any problems with an influx of fresh talent in any area of the club, with new volunteers coming forward to help with plenty of tasks, right down to selling raffle tickets on matchday.

'There are people out there who care about Doncaster Belles, who want to help, and will give us that support, however little it is,' said Chipchase. 'I'm a big believer in those little bits and pieces, they help with the big stuff.'

'They're vital.'

'Without them we wouldn't run,' continued Chipchase. 'It does give me belief that there are people out there that do want us to succeed, do want to get us back on the map, and are willing to do their bit to help.'

Ever the optimist, Edmunds developed Chipchase's thought even further, saying, 'Sometimes you lose those people when you go up, because the parent club takes over all that, and these people get forgotten a little bit, and revert to being a parent or a supporter – but they have a major role to play. I'm from a background where everybody's got equal value because they're a cog in a wheel, and if you take one out, it won't work. So the guy who's out there helping is just as important as Zoey who's managing, Chippy here who's director of football. Everyone has got equal importance.'

The Belles community were truly pulling together, and their leaders were certainly inspirational, but they were under no illusion about the toughness of the task in front of them.

'We've had knocks, many knocks, along the years, but I don't think we've ever had one as bad as this,' admitted Edmunds.

'This is probably the hardest of them all,' agreed Chipchase.

Edmunds grinned. 'But we're still here.'

6

Queens of Orient

LIFE AT Leyton Orient Women had changed immeasurably in just two years. Promoted to the FA Women's Premier League London and South East at the end of 2017, they enjoyed a successful maiden campaign at their highest-ever level, finishing fourth, and securing their place in the newly-named FA Women's National League Division One South-East for 2018/19, alongside a run to the Capital Cup semi-finals.

Their fortunes contrasted greatly with their brother club. Leyton Orient had been relegated out of the Football League in 2017 amidst a lot of behind-the-scenes chaos, including ownership issues. It would have been understandable and unsurprising had they just ignored the women's team altogether. Yet the women remained an integral part of the club, with plenty of media coverage in the local papers – and had their end-of-season prize-giving along with the men too.

Coach Chris Brayford, still heading up football operations, was more than happy with the prospects for the year ahead. He had organised two pre-season trial matches for potential new players and was expecting his squad to acquit themselves even better in 2018/19. As always, with amateur teams and limited contact time, much of the onus was on the players to keep up their fitness and strength in their own time, leaving team training sessions as a focus for group work and to measure progress.

'We traditionally place the emphasis on people keeping their individual fitness up,' he explained. 'People work around their schedules, and if they weren't fit enough they didn't play, but we've tried the last couple of seasons to change the way we manage that – we now have specialist conditioning sessions this season, so we've been working hard on the fitness. What's also been marked is a couple of players who have had their best seasons are also in their best physical shape, and that's a good message in terms of encouraging people.'

It would be difficult to imagine Brayford losing his temper with players; he is the type of person who always seeks the positive aspects in a situation.

'I'm always optimistic! We're happy characters!' he laughed, before considering the realistic prospects for the year ahead. 'One of the things I think hurt us last season was maybe a little bit of squad depth, for injuries – but really any football manager will say that. We've brought in a good sports therapist to work with the [players] and just to try to reduce instances of injuries, I think that will really help us. You never know for certain until the league kicks off.'

* * *

When the league did kick off, the O's found themselves scoring plenty of goals, but conceding quite a few as well. By the start of October, they had two wins, two losses, and a draw on the board in the league – and they were looking to bounce straight back from a disappointing FA Cup defeat, losing 5-4 in an enthralling game to Cambridge City in the second round of qualifying.

They were still housed at Mile End Stadium, and even in an autumn midweek, it was notable that there were fans in the stands to cheer both sides on. Of course, some were friends and relatives of players, but others were simply football supporters, wanting to watch a good quality and competitive match.

They were guaranteed that when Orient took on AFC Wimbledon. The teams had established a rivalry in recent years, as they both battled for top slots in the league table. Their first encounter for 2018/19 was an intriguing one, with the visitors going ahead after a goalkeeping error, Orient equalising just after half-time, Wimbledon moving in front again on the hour, and then the O's securing a point with a soft goal of their own. Either team could have grabbed a winner; a point apiece was probably fair, putting an end to Wimbledon's consecutive victories and maintaining dignity for the hosts.

Captain Danielle Griffiths was reasonably satisfied.

'I think the first 25 minutes was the best football we've played this season so far,' she said immediately after the match. 'I think we just lost our heads a little bit after the goal – I'm not sure what happened. But then [we came] straight out the second half, we composed ourselves. A point's a fair result – they're a good team, they'll do well.'

She was adamant that their standard of football had not been up to scratch so far, and put it partly down to nerves.

'There were quite high expectations at the start of the season,' she said. 'We did so well in our first season in the National League, so I think we all came in thinking, "right, we can push for the title this year". That maybe distracted us from playing our football and getting the results. I think we're settling in now, we're taking it game by game, point by point.'

She grinned, and pointed out that this was the first time Orient had had a full squad available, saying, 'We have lots of teachers who like to take their holidays in August, and then you have the August bank holiday when everyone decides to have a long weekend, so we've now got our consistent first-team squad, which is a lot better.'

Griffiths herself worked in law and had been balancing her long hours and high pressure in the office with her football for years, and continued to take her captaincy duties seriously. She had managed to get to plenty of the pre-season training and fixtures, but work had become much busier in September.

'I have to admit I hadn't even thought about this evening's game until I turned up,' she said. 'I've been flat-out, getting into work at seven in the morning, leaving at ten o'clock at night, doing the same again. Tonight was a struggle, but actually I don't think it disadvantaged me, it's just a bit of intuition I had to play off rather than preparation. I would have dwelled [on the FA Cup result] if I didn't have some kind of distraction. It is good in that way.'

Midweek kick-offs at 7.45pm have long been the norm – but if you have a day job that does not finish until six or later, or you need to be up at 5.30am to go to work, it can be very gruelling.

'These evening games are the most difficult in terms of work-life balance, and I know a lot of people can only get here 30 minutes before kick-off because they don't finish work,' said Griffiths.

She looked around. The floodlights were still on, and the smattering of fans were making their way out of the ground to the tube station or to the pub – somewhere significantly warmer, anyway – while the teams finished up their cooldown exercises.

'Some people don't quite understand the sacrifices some people have to make, the shift-switching that goes on, begging your boss to leave early and promising to come in early the next day – it's the not-so-glamorous side of women's football.'

* * *

Griffiths and her team had adjusted their expectations for the season but were still hopeful that they would have some success.

'We're still within touching distance of the title and the top of the league,' she said a few days later. 'We're only four points from second, and there are three points between second and sixth. There's still everything to play for, and a lot of games to go, we've still got to play a lot of teams. The aims are still set very high for this season at this stage, and, given our recent performances, I think that's realistic.'

The captain described her squad as one in transition, settling down with some new additions, and she thought it had taken time to get used to the personnel – as well as a niggling feeling that they should be winning every game in their quest for the title.

'At the start of the season we were putting pressure on ourselves,' she admitted. 'We saw how we did in our first season and thought we know what we're up against this year, but there's been a lot of change in our league, teams have recruited very well in the summer, it's a lot more competitive than last year, so I think probably our expectations at the start of the season were too high, but we think we can still do well – we can challenge.'

The core of the Orient team had been the same for several seasons, and Griffiths had been playing alongside some of her team-mates for more than half a decade. Now 29, she was not thinking about retirement immediately, but it had certainly crossed her mind from time to time.

'I'm coming to the tail-end of my career, and there are a lot of good people in our team who are young!' she laughed. 'Things are going to start to get more serious career-wise. I want to play for as long as I continue to enjoy playing, which I am, at the moment.'

Her employer had been extremely understanding for years, but she was well aware she was fortunate.

'My work is quite good, they've always known that I play football, and that I play to quite a good standard,' she said. 'They trust me to manage my own workload and not to be nipping out if something urgent is on my desk. It's in my control to a large extent. Sometimes there is a [training] session I can't make.

'It's harder for other people – I do not have the hardest job. There's doctors and nurses and other people like that in our team, I'm in awe. The people with shifts and who have less flexibility who are required to be in a certain place at a certain time, it's really difficult for them, and it's difficult for them to play consistently sometimes.

'I know a couple of people who are playing in the Championship at the moment with full-time jobs in the city. God knows how they do training multiple times a week and travelling all over the country at the weekend. It is a big ask and it takes up a large portion of your life. You're working and you're playing football, and there's not too much time for much else.'

After spending 20 years playing football, Griffiths did allow herself to wonder what she would do if and when she did decide to hang up her boots.

'I'm not sure if I would immediately go into coaching,' she mused. 'That might be something that comes with settling down and having a family and getting involved from the bottom upwards, but I've always enjoyed going to watch the development team and try to speak to some of the younger players and see what they're thinking and what we can help them with. It's always an interest of mine.

'I'm sure I will miss it when that time does come, I'll have free Sundays and I don't know what to do! I'll probably be a bit lost, to be honest. I'd imagine I will always be interested in football and I'll have some involvement, whether it's watching, playing or whatever.'

7

Following a dream

WHILE HER friends travelled up and down the roads of England competing for their Women's Super League and Women's Championship clubs, Ashleigh Goddard had taken a rather longer trip. Most recently of London Bees, she had made her desire to play full-time football very well known, posting about it on social media, and asking for people's help in circulating her details. The attacking midfielder didn't expect to get offered a contract; all she wanted was a chance to prove herself during a short trial.

It had all begun at the turn of the year, when she dislocated her shoulder and had to wait until the end of February for surgery. That ruled her out for the rest of the season – when her contract with Bees expired. She was offered an extension to her deal, but at the age of 26 she felt she had to try her best to step up and compete as a full-time footballer.

Being a footballer had always been her ambition. She spent her childhood playing in the Arsenal youth set-up, and then headed to America on a four-year scholarship, enabling her to keep up her football to a high standard while getting her degree. On her return, she found that her name had been forgotten a little.

'When I came back from America, it was incredibly difficult, way more so than I thought, to get hold of a team, because, as amazing as it was, in England we don't understand that very well,' she said. 'You're at Arsenal, then you disappear for four years, so it's hard to get your foot back in the door. I trained with Chelsea for quite a while, trained with Arsenal, I signed with Reading for a little bit, and then I ended up at London Bees.'

She had always balanced study and work with football, meaning there was little time for socialising, but she didn't regret that.

'Football has always been my number one,' she said. 'I think I went out with my friends once in my entire secondary school life, but I don't miss that, or feel sorry for that, because I chose that life. I chose to come home and get my mum or dad [to] take me training every day. If there wasn't training, I would go running, it was something I had to do.'

But she admitted that at Bees she fell into a comfort zone and was no longer challenging herself, nor making any effort to achieve her dreams.

'I was watching people I grew up playing with playing in WSL1 and for England, people I played with are on the next level, and I've settled,' she said. 'It's a good level, WSL2, but I was stuck there, and I thought if I do it when I'm too old, nobody's going to want to sign me. If I don't do it now then I'm going to regret not really going for it.'

So she did.

'I loved it at London Bees, I'm from Barnet, I've always been a fan, and to be captain for a couple of years was an honour, I loved it, but it was just they weren't getting promoted and they weren't full-time professional and ultimately that's what I want,' she explained.

It wasn't just Bees she was leaving; she also resigned from her job as a teacher, and moved out of her house, knowing that she would have to move to pursue her dream, and sending out emails to clubs she thought she might be able to slot into.

It was a major life change, and Goddard was grateful that her parents had supported her.

'My parents are amazing,' she said. 'From day dot they've always driven me everywhere. I didn't learn to drive till I came back from America, [at the age of] 22, 23, so up until that age they were driving me to every training session, every game. Wherever I was, they would come and watch the game. They'd drive up there from London. Then to allow me to go to America at 18, I'd never been to America before – I'd never been – and suddenly they're trusting strangers to take care of me while I'm there! I feel I'm incredibly lucky to have such an amazing supportive family. Whatever pain I feel or struggles that I get, I know they're feeling the same. They're awesome. They lift me up when I need lifting and I'll never be able to say how much I appreciate them.'

Goddard and her family were also well aware that finding a club might be a lengthy process.

'I just wanted to get my foot in the door, have a chance,' she said. 'I never asked to sign straight away, I just wanted a trial – anything to try and prove myself, get in the squad, anything to train all the time and with better players – that would be it.'

As fortune would have it, Goddard was offered trials with two clubs; the first made her an offer immediately, but she wanted to honour her promise to play with the second on a pre-season tour. By the time she returned, the first club had signed someone else in her position, and the second had budget restrictions meaning they could only sign one player, and that had to be a striker.

At that point, the transfer window in England closed, meaning WSL clubs could no longer make any further signings for the season.

'One week I had both of them, the next week I had neither,' she recalled. 'I was very unlucky with that. Then the window shut, and I put out that tweet, because I realised that my only option really was WSL2 [now the FA Women's Championship], which is everything I had already left, quit and gambled, or I look for a new experience.'

So she posted on social media, and benefitted from retweets courtesy of her friends already playing in the WSL. It was that message that changed her career path.

'Funnily enough, an ex-Yeovil captain contacted me,' she said. 'We'd obviously played against each other at some point but didn't know each other very well. She contacted me and said she played for a team in Denmark.'

That team was FC Nordsjaelland – in the second division, and fighting for promotion. They were the first team in the country to be linked with their equivalent men's club and were interested in taking Goddard on a short-term arrangement until their season ended in November. She wouldn't receive a wage, but she would get accommodation and food, and she would be able to train full-time – she would be able to concentrate on football.

It was an easy offer to accept.

Goddard was happily housed in a hotel attached to the club's home ground, with access to the gym facilities there.

'I have a fantastic gym basically down the corridor from my room,' she enthused. 'I've got all the pitches, all the equipment, everything you can imagine at my disposal, which is amazing.'

She didn't have to get up as early as she did back at home because her time was her own. Her usual routine was to rise, eat breakfast, catch up with her parents, and then start on morning training; if the team had a session scheduled for the evening, she would join in with that too, or if they didn't, she would put together another session of her own. There was also a bit of homework involved; tactics in Denmark were very different to what Goddard was used to back at home.

'It's just trying to be a bit smart and be a bit of a sponge and take on everything,' she smiled.

It was the middle of September, and Goddard was still adjusting to the excitement of the move, but never lost sight of her ultimate aim.

'My focus is still to get as fit as I possibly can, play as much football as I possibly can, I'm basically doing full-time minus the money,' she said. 'We all moan about the money in women's football – I'm literally earning no money. Everyone says teachers' pay is terrible, and it is, but as terrible as it was, I always appreciated it and thought it was half-decent, so to go from that to nothing … I risked it all for the love of the game, as cheesy as it is.'

She was already reaching out to teams in England in preparation for her return later in the autumn.

'A couple of other teams said that if I didn't have a team at Christmas then I could contact them and see if I could have trials again, so they're the teams I'll be targeting to start with,' she added. 'I'll also be looking at how the league's going, and [contacting teams] if I can help in any way.'

It was a relief for her that clubs had already shown an interest in signing her.

'The worst-case scenario would be that everyone thought I was terrible or that I didn't make it or nobody wanted to give me trials, and I'd end up homeless and jobless – but even as a very worst-case scenario I would stay with my parents and figure things out, or I'd go abroad, and that's what I've done,' she said. 'Now I'm here in Denmark I think it's a blessing in disguise because it's given me a chance. It's put that little bit of fire back into me, and you know what, I know high standards. I was at Arsenal for that long, I did England youth, I've done everything but lost that bit of fire to be one of the best. I've watched everyone else step up and I sort of didn't, so now is my time. I've taken the scenic route, but now it's my time. I have no excuses. My only focus is football so I've got to train as much as I can and get as good as I can and hopefully a team will take me. I'm not scared of hard work and working hard. I need somebody to take a gamble on me, give me a chance and see what I can do.'

8

New ground

FLEUR COUSENS worked in television. It was no surprise that the founder of a women's football club, Goal Diggers, had decided to make a documentary film about the history of the game. She and her collaborators premiered *Who Moved The Goalposts?* in East London during the summer of 2018 – at the height of World Cup fever for the England men – and she was hoping it would be viewed more widely. Covering the past century of the women's game – from the 50 years in which it was banned in England through to the modern day – she also found it was becoming an easy way to explain her determination to grow her club even further.

'Lots of people who were involved in Goal Diggers or involved in football, even they didn't really know about [the ban], so it's been quite exciting,' she said. 'There's been some players who really want to just show their family and show their friends, because they were like, "This is a narrative that we find it quite hard to explain, because it's the way we've had to experience football for years, it's too much, it's nice to have a thing where we can signpost and then have the whole history exposed and have a few things cleared up." But there are still so many question marks. We call it Who Moved The

Goalposts?, but you can't really point at one thing, there are just so many different factors, and the history is a huge one. It's just so sad that we are playing catch-up.'

Cousens thought a lot of people were still not aware of the ban that had put such a brake on the development of women's football; and she acknowledged that although there had been mainstream media coverage of the history of the game, most notably in a programme presented by Clare Balding, only those already interested specifically in women's football would have watched in the first place. She hoped that the FA and clubs would start to talk about the century of women's football in England prior to the launch of the Women's Super League rather than gloss over its prohibition and the struggles faced by its players; and she wondered if there was too much pressure on the current generation of Lionesses to progress the game singlehandedly.

'One of my friends was quoting the fact that after we went out [of the men's World Cup] one of the [television] presenters was quoting the fact that, "Oh, we haven't been in the semi-finals for 28 years,"' she said. 'She was like, "We literally were in the semi-finals at the last Women's World Cup, and we were in the Euro semi-finals with the women's team." The England women keep performing and keep getting these amazing achievements, and it's not recognised.

'When we interviewed Jordan Nobbs for the documentary, you could tell how much she knew winning for them was more than just winning a trophy. Winning changes the whole game for women in England. It'll make people wake up. It is so weird, isn't it? A semi-final doesn't quite do that. You need to have that whole trophy moment – you need to have that huge win for people to reassess what's going on.'

And she was concerned that top players were worried about speaking honestly about anything that was not going well, for fear they would personally hamper the development of the sport.

'They have to be extremely party line,' she said, and gave the example of one player who now refused to discuss anything to do with her life off the pitch, having previously spoken openly about it. 'It's interesting. I suppose for them, all the positive things that have happened have happened due to their fame. They're not fighting that they have the biggest pay gap in the UK, they're just happy they have a pay cheque.'

Cousens created Goal Diggers as a place for her and her friends to play football. In the middle of London, it is not easy to find pitch space or build up a grassroots club, but she did it. Her club spent a few very happy years competing in indoor leagues, with a steady number of attendees.

And then it grew. Goal Diggers is now surely one of the most successful grassroots women's clubs in England, and it was all done without FA funding or support – just through sheer hard work. Player numbers ballooned without the need for advertising; simple word of mouth brought new members to the dressing room.

'Even this [men's] World Cup fever has made a difference,' said Cousens, a few months after England's men had reached the semi-finals in Russia. 'One of our players had some friends she'd been telling to come along for ages, but now they want to be Harry Kane. They should really want to be Jordan Nobbs. That's who I want to be!'

On an average week, they could expect around 80 women to turn up for training – just with two coaches on a nine-a-side pitch. And there were still more plans for the future.

'This is a new way for grassroots football,' said Cousens. 'We probably are now the biggest women's football team in London. Why aren't the FA coming to us to find out what we're doing right? Two weeks ago we had a committee meeting and we were like, "OK, we actually need to put a limit on training," which is the saddest thing – the limit is 60 people at training. That's still a lot of people on a nine-a-side pitch, but that's the only way we can still have a successful training session, enough ball time, enough match time at the end, and also for health and safety reasons. But it's so sad to have this week 25 people who have signed up and can't come – there could be 30 people who want to come.'

It was access to facilities that Cousens thought was the primary problem, something that was a particular issue in London, with its high population density, lack of green space and high running costs for everything. She was in negotiations with her local council to try and inveigle some time on full-size pitches for Goal Diggers; after some investigations, she had found that many of the 11-a-side pitches had been block-booked for men's teams, who neither required nor utilised all that space.

'They take it for granted,' she said. 'They've had it for years, because they don't realise how hard it actually is to get that space. They play in these expensive 11-a-side leagues, there's one on a Wednesday night in Market Road, and there's 22 of them who turn up. We would bring 100 people to that same space. That's five times as many people playing on this pitch space! When we go to our nine-a-side pitch on Wednesday evenings at training, we get there half an hour early and do our warm-up outside the pitch to make sure we're ready to go for our hour-and-a-half session when we get on. There's always about 14 men using the pitch and they trot off and 60 of us trot on. Come on! We're using this space to its maximum capacity. Somewhere like London, you should be prouder of the groups who are doing that kind of stuff.'

Cousens was slightly wary of some of the men's teams who shared their space, suspecting that they did not want women encroaching.

'Sometimes they kick the ball into our space during the matches,' she revealed. 'I don't think they'd be doing that if men were playing there. Whenever it goes near me, I boot it out of the park. Get off our space. This is our time. We're serious footballers doing a serious match – if you want to kick a ball on to my pitch when I'm playing, I'm kicking it as far away as I can. I can kick it far because I'm a footballer. It annoys me so much. Don't disrupt our match!'

Although Cousens and her colleagues at Goal Diggers had built the club themselves without any support from the authorities, there was also a slight glimmer of thankfulness that they were independent, without too many forms needing to be filled in; they organised their own fundraising functions in association with a bar, and snippets of media coverage created more interest around them. They were hoping that in the near future they would have the funds to be able to offer membership on a bursary system, allowing some women to join and represent the club for free. They would have plenty of opportunity to secure themselves match time.

'No more school hall or wooden floor!' exclaimed Cousens, thinking back to the seven-a-side indoor league in which Goal Diggers had initially competed. 'We're currently in a Tuesday seven-a-side league, a Sunday five-a-side league, and then a Saturday 11-a-side league, which is twice a month. There's lots of football out there.'

She punctuated her descriptions with grins and laughter, clearly gleeful and proud that so many women were getting their chance to play. More than that, the Goal Diggers ethos meant that coaches did not pick the team per se; instead, players indicated their interest in a particular match, and reserved themselves a slot on a first come, first served basis. That relaxed set-up was very attractive to players of all kinds of standard.

'They don't want to be pressurised into playing weekly when they might not necessarily be able to do that,' said Cousens. 'Living as an adult in London is a busy time. You can't necessarily commit to being able to play every Saturday morning. We do have a lot more beginners than we used to have, but we also have a lot more experienced players than we used to have because they've found something in Goal Diggers that other teams don't get – a casual relationship with football, but one where you can always get game time when you want it.'

Players might opt to compete in just five-a-side, or just seven-a-side, or just 11-a-side – or all three, depending on their preference. (Cousens played in all three. 'Normally there is football on offer at least twice a week for everyone – I do more than that because I'm keen,' she beamed.)

'These leagues are quite high level, so even though selection is done on availability, not ability, some beginners still are turned off because the teams we're playing against are good, so they're a little bit scared,' explained Cousens. 'For the last year I have been trying so hard to find beginners' leagues, but there aren't beginners' teams to play against – until recently. This is one of my big excitements about the changes that are happening – there are now other beginners' teams in London! There are two beginners' leagues we might be able to join next year! Two years ago we couldn't. That wouldn't even be possible because there wouldn't be people to play against. It's really nice.'

Some of the new teams and leagues had even told Cousens that they had been inspired by Goal Diggers' success, which, she said, was 'exactly what we want'.

'A lot of women have missed the boat in many ways,' she said. 'Football wasn't offered to us growing up, so to have lots of 20-plus year olds take up a new sport ... football is a sport that everyone should be playing, it's so exciting.'

The special ethos permeating Goal Diggers' operations was a surprise to some women who were used to a more traditional football club set-up, and did not buy in to teams where selection was not ability or effort dependent.

'There sometimes are players who are extremely experienced and they've been used to a certain relationship to sport and football, and who will come – and won't come again,' said Cousens. 'They are the minority – but also there are other teams for them. There are ability-based teams that they're always going to make the first team in, that they can join. Sometimes they come to us because they've heard of us, and they don't really understand what's going on – but often those people, I'm hoping they're going to not come back. We've had issues with those kinds of people who shout at other players during the post-drill or the training matches. The kind of player who does that and doesn't support everyone in the club isn't someone we really want to have around, because we've got enough players to not have people like that. It's so hard to create the kind of supportive atmosphere we have that often one extremely negative voice can take away from that, and it's not worth undoing all that sort of stuff.'

The input of the membership was vital to the club's operation. Cousens explained that initially all the players had trained together, with the reasoning that experienced players could help and support the beginners. After comments from players, three years later training was running in two groups, because the less experienced players had asked for more detailed, in-depth technical drills, and a smaller group would also give them more time on the ball in training matches.

Goal Diggers' growth had also meant that Cousens needed help from other club members to keep everything running; she was now part of a committee of 14 that made the decisions, with each person having their own responsibilities.

'In the very beginning stages, there were so many things that were just up to me: stuff like hiring coaches, finding pitch space,' she said. 'At that point we were playing on a concrete community pitch in King's Cross, and it wasn't ideal. It was free, but it wasn't a beautiful space. Even stuff like having to transport equipment to the pitch, I had to do that kind of stuff – and then also general organisation, I was doing everything, so things are a lot smoother now. There are so many things that having a committee and having more of an established idea of exactly what we want has helped so much.'

Cousens was pleased with the club's achievements, and looking forward to the season.

'Three years ago I did think the work was paying off, but it was a whole different club,' she recalled. 'Back then it was once a week, a football club, and it was lovely, and I think it was what we needed then, but now it's a community and it's become so much more, and it's so exciting. I do feel very supported by everyone, the committee, and it's an exciting time. All we need is that big pitch and then we'll take over the world!'

Since its inception, Goal Diggers relied on a two-coach set-up, with one of those coaches being female. Coach Ruby had departed, replaced by Coach Ciara, who worked in tandem with the long-serving Coach Josh.

'Coach Ciara has been such a positive presence at the club,' enthused Cousens. 'She is amazing. 'Josh, since the very beginning, has been such a positive force for me. The club is shaped with both of our help the whole way, and we haven't argued in the whole three years. Obviously it's quite hard, he's my coach but I'm technically his boss; if I tell him to do something he's got to do it, but also when he's my coach he's completely in charge, so it's finding the right balance, and it's just worked so nicely.'

She paused.

'Maybe he hates me, I don't know!'

Another smile stretched across her face.

'Having him has been so great because he has been the exact right level between gaining complete respect from everyone in the club but also being able to attend the post-match pie and properly be able to have friendships. If we go to a match he'll be there immediately, with all the boards, ready to do all the warm-ups. He'll have created a message for the whole team, he'll have formations posted to everyone before the match so they all know what they're doing, and he's not getting paid for that time, but he always goes the extra mile.

Someone like that has made my life so easy – not easy, it's a lot of work, but so much easier. I respect him so much. Three years later it's a nice thing that he's still such a huge part of it.'

* * *

'It's wild!'

Josh Pugh still found it a little hard to believe how quickly the Goal Diggers project had grown, nor how many players he got at training. With scores of players turning up ready for a session, and more members showing an interest in joining all the time, he and his coaching colleague had to think creatively about how to plan their evenings.

'It's exciting and challenging to think about how you can get everyone enough time on the ball to work on it individually,' he explained. 'Then oh, we've got a game on Saturday, so we should probably run through the shape of how we're going to try and set up. It's constantly thinking about how you can make it fun and informative, I guess, which is a balance. We're on that pitch for an hour and a half: we want at least 45 minutes of that for mini-games because that's where you learn the most, particularly if [the players are] not as used to [playing in] games. And we want everyone to have a session with each of the coaches.'

There were plenty of variables to consider then – even before the limitations of pitch space had to be taken into account.

'We're on a seven-a-side astro pitch, which is hard, it just is hard,' admitted Pugh. 'Even if we just had an 11-a-side pitch we could split that into three and we could have three coaches there. We'd improve so quickly.'

He accepted that on an astroturf pitch intended for a small-sided game, not everyone would be able to train due to the lack of room and the potential physical dangers from too many people on that surface ('Astro, it's fine, but it's not great – there's a reason pitches have moved on from being sand-based'). Despite those potential glitches, he estimated that about half his regular training attendees were also regularly playing in competitive matches.

'The other half might play once a month because they just want to dip their toe, they're just getting into playing football consistently,' he explained, 'and then there's some others who might not be around that much and will train but not play, but if they have to make a choice between training and playing they'd rather play because that's more competitive and it's more fun.'

Pugh had noticed a slight change in the constitution of the regular Goal Diggers players over the previous three years, both in terms of the on-the-pitch standard and the demographic.

'Where [the club has] really evolved is there isn't like your average Goal Diggers member any more,' he said. 'Some of the players who came in, they have played for county and all the way through university, and now just fancy a kickabout, and we have two beginner teams so there's this whole new group of footballers who will play once a week, and it's going to take them three months before they feel like they're ready to play a competitive game.

'I don't feel like we've lost anything – I feel like we've progressed. You grow and you evolve. We're able to compete with teams in a way we couldn't before. We've not lost anything there, it's very much a good thing, very much a win. When it got going, it was a group of mates or mates of mates who just wanted to get together and play and train and work on some stuff and play once a week in a league. Now there's this whole infrastructure, or brand, I guess, and they see it or hear about it and want to be a part of it because of what they've heard or what they've seen. People have seen us playing and come over and said, "Who are you, how do we get involved?" Then the way that word gets out has changed, so we're attracting types of players we didn't used to attract.

'As one of the coaches, getting better is one of the best things ever – it means we can rely on quality to move up a level. Tomorrow there's no way we'll be bad, the squad we've got is really good, so even if we've got to grind a result out, or we take a while to get going, the talent that we have will take over and will probably win us the game.'

He felt that the standard of every squad had improved tremendously, not just with the new players but with the progress of the less experienced ones. That meant better results across the board, regardless of who secured themselves a spot in the team through the sign-up process.

'We're competing with every team that we play against,' he said. 'We're playing against teams with players who used to be in the England set-up, and have been playing county and borough football for five-plus years. I feel like we've got to the point now where whoever's involved we're going to give whoever we're playing a game. But there are also times now where all we have to do is turn up and we'll beat teams, whereas before we weren't in a position to do that. The ethos didn't really change, we just had the players to do it better.

'It's definitely improved. That's probably because the more you play the better you get, and everyone is playing more. There are a handful of individuals who have come in and really embraced it and really brought up standards, in a way you can only do if you've had a scholarship to play [college football] in the States, you're going to bring the level up for the players around you, playing with players of your level or thereabouts.

'Because the squad's never the same two games in a row, there are certain principles. Anyone who ever plays for us needs to be able to do these things more or less, and if you're playing for us these are the things you need to try and do. Other than that, we'll see how we are. I've just been getting the squad for tomorrow sorted. We've got a really attacking team. For the first time in a while we're probably going to play with two box-to-boxes, a midfielder and a centre-back just in front of the back four – we've never been able to do that before. We'll just try it. We'll give it a go. That's who's around, that's who's around. You can do that with really good players, which is basically what it all comes down to in terms of getting results.'

WINTER

9

The best-laid plans

IT HAD been a tough few months for Lee Burch and his Yeovil team. It took them until November to secure their first-ever win in the top flight, beating Everton by a single Hannah Short goal. Although the start to the season had been hard work, the coach was clear that it had not seemed like a never-ending slog.

'Time flies by in football, I think,' he said. 'You're always looking for the next game.'

He felt that his side had been close to victory many times in their opening matches ('It just wasn't going for us,' he recalled) and was proud of his squad's tenacity and dedication.

'They had to gel quite quickly because obviously we were struggling,' he said. 'The full squad wasn't put together until quite late and then we've added a couple in the season; they had to pull themselves together quite quickly and they've done that well, they've continued to get strong with that. Things like the first victory and the positive performances are how that happened.

'The last month ['s matches have] been very similar. We just believed that if we kept doing the right things, we wouldn't keep losing games of football, and we felt that a little bit of luck would go our way at some point.'

He corrected himself. 'You've got to make your own luck. We did that this weekend, and hopefully it will start to even itself out a little bit more.'

* * *

There were five days to go until the end of the Norwegian football season, and FC Nordsjaelland were poised to secure their place in the spring play-off to win promotion.

Ashleigh Goddard had played a crucial part in their push, but was packing her cases ready to return to England two days after the final match.

'The team has done very well,' she said with a typical footballer's understatement. 'Each year they've got promoted and are hoping to do the same this year. It's a bit different from what they've normally done, but this time you get put into a mini-league where they battle for promotion again. I won't be here for that – that doesn't start until March or April. My aim was to try and help get them to this point and get fit myself, so I'd say it's been pretty successful.'

After her shoulder operation earlier in the year, achieving match fitness had been her aim, although it had been trickier than expected.

'I have no problems in going to the gym, I love that, so that's not been the problem, but when I say this people don't understand what the issue is – the food, I really struggle with the food!' she revealed. 'Because I stay in a hotel – I don't get paid but I get accommodation and I get all my meals – it's not like a normal hotel where there's a buffet and choice, they'll put it out for everyone who lives here, and if you don't like it then you're stuck.'

The meat-heavy diet proved a problem, so she had found herself eating more bread and therefore more carbohydrate than anticipated.

'Fitness-wise, I came [to Norway] with pretty much nothing and my shoulder was weak, and I can confidently say my shoulder is completely fine and I'm a lot fitter stamina-wise, and my game fitness, definitely, but I haven't really achieved my goal of being an extreme athlete, like Jessica Ennis!' she laughed. 'I've done the best I can, but I've struggled a bit because it's not like I can go to the shop and buy stuff and cook stuff because I'm in a hotel, and I'm not getting paid. When I quit my job, I saved, obviously, and it's insanely expensive here, so even if I could cook, which I can't, I wouldn't have been able to last three months buying my own food without getting paid. It's been a big challenge, I've loved it, I don't regret it at all and I'm definitely in a better place than when I came, by a mile, but I'm very much looking forward to coming back, and still working as hard as I am. When I come back, even a month will make a massive difference.'

Nevertheless, she had proved her worth to the team, slotting in as a utility player and covering whichever position necessary ('I've actually been playing forward for the last few weeks. I hate playing forward, forward is not my position, but if you think that's best for the team, of course I'll do it'), and hoped that she had done enough to impress a WSL club.

'We have our games on a Saturday so when it comes to a Sunday I'm a Twitter-crazy person, following all the WSL games to see how my old clubs and friends are doing, and to see what clubs I could help if I joined or had a trial with,' she said.

She already had two trials in the diary. After her disappointments in the summer, she was apprehensive but also excited about what the future might hold.

'As cheesy as it sounds, this is my dream – to try and play professionally,' she said. 'I got so close to it in the summer, even though I wasn't in the best physical condition. To be so close and to have a team say, yeah, they want me and to have it all fall apart, it was tough, but I like to think of it as maybe it happened for a reason. When I get a knockback like that I try to think of it as just setting myself up for a more epic comeback. I'm 26 now, and I see 18, 19 year olds getting their debuts in professional football. I know I've taken the scenic route, but ultimately, yes, I'm very nervous, I'm very excited, I'll give it everything I can in these trials, and hope that I get something. If I don't, I'll look at my next options. I'm not going to give up on it whatever happens. I'm really hoping this time is the time. I just need someone to take a chance on me.'

* * *

Back at home, the Lionesses camp had been rocked by the news that vice-captain and Arsenal star Jordan Nobbs had suffered a cruciate ligament injury, joining her club team-mate and Scotland playmaker Kim Little on the sidelines.

They were not the only female players contemplating several months in rehab. Though Barnsley's Dani Lea was on the way back, there were still several women beginning the road back from the most serious injury of their lives.

Female players are more susceptible to these kinds of injuries; with less natural muscle mass in the top part of the leg, they also have less stability in the knee joint. They are also more likely to pick up ligament injuries in any part of the body due to hormones affecting ligament laxity. Strength and conditioning work tailored for female footballers can reduce the risk, but for any player it will always be a possible problem. With top-class medical care and access to gym facilities, the route back to match fitness can be made much easier. For those players whose clubs cannot offer those benefits, it can be very, very tough.

London Bees' Katie Wilkinson had suffered a severe ligament injury in her foot when playing for Aston Villa two years previously. Only in the middle of 2018 was she starting to get back to full fitness and compete as she wanted to in the Championship with her new side.

'I was in so much pain,' she recalled. With no ambulance on site, she had to be transported to hospital in the back of her mother's car, with every bump in the road magnifying the agony. Without a brace keeping her foot still, each forced movement was uncontrolled.

'My foot felt like it was about to fall off – just snap off.'

Five ligaments in her foot had broken. She was told that it was possible that she might not play again due to the severity of the injury and the complicated nature of the surgery that could be needed to fix it.

'It could have gone one way or the other,' she admitted. 'I was told that I had to wait a few months for the operation itself, just because they said if they'd have operated on five ligaments, my foot wouldn't have reacted at all – it would have just stayed as it was – and that's not a good thing to do. I had to wait for my ligaments to heal – those that would heal, let them heal, and they'd reassess me, give me another MRI, see where I was at.

'It turned out two or three healed on their own, but two needed operating on, and at that point they said they'd be happy to do the operation, because it wouldn't need as much work and my foot would hopefully react to it OK.'

Even after the operation, a return to the pitch was not guaranteed because so much rehab would be needed. Wilkinson was essentially immobile and missing football, which had been her outlet for most of her life.

'My bum was permanently stuck to the sofa,' she said. 'I was doing a degree at university at the time as well as trying to run a business. I still managed to get a first-class honours degree at uni, which was unbelievable, and I got back playing again, and the business was still going. It all kind of works out in the end, but you've got to keep going, really. At times I was so high off the medication and all that stuff, I couldn't even see the piece of paper in front of me let alone do the work.'

Looking back, she gave credit to some of the Villa Ladies backroom staff, who gave up their own time to attend appointments with her and support her in her recovery. She did not have access to the rehab facilities or the gym at the Bodymoor training ground, like an injured player on the men's side of the club would have done, which was disappointing to her, so she did what she could with the resources she had.

'You can imagine me, knowing for 18 months I'm probably not playing,' she said with a slightly embarrassed laugh. 'I was grumpy, going in [to the physio], knowing I wasn't playing. With what they had, the budget they had, they were unbelievable.

'The facilities they've got at Bodymoor are unbelievable, but we weren't allowed to use them. It wouldn't have cost them anything. The hydropool when I was rehabbing, that would have been unbelievable for me.

'I don't know what their reason for it is, I don't know, who knows? It wasn't the best. But again the physios that were there, I'm forever in their debt for what they did for me, because I probably wouldn't be playing now if it wasn't for them.'

Wilkinson wanted to get back to match fitness as soon as she could, but a change in club management meant she was not in Villa's long-term plans. She chose to move to London Bees after manager Luke Swindlehurst made an offer for her to head to Barnet.

'It was difficult to come into a new coach's department,' she said of the end of her time at Villa. 'I wasn't really getting given the opportunity to play. They're saying, "You're not fit enough, you need to get match fit," but how do you get match fit without playing? It was just going round in circles really. It was a difficult decision, but Luke came in for me at Christmas and as soon as he did I knew it was the right decision. I want to be playing.

'I tried my hardest, I was staying after training to do extra fitness – and that again, the physio or a coach would stay with me after training to do fitness with me, to try and get me back fitter. I was training probably two, three times a day – too much, probably. I was trying too hard probably,' she added with a sense of realisation.

One of her first goals for her new club came against Villa, and she was willing to say that it gave her a sneaky feeling of satisfaction, although it was strange to score against the team she had represented from the age of nine and some of her closest friends.

'I had a point to prove,' she said. 'That was definitely a really sweet moment, and one that I'll probably not forget.'

Her 2018/19 season had been interrupted by an emergency operation in October to remove a large ovarian cyst, measuring ten centimetres by eight centimetres, that had twisted round and was causing her agonising pain.

'They showed me the pictures of it where it had twisted round, and they said, "For it to twist round three times, you must have been playing rugby or something,"' she recalled. 'I said, "I feel like I do sometimes when I'm on the football pitch – I do get knocked about a little bit!"'

It meant more rehab was in her future, but she was hopeful that the London Bees facilities at the Hive – another space shared with a men's team – would help her to return to the pitch as soon as possible, and that the backing of all the staff and her team-mates would be invaluable.

'A few people who are involved with Bees from the outside a little bit always say what a great team environment it is,' she said. 'There's no cliques, people get on, it's like a little family. It helps being at the Hive, because that's just our little base, where we know where everything is. We train there and play there, and it is nice – we get treated really well.'

Katie Wilkinson's new captain on signing for Bees was Emma Beckett, the Ireland international midfielder. The

31-year-old had set up a crowdfunding page after three of her players suffered serious knee injuries within a few weeks of each other; she knew that asking for donations was not ideal, but she did not want to see her friends and colleagues financially impacted as well as in pain.

'We've got three players here who really do need help, and that was my front-running intent – to make sure the players got the support they need,' she explained. 'One of the girls in particular will need specialist treatment, it's not a standard injury. The second [motivation to set up a crowdfunding page] was to raise awareness in women's football. I'm sure they're not the first you have heard of to suffer a knee injury, but it's disappointing. During my time at the club I think there's been seven ACL injuries, and that's in two and a half years, which is a huge number, really. There's a lot of talk about the boost in the quality of the league, things like that, which is going to be impossible to do if your best players are sidelined with injury for a year. That's my driving force too. Seeing the girls, knowing that every one of us works or goes to university, in some capacity – football sadly is a pastime at the minute. For me it's slightly different as I'm winding down in my career, with the full-time job that I do it's a different story for me. The majority of my team-mates are a lot, lot younger. They're early 20s, not even that in some cases; promising players, they've been involved with England under-age groups, top clubs and academies, and to see them, their promising careers, put on hold because they're not getting the relevant support, it's a bugbear of mine, it really is.'

Although at the Hive the Bees players could see a doctor and have an MRI scan almost immediately, the problem they faced was the delay after that. One of the injured players had been waiting for over six months to get an appointment on the NHS.

'For me it's a whole process: it's not one stage at a time, we have to figure things out, we need to make sure there's a good physiotherapy plan in place, there's a rehabilitation course that's been thought out ahead of time, the players are strengthened and built up prior to surgery, whenever that may be,' said Beckett, 'and it's difficult. It's not something I just see our club suffering with. I don't think people outside of it in the women's game really understand how difficult it is. I've seen all three of these girls suffer emotionally, mentally. You read about Premier League male footballers and they have every type of welfare, wellbeing coach within the club; there's counsellors, there's psychologists, and obviously as females that's not something we have access to [via the club].'

Beckett was sure that lack of understanding and awareness of the women's side of the game was widespread, and had been to see senior figures at the FA to discuss the problems they faced – from injuries to the quality of pitches they were expected to play on. She was also concerned about the attitudes and abuse female players continued to face, and pointed to the recent revelation that England winger Karen Carney had been sent rape threats via social media.

'It's not delusions of grandeur, but at the same time in order for clubs and women's football to actually regularly turn out revenue and profits, things need to improve all round – it's kind of chicken and egg,' she said. 'I think certainly when you speak to people not in women's football, it's like, "Well, you're fortunate to be able to play," almost. The Kaz Carney thing recently on social media, unbelievable, and, sadly, she's not on her own. Thankfully, I've never suffered that level of abuse, but so many players get comments about their physical appearance, derogatory things about disease or rape, it's unbelievable.

'You're not only fighting against the status quo to play football, but to make a living out of it, to sustain yourself within the world. If you're living in London the cost of living is much higher and it's difficult to do that in a football way. For me, that's the reason I didn't go pro. I played pro in Norway for a year, because I was able to juggle work simultaneously. This is the case for many girls in our team – what they earn [in their day jobs] at the moment outweighs what they would earn in a top league. Only a small percentage [of female footballers] are on real decent wages, some of those being six figures, but other than that there's such a gulf, and it's not right.'

Beckett wanted her players to know that she was on their side and trying to make things better for them.

'As captain, as someone who's a little bit older than the girls, who gets to see it first hand, these girls really suffer, and I'm not just talking about these three [with the serious knee injuries],' she said. 'I needed surgery on my wrist following a tackle on [an artificial pitch]. I was in a cast for seven out of 12 months at one point. I'd fractured my scaphoid, which is a tiny bone, the size of a peanut, in the back of your hand, and I'd done it playing football, playing for my club at the time. I had to go down the NHS route – unfortunately I wasn't offered anything privately – and I missed one game. I had it operated on, missed that [game], and played in a cast for the rest. I love football, I'm probably daft enough to continue playing whatever the weather.'

But she knew that was partly because of the stage she was at in her playing career, acknowledging that she could well be in the final years of being able to compete at a high level, and as a self-employed consultant she had some measure of control over her schedule. For younger players, playing through injury would be tougher to take, particularly if they also had to balance it with study or an entry-level job.

'I had actually had a message from someone in response to the crowdfunding page, from a girl who plays football in a lower league but is actually a surgeon,' she revealed. 'She said, "I feel like you're trying to put a band-aid on a bigger problem." I said, "In all honesty I am." For me as a player within this club, for these three girls, I just want to help them, that's all I want to do. I want them to feel like there's hope because at the moment the girl who's been injured for weeks on end, she's still no closer to her operation; the girl who's done [the same injury] three times, she's obviously beside herself; and then the girl where the NHS have said, "Do you know, I've never seen anything like that, I'm not sure how we'd go about treating it, yet I really do hope you make it back to football." I really do want to give them a sense of feeling that someone is actually fighting for you.'

* * *

One of the issues with the serious injuries to the Championship players was that as part-timers they were not entitled to full union membership.

'Where do we draw the line of how we support players who are injured. Does it come from the PFA? Does it come from the FA? If clubs haven't got that money, where does it come from?' asked London Bees' Katie Wilkinson rhetorically.

'You look at Bees at the minute. We've had injuries here and there. If it carries on the way it's going, we ain't going to be able to put a starting 11 out, so at what point should the FA be saying in [licensing] applications [to compete in the WSL or the Championship] a club should be able to support any player who does get injured and they'll pay the fees for that?'

Wilkinson had been a member of the PFA during her spell at Birmingham City and had tried to renew it on joining Villa, but was unable to – although she was told that she would be considered a member anyway.

'It seems like you don't have to pay your [membership] fee – you're entitled to it,' she explained. 'Once you're a member, that's it. But I didn't realise the PFA supported you with operations and stuff. If I'd have known that, would I have been covered? I don't know. I was in the league below so whether they'd have covered that I'm not sure. But if all these people that have once been a professional footballer and are still a PFA member just because they've been a member for one year, and are still getting the support from the PFA, why is it so difficult to allow another ten teams to have their players as PFA members?'

Indeed, these kinds of problems received additional media attention when national newspapers reported that the standard WSL contracts were set up to allow clubs to release players should they incur an injury or illness which kept them out of action for three months – a very small amount of time considering the length of recovery that may be required for a serious football-related injury, and especially compared to the contracts in the men's game, where players would receive up to a year's notice of intent to terminate their contract if they were absent for 18 months. The FA responded to criticism by saying that the clauses were necessary for women's football at this point, describing them as a 'bespoke measure to support the sustainability of elite level women's football in England'. They assured observers that these clauses would be reviewed – and that they had been initially written with the help of the PFA.

Certainly the FA were right to have a certain amount of wariness; for all the increased publicity centring on the top names in women's football, the sustainability of the club set-up, particularly with a fully professional top tier, had yet to be proven still. With the repeated and rapid changes in the domestic league structure, and the relatively truncated seasons along with big gaps between matches, it was difficult to tell which strategies had actually reaped success. As such, it should perhaps not be entirely surprising that external companies and men's clubs alike have been reticent to invest money in women's teams until they have been convinced that there might be some return – whether financial or a less tangible benefit, such as community engagement.

Millwall Lionesses were more settled after a new board of directors had assumed control of the club, and Chris

Phillips and Pedro Martinez Losa had taken over the reins of the squad, but money was still in short supply for many teams.

One national newspaper splashed a story across its pages in September revealing that Crystal Palace players had been asked to raise their own sponsorship to cover their costs; apparently that paper had been expecting shock and horror from readers, when in the women's game it is well known that sponsorship on a relatively small scale is essential – and when players are not fully professional, match fees (essentially 'paying to play') are still required.

More than that, however, the story was not quite right, suggesting that Crystal Palace Ladies required each player to contribute £250 – either through sponsorship, or from their own pockets.

But a source close to the club explained in October that the story that ran in the national media was not quite accurate, and, as she understood it, the request for contributions applied only to some members of the development side after a league restructure affected their funding.

'The men's club are very good,' she said. 'It's important for the women's side that we go out and seek our own sponsorship.'

Even more headlines were grabbed a few days later when star of the men's side Wilfried Zaha wrote a sizeable cheque to fund the women.

'It's amazing that he did that out of his own pocket,' said a Palace Ladies first-team player. 'It's so generous of him to do that to ensure that these girls haven't had to pay their registration fee or the money for their kit – but it is quite common for players to go and get their own kit sponsorship.'

This player revealed that she did not pay and had never paid a single penny to represent the side – everything was covered for her, including travel and accommodation for away games, along with a wage.

'There's nothing wrong with the club – if anything, they're going above and beyond to make sure they're pushing us on in this league,' she added.

* * *

Barnsley manager Chris Hamilton was quietly, undemonstratively content with the way his team had responded to a shaky start to the season; they had strung together some wins, going unbeaten through the months of October and November.

'They've been brilliant,' he said. 'Obviously some of the results weren't going our way the first four games, but the performances were good, and then it's just clicked for them now they've got that first win, and they've just kept it going – they've been brilliant.'

He, Glossop and the squad had not done anything differently after the disappointing results; they had talked about the performances and agreed they did not want to spend their season discussing their bad fortune, or how they really should have won their matches. Hamilton was certainly happy in his new role, despite the hours in the car.

'I'm not minding the travel, to be honest,' he said. 'It is long, but I get to plan my sessions and think about the games. It's actually a good time to reflect, to be honest.'

He knew that there had been too much hype around their pre-season results, and that for a squad that avoided relegation by a goal last time around, the objectives ought to be a little more down to earth.

'When I go to board meetings we talk about a certain area where we'd like to finish, but when I speak to the players we are literally just taking every game that comes up and trying to win it,' he explained. 'Teams that play in this league, they all seem to beat each other, so you're not going to have a team that's going to win every single game. As long as we keep ticking our results off, we'll just see where we end up.

They had 17 points at the end of last season, and we've got 18 now after ten games, so we've smashed that already. It's setting little targets like that along the way, and it seems to be working.'

Hamilton praised the professionalism of his team – despite the fact that they were all resolutely amateur. Most of the squad were aged under 25, with a few teenagers progressing from the development set-up.

'It's honestly a fantastic place to be,' he said. 'I enjoy going to take the sessions, and the assistant manager enjoys it as well. The players look happy at training, they're having a laugh and a joke, then as soon as the warm-up starts they get their professional heads on. It's a happy place to be.'

As always, others were drawn to their success, and Hamilton was especially pleased that the local media had started to cover the women's matches.

'That's coincided with us winning seven in a row,' he admitted. 'I don't know how much they would have done [without that run of results], but now everything's going right they want to be part of it.'

So all that Hamilton and his team needed to do was keep winning.

He chuckled.

'That's not hard, is it?'

* * *

It was a surprisingly warm December day in South Yorkshire, although light grey crowds hung ominously over the hills, pregnant with the threat of a swift change in weather. The previous 24 hours had seen a downpour of freezing rain as well as gusting winds, blustering all over the United Kingdom as a result of Storm Diane, and forcing the postponement of plenty of fixtures in the women's football calendar.

That wasn't the case in Barnsley. The Ladies were all set for a match on the astroturf. It was not, however, a competitive game. Although they had had a County Cup match scheduled, their opponents had forfeited a few days previously. Hamilton had been quick to get on the phone and arrange a friendly with Wolves Women – an encounter he was sure would prove more valuable in terms of learning about his players and keeping them playing at the top of their game prior to the Christmas break.

Director Natalie Jackson was in the stands, with her baby Lexie. Since taking on her position, she had also assumed the responsibility for the club's marketing, and had big plans for the future.

'Marketing is where I think my strengths are, because it's about managing the message that we want to put out,' she explained. 'Women's football has come a long way since I was a kid. My walls were covered in posters of the Man United team and it didn't cross my mind that they were men, but it also didn't cross my mind that I could play football, so I never asked to play football. I never looked for a team, I never asked my parents, I watched a heck of a lot of football with my dad, I probably watched two football matches a week on telly, it didn't cross my mind that it wasn't women.

'So I'm keen with everything we do here to create a different world for the girls that I coach, and for Lex.'

Jackson's business partner, a former Olympic athlete, was keen to introduce Lexie to different sports; Jackson admitted that if her daughter were actually aware of sports at all, she did not even know that men also played football yet.

'Every week, with her around, I'll be watching the *Women's Football Show* [the BBC's regular magazine show], and she's down here – this is probably the tenth game she's been to since she was born – and she's been to the women's England game, so actually everything that she sees is women's football,' she said. 'She won't think it's weird, and I'm going to make a point not to say, "Look, it's women playing football!" and I don't want anything at Barnsley Women FC to border on that. That's 20 years out of date for me, and it should be even more out of date.'

Jackson had taken her girls' team to the England match as well as her baby, and had thoroughly enjoyed the atmosphere, contrasting it with a big men's fixture, and thinking it was a great way to get children engaged with football more broadly as well as Barnsley specifically, which she thought was part of her job as director.

'The key things that I've tried to do so far with the marketing for the first team has been about increasing the fan base, because I think there probably wasn't very much of a fan base to speak of before this season, and it's growing now,' she said. Part of that was building the links between the 13 junior teams at the club and the senior first team, and she was really pleased that her charges could name their favourite Barnsley Women player.

Instead of the usual selection boxes for Christmas, Jackson had got the girls an issue of a women's football magazine, partly because she knew they would love to read it, and partly to send an important message to parents, showing them that media coverage for the sport did exist and could be accessed easily if they knew where to look.

'The first thing they say to me at training sometimes is a fact about a female footballer that they've found out – I love that!' she smiled. 'So yeah, I think a big part of my role and the role of marketing for the club is to create a fan base, tell people that we're here, and link up with the junior teams in a way that lets them have these guys,' she gestured at the pitch, 'as role models because I think a lot of people from my generation missed that.'

Jackson's day job meant that she was much in demand as a public speaker, and she and her company had launched a campaign to promote more equal media coverage for women's sport, with the tagline 'See Sporty, Be Sporty' – with the intent that if girls saw women playing sport, they would be more likely to participate in it themselves. They were now working with schools to raise the profile of sport for girls and women – and to increase the opportunities for their female pupils so they were treated just like the boys. She knew this would be a massive challenge, because it entailed not just getting buy-in from senior staff, but also changing some deeply-held stereotypes for some people.

'A lot of people will say, "Oh, we treat girls and boys exactly the same." My answer is that given what we know from 'See Sporty, Be Sporty', and the media research that we've done, actually if you're treating girls and boys exactly the same, you're treating them very differently, because the world is treating them differently. We are still bringing girls up as girls, and boys up as boys – if we ever find a situation where people are just people rather than girls and boys, that would be my ideal, but actually that's not the way it is. Whilst the world is still not treating girls and boys the same in sport, my view is that schools shouldn't be treating girls and boys the same in sport. We have some primary schools saying things like, "We offer football to girls and boys." We're still not at a point for me where that's treating them with equity. We might be treating them the same – but that's not giving them the same opportunity.'

Jackson wanted teachers and parents to think about several everyday situations that might be restricting sporting chances for girls – for instance, how classes were divided when group work was necessary.

'Are we splitting boys and girls up? Sometimes that's appropriate but actually I think a lot of the time we're split into girls and boys because we haven't thought of a better way – it's easy. Are there other ways we could split them that aren't saying girls and boys are different?'

She also pointed to the way sporting achievement was recognised in schools – sometimes with photographs displayed in school receptions.

'A picture is worth a thousand words. What message is it sending if in our newsletter or up on walls or in reception we do only have pictures of boys, which unfortunately is what we see sometimes in schools? The other thing, sometimes we've got pictures on the wall of a boys' football team and we're calling it the Year 6 or Year 7 football team. Any message like that is making a sport a default male.'

Of course, the governing bodies of the sport also did that. The men's Premier League has no gender identification; the Women's Super League does. The men's World Cup does not; the Women's World Cup does.

'The gamechanger would be if they started calling the men's teams men's teams,' said Jackson with a serious look.

Barnsley had recently received an email from a local school asking them if they would be able to send down a couple of players to talk about getting involved in sport – and they wanted both male and female footballers to attend if possible.

'I think that's brilliant!' she enthused. 'It's exactly what we need, and it's exactly what the players need. There's an opportunity now with this generation of players, where they aren't coming from the generation that I was coming from. Most of these players have played their whole lives, and it's been fairly accessible to them in a way that it wasn't quite as accessible to my generation. I hope that by the next generation it'll be even easier. We've got hundreds of girls down at Tuesday night training, so it's very straightforward if you're in Barnsley to join a girls' team now. It's as easy as it is for boys. It is important to get role models, it is important to treat these players as professionals, in a sense; they're not second-class citizens playing football. We need to give our first-team players the opportunity and also the responsibility of being role models for others, because that will help them be the best versions of the players they can be.'

But the Barnsley Ladies were not professionals. They were amateurs, giving up their free time to play, and not receiving any financial reward. Nor were they receiving any money to go and speak to schoolchildren, or attend their prize-givings; nor to mentor one of the junior teams, which each of the first-team players was doing.

'I fully appreciate it isn't their job, and I don't want to make it their job,' Jackson acknowledged. 'They play football because they enjoy it, but also I think they are getting something out of it, and I love that.'

Jackson herself was also a volunteer, as were her fellow directors, and the local student who had just taken on some of the work of managing the club's media, both online and in print.

'We're all here because we want to make a difference to women's and girls' football in Barnsley,' she said, 'and actually there are a lot of people maybe studying for things who want to get more experience, and it's a really exciting time to be part of something that will develop and will be important in the next five to ten years.

'We are all just volunteers, we are all here because we want to make a difference, and I think that does show through in how much we've achieved so far. There's a lot we still want to do.'

* * *

Barnsley Ladies had grown thanks to the efforts of volunteers over the previous decade or so. Rachel Jardine had handled the majority of the club's paperwork since her nine-year-old daughter had started playing for one of the junior sides. Then, Barnsley had only had four girls' teams and two for adults, but a cursory web search had suggested that might be the best fit for Jardine's daughter, who had lost interest in tap and ballet classes and wanted to try something else.

'She pretty much signed up the first night we went,' recalled Jardine, 'and then because I was a single parent at the time it was my job to take her to training, my job to take her to matches, and I just got more and more involved.'

First she served as treasurer, and then took on the role of club secretary; with only a handful of teams the administration was reasonably straightforward, but as the club grew so did the workload. Jardine's efficiency was obvious and observed, leading to invitations to help run the girls' league itself as well. Working full-time in the supply side of a global lingerie brand, she found herself trying to get her football tasks done in her breaks or lunch hour, and it ate into her evenings as well, stopping her from pursuing her own favourite sport – long-distance running.

'It was just getting to the point – because I wanted to spend my evenings going to running club – I didn't have the time to grow the football club any further,' she said. It was at that point that she stepped back from her involvement in the club, handing over most of her duties to people with more spare time, although she remained treasurer. She had handed over plenty of plans to take forward, including more pitch space and a clubhouse, as well as a close relationship with the community department of the men's club, which gave the women a page in the matchday magazine, and was really proud of what had been achieved.

'It was sad to have to let it go, but I thought it was time for fresh people to come in with fresh ideas,' she said.

Even so, she was still combining her love of running with her commitment to the club; she had completed the London Marathon three years on the spin, most recently raising money for Barnsley Ladies, with the aim of covering the cost of a defibrillator on site.

Jardine's daughter was now grown-up – 20 years of age – and no longer played, although she managed a side of her own. A decade on, Jardine was also able to answer a question – had she been interested in football at all before her little girl pulled on a pair of boots?

'No!' she laughed. 'No.'

10

Rising East

IT WAS the week before Christmas, and Danielle Griffiths had nipped out of the office for a quick coffee in the Liverpool Street station complex.

It was chilly, but not yet icy, and most of the bars in the area were full to the brim of revellers, even at 5pm, before work officially finished for the day.

Griffiths was intending to go back for another few hours of work after her swift break.

'I'm off tomorrow because I need to go Christmas shopping,' she was quick to point out. 'I think most people in my office have still got Christmas shopping to do.'

She was scheduled to have two weeks of holiday over Christmas, going back on the first working day in January, but knew she would have her laptop with her and that she would be checking emails before the turkey got cold. As always, she pointed to the number of her team-mates who had tougher and more important jobs than hers, but she did admit that hers did rely on a lot of long hours when other people would not be expecting to work; there was no such thing as a working schedule, and she needed to be contactable whenever a client wanted her.

Fortunately, over the festive season, she would not have a packed fixture list with her Leyton Orient side; a winter break gave them all a break from playing. With amateurs, the schedulers were kind; players needed time with their families and were likely to travel.

'We're a ridiculously international team, so everyone flies off to these exotic locations – Panama, Spain, America – for their Christmas holiday,' she explained, and then laughed as she counted out the number of players who would not be able to attend a match at the end of December. 'You'd probably just have me turning up on Sunday!'

Not only that, it would be difficult to find pitches able to hold up to the vagaries of the weather; Orient had been through a spell a couple of years previously when they had an extended break because of a series of waterlogged or frozen pitches, and, a few weeks prior, they had an away trip cancelled due to excessive rainfall.

Nonetheless, Orient were still near the top of the table, and Griffiths had her eyes on league leaders Crawley and Billericay, who she thought had benefitted from the changes to the top of the domestic competition.

'A lot of the players in the Championship have come down to the third [tier], and a lot of the players from the third have come down to our league, so Billericay and Crawley have done really well with that,' she said.

'The standard is higher, it's pushing everyone else on. Billericay and Crawley are the two teams who got promoted into our league, and they're the ones that have raced ahead. At the start of the season we were thinking we were in with a chance if we do what we did last year – actually we need to keep improving.'

Orient themselves had recruited a few new players, although not too many. Two of the additions to the squad were women Griffiths knew from some years back.

'Hannah Porter, who joined last year – I played with her when I was at Colchester, we came through from the centre of excellence all the way up to the ladies' team,' she explained, 'and Kat Nutman, who's just joined, she was at Colchester. She's a few years younger than us, but I played with them both, so it was nice to see them.'

They had slotted in well to the squad, and the team were currently fourth in their division, although they had not yet faced top-of-the-table Crawley, which Griffiths thought would be a real test. She was enjoying captaining a side that was taken seriously by the men's club.

'Having the same kit – women's fit kit – as the men; going to the games; being part of the presentation awards; having our match reports on the men's website; being in the men's programme; having a dedicated reporter who comes to all our games, it all just feels a bit more professional, really,' she said, adding that more and more fans were attending the women's matches, even away games.

'It was mums and dads only in the crowd [before the club became part of Leyton Orient],' she explained, thinking back to when they were known as Kikk, and ran the club entirely by themselves. 'Now mums and dads have got better things to do because we're all grown up! A few seasons ago, before we were Leyton Orient, we had no fans really, we didn't have a following, we were an independent club, so to have a core group of people who all know our names …'

She trailed off. She was clearly thinking about the old days, when they were that independent club. Did she feel like anything had changed for the worse since becoming part of Leyton Orient?

'No.'

She was insistent. Leyton Orient Women might be part of that club, but they were a team with their own identity, run by players for players. 'We obviously abide by all the rules Leyton Orient want us to follow with their brand, which is correct, and we make sure we do that, but we still decide how we want our women's club to run.'

Griffiths previously mentioned that she was thinking about what she might do after she opted to stop playing, and wondered whether her day job and her footballing career plus her captain's responsibility as a role model might have given her a few ideas.

'As part of my job I work with schools as part of our corporate responsibility, and I was always be interested in giving young people ideas about what they might be able to do in future,' she said, thinking about her own experience as a little girl and knowing that professional football was not a career option in England, and how that had changed for the next generation. 'I really enjoy that, going to events, handing out medals, things like that, it's exciting. It's changed the game for them. Whether I'm ready to be a coach or a manager yet, it's probably a long way off, I've not had time to do any of my badges – unsurprisingly perhaps.'

She was expecting that one day she might be a parent, and if her children started to play football, she had already considered that she would probably end up getting involved whether she liked it or not.

'Yes, kids are in my life plan – not yet,' she was quick to say, wondering whether motherhood would be the thing that ended her playing career, or whether she would want to come back to football afterwards. 'I played against Katie Chapman after she'd had three kids! She scored two goals against us. We were like, "You're ridiculous." I'm not sure I'd be bouncing back after I have a family. You never know. People seem to think I won't be able to give it up.

'It'll be a loss. I'm sure I'd find plenty of things to do, but whether they would fill the gap, the social aspects of it … I love hanging out with the girls, it's so much fun.'

It would not just be a loss, it would be a complete lifestyle change. Griffiths had spent her entire adult life and most of her teenage years playing football at an incredibly high level. Her weekends and holidays, plus her weekday evenings, were all organised around it.

'Two-thirds of my life,' she nodded. 'It's scary. I'm naturally competitive, and it's my kind of relief from the stresses of day to day, so if I wasn't doing football I'd have to do something similar.'

Griffiths had a ring on the fourth finger of her left hand; her wedding was planned for six months' time, at the end of May. Theoretically, that was the close season, but she had a wry smile on her face as she acknowledged that it was possible that cup runs and weather postponements might extend the season a few weeks, clashing with her marriage, and meaning that her team-mates would attend that rather than play.

'Chris would kill me,' she grinned.

* * *

Before Orient Women got on to the Stepney Green astroturf for training at the start of January, other teams were completing their sessions. There was one large squad, running around with enthusiasm – a group of young girls, rowdy and excited – and one smaller squad, intent and focused – their mothers, who had decided to try out the game for themselves.

First of the Orient set-up to arrive was as always Chris Brayford, dragging the large bags full of kit, equipment and folders with session plans. He had not been best pleased with his team's performance on the previous weekend, when they lost 3-2 at home to Stevenage.

'The first half-hour, we played them off the pitch,' he fretted. One of his players had suffered what looked to be a serious knee injury, and that substitution affected the rest of the team. 'Even though the player we brought on played great, it wasn't her fault in the slightest, we kind of lacked a little bit of confidence, missed chances, it's one of those ones you spend a bit of time shedding a metaphorical tear – and then you start thinking, "For a chunk of that game, we were ten times better than them." It's frustrating that we didn't get the result, but at least we know. We played Tottenham last season, and you play certain teams and you think they're just a better team. Those defeats never hurt, it's the defeats where you're thinking, "How?"'

Brayford had not brought in many new players. His squad had done well in the previous years, and he wanted to give them the opportunity to succeed. If someone were to join them, they would need to fit in to both the style of play and the spirit of the squad.

'It was interesting in the summer, because we had trials, and we had a lot of quality players, but we didn't want to bring people in and give them false promises and stuff,' he said. 'The vast majority, we said to them, "If you come in, you'll be playing for the development." There were two or three we were working to sign, and actually of those two or three one's starting in the Championship for Millwall Lionesses. They were good. We could easily have brought 20 players in, and [then if a player does not get in the first team she thinks], "Oh, the manager doesn't rate me, that's why I don't get in." I think it's much better that we've got faith in them and they've got to perform. They never performed on Sunday, so they can do better, but they didn't become bad players overnight.'

The huddle outside the tall fences encasing the pitches grew as the Orient women began to arrive. Goalkeeper Jette Larsen was there for the first time, having watched the match on Sunday. She was looking to join the club for the rest of the season, moving to east London from Denmark as part of her course of study, social education.

'She played national league in Denmark,' explained Brayford. 'Social education, is that like social work or sociology?'

'I don't know how to explain it in English,' replied Larsen. 'We're working with children, and the line that I'm in is from zero to five years. In Denmark it's just before they go to school that we're working with them.'

'That's a very hard job,' mused Brayford. 'I have nieces and nephews who are under five – very entertaining but I wouldn't want to be psychologically understanding them, I'm not clever enough!'

Larsen had left a five-year-old niece behind in Denmark too.

'One of the things that my niece was saying to me before I came over here – "Why are you doing this?" And I was just looking at her.

'"Why am I doing what?"

'"Why are you going to London for six months without me?"

'"Because I want to?"

'She was just, "No. You will miss me and I will miss you."'

Larsen had been seeking a club in London ever since she had heard about her trip, even though she had not known where exactly she would be living. She found herself a flat in Limehouse, and took herself out for a walk one day; her route happened to take her past Mile End Stadium.

'I went in and asked if they had a women's team here and that was it,' she said. 'I just want to play.'

One of the youngest members of the squad was 18-year-old Camila Pescatore. She was living in west London and commuting across for training and matches, but did not want her stay in England to be a particularly long one; while working in a chain coffee shop she was also applying for scholarships to study and play in the United States. New to the team in the summer of 2018, she was also new to the country, emigrating with her entire family to the UK from Venezuela, which had interrupted her professional career.

'I'd finished school already in 2017 – just when I was finishing they were starting the professional league,' she said. She had started to play as a six-year-old alongside a group of boys who had been playing together for the previous 12 months.

'It was quite difficult at the beginning,' she said. 'I had to get used [to it] and win my spot in the team and when I finally made it, actually my first practice I went to the coach and told him, "They won't pass the ball to me, what should I do?" And he said, "Earn it. You have to earn the ball."

'That's what I did, and then I became the captain of the team eventually, so it was progress for me.'

Meanwhile, striker Sophie Le Marchand was using her time before training wisely, grabbing her team-mates and asking them to do short video interviews that she could post on the club's social media accounts. This important work was interrupted by a yell.

'Let's go!' shouted Danielle Griffiths, who had been watching the time and called her squad on to the astroturf as soon as the clock ticked over to 8pm. It was a freezing cold January night in east London, with the bright lights of Canary Wharf dulled slightly by the encroachment of the Crossrail construction project, building floodlights right up against the pitch.

* * *

It was much warmer four days later, when Orient hosted Luton Town Ladies at Mile End. Goalkeeper Larsen was in the stands, in a tracksuit and long warm coat. In the middle of training on Wednesday she had spent some time with the physio, who had been taking a look at her knee.

This was no new injury. Larsen was another player who had suffered a cruciate ligament tear. This had happened early on in her career, and 12 years later she was still feeling the effects. It was another incident that was entirely accidental; her foot had caught in a dip in the pitch.

'I could just feel it right away that there was something wrong,' she remembered. 'I was trying to get up, and I put my foot down – my knee was just going like this.' She gestured with her hands, indicating looseness.

'When I was laying down and my coach came over, the first thing I said was, "Don't touch my knee," because I could just feel it right away.'

The injury had happened just a few minutes before half-time and Larsen was hopeful that she might be able to continue after gathering herself.

'I told the ref, "Oh, I just need to run a bit," and then I got up, and tried to run, and my knee was just going like that again' – she repeated the movement with her hands – 'and I was like, "OK, fine, no." One of the coaches that was on the team was looking at me and called the ambulance to get me.'

But it still took several months before she got a diagnosis. The injured knee had been treated by putting it in a brace, allowing the ligaments to begin to mend while the joint was immobilised. Larsen spent six weeks on the sidelines, and once the pain had gone she decided she might as well begin training again. After that went well, she returned to the starting 11. Her pre-match warm-up was fine. Once the whistle blew, her knee gave way again.

'In the first minute, I was going out to kick the ball away, and that time I could just feel my knee was just doing something,' she said, 'and there was just pain afterwards. I was looking out for my coach. I couldn't play any more.'

She returned to hospital, where the doctors suggested it was an anterior cruciate ligament tear as well as a problem with the meniscus. Six months later they took a closer look through surgery, fixing some of the initial injury.

'It was not that big of an operation,' she said. 'They said to me, "You can live with just one ACL, just have the right training and so on."'

That meant plenty of rehab in the gym, and Larsen committed to it.

'I was at the fitness centre doing some of the things that I had to, I was on a bicycle, and my knee didn't do anything, it just locked, and I fell down on that bicycle because my foot was locked on the pedal – I couldn't get out,' she said. 'My trainer who was there was just standing and looking – then she came running because I was crying, I had hit my head on the other bicycles! She said, "You know what, you need to have the ACL operation.'"

She had the full reconstructive surgery, a year after she had first suffered the injury. Of course the operation caused physical problems, but it also affected her psychologically; she did not even want to walk on to a football pitch, and certainly did not want to return to the ground where the injury happened in the first place. Instead, she decided to go back to playing basketball, a sport she had enjoyed when she was younger, and after some time she tried football once more, just for fun.

She still found herself in pain, though, but had chosen to ignore it as best she could.

'When I have to do the goal kick, I can't do it – there is something in my head that's blocking it,' she said. 'Even though I have played national league in Denmark, I have always got one of the defenders to do it.'

It was a tentative performance that Larsen was watching unfold in front of her. Orient looked timid in front of goal, although their build-up play remained excellent and incisive. It was clear that this was a psychological problem rather than anything to do with their team or their tactics. An unfortunate own goal, as the Luton defender attempted to clear the ball off the line, looked set to be the only strike that would put the hosts ahead at the interval; multiple shots on target and goalmouth scrambles proved unfruitful.

That was until a few minutes before half-time. The relief was obvious. Chloe McNee took a chance on herself and had a shot on goal from inside her own half; clearly it was a goal nobody had expected, but one that everyone was delighted to see. Camila Pescatore, who had come on as a first-half substitute, scored Orient's third of the afternoon after skipping down the right wing. Not only did it mean an instant response to the disappointing result against Stevenage the weekend before, but it also meant three points that moved Orient up to third in the league table.

Pescatore left the club soon afterwards. She had achieved her dream of an athletic scholarship to the United States, courtesy of an agency who had circulated her video highlights to colleges across the country, enabling her to study and play football to a high level.

'They wanted me to come in February – it all happened really quick!' she said via Skype. She was enjoying being able to select which courses she took every semester, allowing her space to train every morning from 7am, then head to the gym for weight training two hours later, before going to the classroom. She was also studying for the first time in two years – and in her second language. She was grateful to her tutor for her patience, and was proud that she was passing all her courses so far.

'I'm tired – I had six months without doing training every day!' she admitted. 'When I was in England we trained only once a week. I'm getting used to it, but it's nice, I really like it, I really like the team. The girls are all nice, and it's a really international team, we have girls from Brazil, New Zealand, Mexico, Spain – lots of nationalities.'

She spoke or FaceTimed with her family every day if possible, and added that her mother was liable to cry during these calls ('they are happiness tears!' she explained); and she also kept in touch with her Orient team-mates. She was still on all the group chats, and followed their progress via social media on matchdays.

'I was really sad, I felt like I left in the best moment [of the season so far],' she said. 'I was getting on so well with my team-mates, I had made new friends, I was getting into it. That feeling of leaving in the middle of the season, when we were doing really well, it was really sad. I didn't cry – but I was sad!'

* * *

One of Orient's senior players had stepped back from the club altogether the previous year. Olympia Diamond, a cross-Atlantic transplant, had served as liaison for new players, taking on the responsibility of welcoming any newcomers and helping them to settle in to the group. Now her boots were well and truly in storage.

Partly it was due to circumstance. She had spent a year commuting to Liverpool for work, and although she made it back to London for most weekends, she did not get a great deal of time on the pitch.

'I was like, "I'd like to still be part of the team," and having been a coach before in the US, I'm quite pragmatic – I'd like to still play but I can't come to training so I'm well aware of the fact that I might not start, I'm not expecting anything, so I did that for that season, and it was really hard, I'll be honest,' she recalled. 'It was really hard just for travel. In theory, it was good but in terms of reality, in terms of where we were as a team, it wasn't really an ideal situation. A couple of times because I wasn't playing a lot I was like, "I'll play for the development," and Chris was like, "No, you want to come down and be part of the team, we want you there," but I wasn't really playing, and it turned out our development team at that time wasn't really well organised yet. It was a tricky season that way because I didn't get to play a lot in terms of football, but it was important in terms of being part of the group of women who I've been friends with since I moved to this country. That was a really big season for us because we won the triple and got promoted. I'm really glad that I stayed and kept going, but from a personal perspective it was challenging. I didn't really get any football that season.'

She had looked for a club in Liverpool, but that proved more difficult than she had expected. There were no teams in the city centre, and without a car she could not commute to any of the clubs on the outskirts. She would have been happy with a recreational league or simply training with a side, rather than expecting to join somewhere of an equal standard to Orient, but she found it impossible. When she returned to London permanently in August of 2017, theoretically she was able to pick up where she left off as a player. Instead, she found herself in a new and challenging role – asked to take on the position of player-manager of the development team.

'I had been an assistant coach in my previous career path for a couple of years, and Chris thought it would be a good way for me to get back into things, since I hadn't really played that much in the previous season,' she said. 'I do really like coaching, so I was down to give that a go, and it turned out to be really fun, actually, and it was really hard. It was fun in terms of me getting to come up with training sessions and things – that's my favourite bit, actually, coming up with themes for training and how it was going to benefit, and organising teams, I get super into that kind of stuff – but it was really hard, it was really, really hard.

'At first Chris was trying to do both sessions, which was fine, but then obviously more and more people show up, and he can't organise a training session for both teams because you do have quite a level difference, but also like realistically when you've got to prep for a game, you're playing completely different competitions. For the first team, the preparation and training session that he needed to do is not at all appropriate for the game that we're going to have on the following weekend, as well as personnel. Someone who I have on my team who I'm going to be playing as an attacking right mid, if they were playing on the firsts, that's not where they would play, so realistically that's not a good system. So as the season progressed I started taking the development more for training sessions, which I really enjoyed, like I said, because I like doing training sessions, but in a personal sense it was a really good challenge.'

Diamond was getting to training on time and loving being back on the pitch as well as coaching – but she still had issues with work, even though her new job was in London. She had a lengthy trip on public transport from her new home in north-west London to her new job in north-east London, and then she travelled down to east London for training and for home matches before heading home again.

'It was a pain in the ass, I'm not going to lie,' she admitted. 'And then on the weekends the development team plays at Hackney Marshes. Luckily some of the other women on the team had cars and they'd take the nets and corner flags and stuff, and I'd have all the kit and medical stuff and someone else would take game balls most of the time, which was nice, so we spread that stuff around, which was good, but yeah, from where I live, Hackney Marshes is a pain to get to. It's awkward to get there in general. Even home games were away games for me.'

Her fiancé booked her on to an FA coaching course as a birthday gift, which she loved, but as she continued her work with the development squad she found plenty of admin as well as tough tactical decisions.

'I'm glad I did it for the year, being player-manager, but it was really hard because there's so much to do in terms of paperwork and organisation and planning, and, being a player-manager, it's really hard to make those judgements of like who's starting, who's coming off, subs, calling out subs during the game, making sure everyone's coming off – "I've got to sub this person at this time, is this enough time?" You know what I mean? That kind of thing – plus pre-game making sure you've filled out your form and making sure everyone has their cards and you've got to set up the nets before the game, there's so much!'

In her previous coaching roles, she had been an assistant, meaning that ultimately decisions did not lie with her. Now, they did.

'All of a sudden it was like getting thrown in the deep end,' she said. 'For me it was a really good environment to do it in. We had a lot of new players, the development team had a lot of new players, but in terms of the people who had been there, I'd known them for years, so I think there was a level of trust. Being a player as well and still playing with them, I felt like we were doing this together: this is what the plan is, this is the team and this is who's starting. I tried to make clear, "This is what I'm considering when I choose people," and I tried to talk to people after games and I tried to keep it all open and discursive as well. My brain was working all the time.'

The deliberation and the dedication paid off, though. After struggling the season before, Diamond led her development team to promotion, missing out on the Championship by a point. Nonetheless, she felt that was the right time to retire completely from competitive football – as both a player and a coach.

'I've been playing since I was six so it was a big decision, but it was weird,' she said. 'I was doing well and I did well in the season, and I was very kindly voted one of the players' players of the year, which I take as a massive compliment considering I was also coaching them, they don't have to do that, that means I didn't piss them off too much! That was massive, that meant a huge amount. But when I was on the pitch I didn't care like I used to, and that's not saying I didn't care to win, I want to win, but I didn't care if I did well or not. I had no impetus to keep getting better, if that makes sense. In every game I've thought, like, "How can I improve?" and before a game I'd set goals for myself, what I want to achieve and how we're going to work in this formation, things like that I really engage with. And now I'd go on to the field and I'd be there and be like, "Someone else will want this more than me." I'm happy to run around but I don't care to make myself better any more.'

Was that because she needed someone coaching her to motivate her? The question seemed to surprise her.

'That's a good point, it might be,' she mused. 'There's no one who's there assessing or critiquing me or my positioning. Yeah, could be. It was hard for me to do that for myself.'

She felt that playing and coaching both needed 100 per cent of her attention if she was to do either job as well as she wanted, and she knew that was impossible. She could not pay attention to her players' performance or any potential tactical switches simply because she was concentrating on her own tasks in the game.

'The biggest kick is when you're coaching the session and you're working on a concept and you're explaining how this works and you see someone get it – you see someone working hard and getting it,' she said. 'I see someone who's worked hard and put in the effort, then I want them to do it on the pitch. I see that and think they should get a chance. I'm happy to go off.'

Recently married, and busy with that new job, Diamond had considered giving up playing and becoming just a coach, but knowing the time commitment that would involve, she opted not to; there were other things she wanted to do with her spare time.

'I miss the girls,' she said. 'They were the first people I met when I moved here – I joined the club two or three weeks after moving to the country. I didn't have a massive social circle at the time! I miss them a lot. But I'll be honest, I don't miss schlepping across London or the south east of the country on a Sunday, I'm not going to lie, I don't miss that. I do miss playing with them and chatting and that fun at training sessions where you're joking around and playing together. I miss that with them.'

She still followed their progress, though, keeping up with their results, and she was still on their social WhatsApp chats, so she was still connected with the club, albeit at one remove. Although her studded boots were packed away, she thought she might invest in a new pair of trainers; a colleague had invited her to a kick-around in a central London mixed five-a-side team.

'It's very social, really mixed level, totally non-stressful and having Guinnesses afterwards at the pub is the main thing, which I've never done before!' said Diamond. 'I've never had just the camaraderie bit!'

* * *

Fleur Cousens was about to fly to Mexico and was missing her seasonal trip to Old Trafford in order to do so.

'With TV, you never know what your next contract is going to be,' she explained in a Shoreditch coffee shop. 'It's a perfect time to get on a plane.'

Eight days before Christmas, she had wrapped presents for the rest of the Goal Diggers committee – long-sleeved black t-shirts with the club's logo. She hoped the gifts would go some way to show how grateful she was for their work.

'I always get such an overwhelming feeling of emotion when people sign up for these roles because they're voluntary, and when you break it down, it's little things,' she said, pointing out the fiddly time-consuming nature of a job like managing the team's Facebook account. 'And what they write in the applications is so nice.'

She was hoping that in the new year a volunteer would take on a rather bigger job – finally finding a bigger pitch for training. The club's fundraising and ever-increasing membership was so successful that finances would not be a problem – they simply could not locate a pitch able to accommodate them. In the face of block bookings and lack of local authority ability to look into what space was being used and what wasn't, and what should be available to a grassroots project like Goal Diggers, Cousens was essentially powerless. She had her fingers crossed that someone with more specific expertise in the area would be able to make that major breakthrough.

'It's just so annoying,' she said. 'It just seems like we've come so far and some people don't think it's a sport for women and we're showing that it is – but we're also not being allowed to play. Back in the day [from 1921 onwards, when the FA banned women's football on affiliated pitches] we were banned from playing on pitches, and it just seems like a similar thing, because we haven't got pitch space. Now that we're trying to make it a sport for us we're just hit with these barriers that have been around for years, because these men have held on to their spaces for so long, they're not going to let go.'

It wasn't just about accommodating more players; it would also mean better quality training for the existing players, with three coaches having the space to work with three separate groups, organised into beginner, intermediate and advanced players. She pointed at the roof of a building opposite the busy Old Street roundabout.

'In America they build pitches on roofs and stuff, I'd love that!' she explained. 'It makes sense. There's no space on the ground. That would be nice.'

* * *

Ciara Monahan had joined the Goal Diggers coaching team alongside Josh Pugh when a vacancy arose. She had played in a few of their matches as a fill-in when members weren't available and had completed her coaching badges through her own 11-a-side club. Then when Cousens asked her to run a trial training session she was thrilled to be able to do so.

But coaching wasn't always her dream. In fact, she was adamant that she loved playing too much to stand on the sidelines.

'I was like, "No way do I want to stand around and coach people how to play football – I want to play football!"' she laughed. But her club director suggested she helped out at a primary school session and see how she liked it.

'I started coaching these really adorable kids – these young girls – and I was just like, "This is amazing," because I remember being that age and there was no such thing as girls-only football sessions.'

So she started her coaching badges with an eye on managing her own under-11s girls' team, and then the opportunity to coach Goal Diggers arose.

'It's like two ends of the spectrum – going from coaching 11 year olds, ten-year-old girls who have never played football before, and then coaching 30-year-old women who have never played football before,' she said.

Monahan started her own playing career as a little girl, kicking a ball around with the boys on the concrete spaces on their estate, before joining a formal team as a teenager and benefitting from the coaching of Kirsty Pealling, the Arsenal and England star. One of the drivers of her own coaching sessions was to think about what kind of drills and practices would have helped her at the same stage of her life.

'All I do all day is just watch YouTube videos about football drills and things that people will enjoy,' she admitted. 'I think being a player myself really helps because I think, "What would I want to work on? What would make me a better player?" So that's what I do in my sessions, I just think what would make people better football players, and that's what I do.'

Monahan acknowledged that coaching Goal Diggers was an unusual challenge – working with women who might never have kicked a ball before, but were hugely accomplished in their lives off the pitch. She needed to find the right tone to strike, and to target the sessions at the right kind of level.

'A lot of them are used to being really good at lots of different things, so sometimes when they come to the session and they're not so good at it they're very surprised, and they're like, "But I'm really good at things!"' she explained. 'Being 25, 26, 30 and trying to learn a completely new skill from scratch is really hard, so it's incredible. In our sessions we split based on ability, where we have an experienced group and a beginner group. That helps a lot, and there's definitely room for overlap, and interchange, and progression in that.

'When I first started coaching them I completely missed the mark and I would give them drills that were far too complicated. You really have to adapt and think, "This is like people learning a completely new language." For me who's been playing football since I was six, it's in my DNA, [but] it's completely unnatural movement for a lot of people, so I really have to slow everything down.

'One of my favourite stories is this woman who's in advertising … she turned up [to training] and looked really glamorous, she had these silver trainers on, really inappropriate for sport, and in one of her first sessions she just looked like she had no interest and she'd just been dragged along. It's four, five months down the line now and she is one of the most competitive footballers you will ever meet, like she's completely just fallen in love with it, and that's because it grabs you. Now she's so committed, she's got a new pair of football boots, she's on board. It doesn't matter what age you are, really.'

Monahan knew that the Goal Diggers ethos was a big part of helping beginners to feel welcome and encouraging them to develop their new skills, and it was something she cherished and worked hard to protect in her own sessions.

'You can feel OK to be vulnerable and learn something new,' she said. 'I know a lot of talented football players who have gone along to coaching sessions where they've just been absolutely torn to pieces by a horrible coach, and they just crumble because they're nervous and they can't learn anything because they don't feel free enough to be able to be vulnerable. I think at Goal Diggers we will take you, whatever level you are, and all we want is to make sure you have an opportunity to play football – hopefully you'll learn something – but more than anything else that you have fun when you play.'

* * *

The final member of the Goal Diggers coaching trio was Kitty Burne, an old school acquaintance of club founder Cousens. Burne began her playing career as a child, representing her county of Middlesex as a teenager, before the combination of a knee injury and exam pressures forced her to give it up. She knew she would not be able to make it as a professional footballer; even if she did find herself offered a contract, it was unlikely to be a sustainable, well-paid career. Instead she opted to volunteer at a sports centre, helping out with some football training, and decided to begin work on her coaching badges. They helped enormously when she took a gap year before going to university, when she travelled to Swaziland and coached a group of boys for two months. It was not the usual choice of activity for a teenage girl looking for work and life experience before heading into tertiary education.

'I just thought I don't want to go and do something … like building a wall, or whatever people do,' recalled Burne. 'I've actually got a skill I'm quite good at, and they'll be quite surprised to have a young girl come in and say, "Hey, guys, this is what we're going to do now – girls can also play football too."'

It was not until after university that she began to play again. She knew that Cousens's team were always happy to welcome new players, so she sent a message asking if she could come along – and also mentioned that she was a qualified coach if her skills there were ever required. She was playing five-a-side and 11-a-side matches, and training a few times a week, loving the feel of the ball at her feet.

Then during one match she took a fierce football to her face. Her head snapped back, causing a whiplash as well as the impact injury. It was a severe concussion and confined her to bed for several months. It affected her speech, causing a stammer, as well as limiting her mobility and forcing her to withdraw from the course of study she was pursuing in an effort to move into a law career.

'I had about half an hour's social energy in me every three days and other than that I just listened to audiobooks and slept,' she said.

When she began rehab, going down to matches was a welcome distraction, even if she could not participate as much as she would have liked.

'I would still go down when I was feeling up to it,' she said. 'I would still go down and watch the matches, and spend a lot of time just standing on the sidelines of a Saturday match, and gradually they said, "We need someone to cover for this game, Kitty, these are the formations, can you come along, help with subs, and be a bit of a coach for a bit?" And I said, "Yes, of course, if you need me to cover training, that's OK," so as I did that more frequently, I'm now part of the coaching rota, I help out. I play whenever I'm feeling fit, and coach when I'm not.'

Knowing her own limitations was key. Despite sustaining that concussion a year ago, she still knew she was not back to how she had been previously.

'I'm a lot, lot better than I was, [but] I still have really bad days,' she said. 'Even the last two or three weeks after Christmas I've been quite unwell and had to take time off work because I just get totally knackered. I still have headaches every day, actually.'

Even so, she felt well enough to relish her new role at the club, and the way it integrated her more into the decision-making process, working collaboratively with Pugh and Monahan to create tailored training sessions. On weeks when she was able to play, it meant that she had extra insight into what needed to be worked on – although that did create its own problems.

'If I play one week in 11s, we can talk about what had gone wrong and what we should work on in the next week's training session,' she said. 'That's when it gets a bit weird – I'll say, "OK, what we didn't quite do during the match was this, so that's what we're going to focus on."'

She laughed.

'And they'll be like, "Yeah, but you didn't do it either!"'

* * *

On the coldest weekend of the year, Goal Diggers had two full-size football teams playing matches on Clapham Common – one in a competitive league, one in a friendly. The snow had been falling in fits and starts all week, with intermittent flurries of sleet and below-freezing overnight temperatures, but bright sunshine had melted the ice, leaving the grass soggy and muddy, with puddles scattered around the playing area. The Saturday morning dogwalkers happily meandered across their usual routes, leaving heavy footprints in the mire, not realising or not caring that in a few hours the fields would be full of footballers attempting to get some kind of grip on the ground with their studded or moulded boots.

By midday, almost every piece of grass on the common was populated by a football team; here a mixed side of under-eights kicking a ball around and squealing with delight; there a match between older boys; carving out a space of their own were a group of friends, men and women, trying to find room to spread out some cones so they could try out some training drills.

The Goal Diggers squad playing the competitive fixture convened in the changing room nearest to the path arcing through the common. With high ceilings and dark wood panelling, decorated only by regular intervals of pegs to hang clothes and bags on, the room was essentially a larger, sturdier, garden shed. The women had arrived with their kit on underneath plenty of warm layers, meaning that all they needed to do prior to kick-off was peel off a coat and a fleece or two and don their boots. In the meantime, they took a seat on the benches around the changing room, ready to listen to coach Josh's team talk.

As Pugh read out who would be comprising the starting 11, each name was applauded. Cousens tried to surreptitiously eat a bar of chocolate while he went over the tactics, using a white wipe-clean board to set out formations and movement patterns.

'We've got the quality, and we've got a structure everyone seems to really understand,' Pugh told his squad. As he listed his starting line-up, each name was cheered, whooped and applauded. 'We are going to score goals. That will happen.'

There was a general hum of low-level chatter and discussion, but everyone still managed to listen and pick out exactly what their role would be; and after Pugh had finished his briefing the players had the opportunity to share their own thoughts, reflecting on their previous match (which had been a thumping 12-0 win) and what they knew of the day's opponents, warning each other of a tricky centre-forward who was likely to channel most of the attacking threat they would face.

The squad jogged out for their warm-ups, which would be more than necessary. Piling their bags on the touchline, most kept their tracksuits on, and several had layers of thermal protection under their usual playing kit, topped off by a beanie hat with the Goal Diggers logo.

Coach Kitty Burne was playing today, marshalling the midfield in the first half, and taking the precaution of wearing a head protector much like the one popularised by Arsenal goalkeeper Petr Cech after he had suffered a skull fracture. Founder Fleur Cousens was playing too, leading the line; and as with most amateur teams, the difference in physical style and appearance between each player, marking her out as an individual rather than the more identikit pro athlete, was intriguing. Cousens had run out for the warm-up with her oversized gold hoop earrings still in place; the winger was sporting a cape the colour of mustard; the right-back's manicure was perfect, nails a glossy shade of dark red, sparkling rings subtly decorating her fingers.

It was not a day for fizzing, intricate, passing football. The pitch forbade it. The ball bounced and bobbled in the mud; the players on both sides struggled to get any kind of purchase on the ground, striving to sprint but essentially wading. When a player fell to the ground following a tackle or some kind of coming together, it was obvious she required attention; nobody would feign injury and voluntarily take to the floor in these kinds of conditions.

The Diggers were 4-2 down at half-time, but they took some consolation from the excellence of their two strikes – one a perfectly weighted chip over the goalkeeper's head courtesy of Lauren Fitzgerald, the other a beautifully executed free kick curled into the net by Verity Phillips. The opposition, perhaps a more experienced eleven-a-side team, capitalised on the short stature of the Diggers goalkeeper, testing her with high balls and using their greater physicality to force errors.

Nevertheless, the Diggers ethos kept the atmosphere positive. Players switched in and out, with the onlookers wrapping themselves in their own coats as well as those of their team-mates as they tried to keep warm, the chill wind blustering across the flat common, with nowhere for spectators to shelter. Every piece of good play was applauded, every player had some encouragement shouted her way by her squadmates; it was in sharp contrast to the bellowed instructions coming from the opposite side of the pitch, where the opposition's coach urged his own team on. It was ultimately a disappointing result, but an afternoon every player enjoyed as she continued to develop her 11-a-side skills. The level of commitment to the Goal Diggers' ethos was such that even with a defeat, even in a chill wind, even swamped in inches of mud, a match was still the highlight of the week.

11

Changes

FOUR MONTHS into the new season, everyone had just about got used to the alterations in structure and names. Carol West, long-time chair of the Women's Premier League, was now the chair of the Women's National League, and had steered her leagues and clubs through a complicated time as the top-two tiers moved on from amateurism.

'I think we're in that transition – it's going to take a few seasons to settle down,' she admitted. 'We've got the clear, distinct levels now. We've got WSL which is full-time professional, we've got Championship which is semi-pro, and then we've got us, which has been renamed, we're the National League. I think the things that the FA have tried to put in place, they're not going to materialise overnight, and some people are quite short-sighted and a little bit impatient about things. We are the biggest league in the country, we've got a lot of players and a lot of clubs. We try to present a platform for competition that allows that progression through the pyramid and hopefully gets people ready, gets clubs ready and groomed – if you want to take that next step into semi-pro, into tiers one and two, then they've had a good grounding on the way up, so that's our job, I guess.'

She paused.

'We're not the Premier League any more, we're not the top tier of women's football, but we're the top of the amateur game, so this is as high as you can go without taking that step forward, and [then you have to be] either good enough in terms of a player, or you're viable enough in terms of a club to take that next step. Anybody can get to us – yes, there's criteria to be met but the criteria [are] quite low, it's more around playing facilities etc. Any team starting at the bottom of the pyramid next season, if they're good enough, if they've got the players, if they've got the infrastructure, they can get to us. There's not really any restrictions or anything to inhibit that outside of their own ability, so I think it is important that we are the top of the amateur game, and clubs have got to come through us to get higher, so we want to make sure that any clubs or players that are passing through us are playing with us to the best they can be as well. It's a very competitive league.'

West was cautious. She knew very well that there were only a certain number of spots at professional clubs, and indeed only a certain number of clubs that would ever be able to compete in a fully professional league; even ones that were brilliantly run at amateur level could potentially acknowledge that they did not have the funding or staff availability or facilities to step up to the Championship should they win promotion.

'Everyone might want to play for England one day, but it's unlikely that they will,' she said. 'There's not many people who will realise that dream, so they've got to be given somewhere to play. They still might be excellent footballers, they just might not be the very top, that's a very small percentage, so they've got to have somewhere viable and credible to play. I'd like to think the National League is run sufficiently well to support clubs and maintain and increase standards, and obviously the reserve section plays a big part in that.'

The National League's reserve competition was an initiative West was spending much of her time on. With no squad caps in the league, a club might have more players signed to them than could potentially be named in a first-team matchday set-up, so a national reserve competition was something she felt strongly about.

'We're trying to do that with a view to trying to underpin and support the first team, and give players that opportunity before first-team football,' she explained. Local leagues did not provide a high enough standard of football to prepare players for competing in the National League should they be required. 'Suddenly they're needed because of injuries or whatever to play first-team football – that gap is quite significant in some cases.'

West never forgot that those running the clubs were volunteers, just like her, giving their time to the sport they love to ensure it kept going. There were rules to follow, of course, but she avoided being officious.

'The reason I got involved in football back in the day was I didn't like how the regional league was run in terms of the committee; you turned up to a meeting, you were shouted at, you got done and you were told to leave, so that's the reason I got involved in the first place,' she recalled. 'From my perspective, we've got an open-door policy, very much; so obviously, yes, we've got the league secretary and all formal process of communications go via the right routes, but even today I've had two clubs contact me directly because they can. I know that goes against the grain in some views about how committees or football leagues should be run, but I think it's important. We do try and get to games and we are visible, people can pick the phone up, or they can ring up for a natter, or they can have a bit of a moan, whatever it is they need to do, and they know they can do that and I think that's really important. Because of that, we've got a really good relationship with the clubs by and large.'

West had been in post for some years, combining the position with her full-time job in the police service, but she still enjoyed the responsibilities of chairing the league, insisting that if she ever tired of it, or found it stressful, she would step down.

'During the day I've got my phone, I've got my iPad. If I get an email I'll answer it, if I get a phone call I'll answer that, so it's not about the slog of "I do 40 hours' work" [per week as league chairman]. When you're not doing the physical stuff of answering phone calls, emails etc, you're thinking about the stuff; you're projecting, you're thinking about next season, you're thinking about cup finals, all the stuff you have to think about. It never switches off, really, and I don't think it can – but in terms of sitting down and tapping at a laptop, there'll be several hours a week of that, but there's also a lot of discussion, a lot of chat. Obviously we meet every six weeks and we speak as a committee on the phone, and I'll talk individually on top of that.

'If I didn't enjoy it I wouldn't do it. I'm not saying it's easy, sometimes it's not easy at all, but I think between us, as a committee, in my experience, I like to think we're pretty good at what we do, which makes it a little bit easier as well.'

* * *

Nobody really expected Barnsley to reach the semi-finals of the Sheffield and Hallamshire County FA Cup. Their opponents in the last eight were Sheffield FC, a club that had spent the previous seasons in the WSL set-up, and even now were in the league above the Reds. A good performance against higher-ranked opposition would be pleasing; a win would surely be inconceivable.

Inconceivable to anyone except manager Chris Hamilton, perhaps. He was always confident his team would get a result; after a run of 11 matches unbeaten, they were second in the league, and in impressive form. He knew they would not be scared of Sheffield – not that they lacked any respect for them, but more that they were secure in their own skill. A 2-1 win took them into the final four.

'I've been to see a couple of games in the league above because I wanted to see where our level was compared to the league above, and I know if our team was in that league right now we would be easily mid-table in that league,' he reflected afterwards. 'I knew going into the game if we played the way we did and didn't play the occasion then we'd be fine, and that's kind of what happened. The feedback we've been getting after the game from people who came down to watch us for the first time – they're saying you couldn't tell who the team in the league above was, or, if you could, you would have thought it was Barnsley. So that's good to hear as well, that people are now coming to watch us and seeing the work that we're doing, and they're impressed with the girls. Yes, I'm really happy with that.'

Hamilton had been in the hot seat for six months, and the progression of the team and the club was almost difficult to believe. He reminded himself regularly that this was a team who had avoided relegation by a single goal the season prior; with such excellent form it was easy to get seduced by the idea of winning the league as well as a couple of cups for good measure.

'I think people are thinking, "Go for the league," but sometimes we just take a step back and look at where we've come from, since the summer, and what we walked into – when I first took the job and where we are now, it's incredible, really,' he said. 'This season was about trying to get a style of play for the club and trying to put my personality into the club as well, and getting the right players, making it a place where people want to play and give them something to play for.

'I think that's now where we're at, to be fair, and I think we're maybe a year ahead of ourselves. We planned to go for the league next year and wanted to get the club running the way I wanted it to be run this year, but now we are where we are, so all we can keep doing now is try and keep winning, and hope that Burnley slip up. At times we get carried away thinking, "Let's go and win the league and win both cups," but sometimes you need to take a step back and appreciate where we are now.'

Hamilton admitted that sometimes he saw his team slip into bad habits from last season, fretting over mistakes made; the way round that was to work on increasing possession and to instil more self-belief.

'When we gave the ball away cheaply was when we were panicking, and we were panicking because some of the players were thinking, "Oh, last season we would have lost this," and you invite pressure on to you, and if you give them the ball then they've got more chance of scoring, so it was just improving how we kept the ball,' he said. 'We've done that, and now they look confident, they don't look shaky. You get little lapses of five minutes in a game, or maybe ten minutes, but overall we're very confident on the ball now. The girls trust in the way we want to play and they know how to get themselves out of pressurised situations now.'

The local papers had even started taking an interest in the team now. Hamilton was shrewd enough to know that it was their success that had attracted that coverage, but nonetheless he felt it was a positive move, as was the increased number of junior players heading down to support the senior side.

'Build it and they'll follow – that's what's happening at the minute,' he said. 'The younger girls are now coming to our games – and their parents are coming. On Sunday we had the under-nines team there, which means all their parents come to the game as well because they can't get there themselves, so then you're getting them along. Then if we've got a team that's entertaining on the pitch, the parents will want their daughters to follow and stay with Barnsley all the way through and be on that pitch.'

It was a club where individual ambition could be nurtured, and Hamilton was no exception. He was just about to finish his UEFA B coaching licence, and was honest that he wanted to be a full-time football coach.

'You always need to have longer-term targets, and I do, because if I didn't then I wouldn't be as passionate as I am now,' he admitted. 'I don't want to be one of them people that settles for being a northern division one manager, because then I'm not giving the girls everything I've got, and we'll just be a mid-table team.

'I want to be full-time in football. Hopefully that's going to be with Barnsley, and keep growing the club, and we can go that way. I want it to be at Barnsley. Everybody's got ambitions. I think if you don't, that can hold you back itself.'

* * *

Hamilton thought it was better to be in the chasing pack, waiting for league leaders Burnley to drop points, and then pouncing. With only one team able to be promoted into the Premier Division, he was treating this season almost as a trial run for a promotion campaign in 2020. Wherever they finished at the end of the season, captain Lucy Turner was already satisfied with the result. She confided that she had genuinely considered giving up football in the summer of 2018 after Barnsley's disastrous season in which they avoided relegation by a single goal; the atmosphere at the club had become so toxic that she did not want to play any more.

'It were definitely an option for me,' she admitted. 'It were either I'd go somewhere else, or I was just going to stop playing and concentrate on my life outside of football, because I just didn't enjoy last year whatsoever, and it's a massive part of your life when you're training two, three times a week and playing. It were quite a big stress and I think quite a lot of people were the same. But obviously when Chris came in, I said to other clubs that came in for me that I'd always give the new people a chance, and just completely loved it from the first training session, so it were quite lucky really that I didn't have to go anywhere else.'

With the new coaches in place, and new personnel joining the squad, Turner was not expecting to remain captain either, and told them as much.

'I think [Chris] just appreciated us more than what we've had before,' she recalled. 'He knew that we needed new players, but he did it in the right way. He introduced everybody, and from the moment that they came they integrated to our team – and keeping me as captain, we had a conversation before that were decided again this year. I didn't think I were going to be the captain, and I said that to Chris. If he wanted to make anyone else the captain, it's his judgement, starting things over, clean slate and stuff. He said he appreciated the relationship I had with the players and stuff, and just wanted to keep that, try and gel everything over.

'I think because we get along with him as a person outside of football, and all the coaching staff, really, we've got to know them, and he were quite fond of doing team-building activities, and in the sessions, getting to know everyone, getting to know what they do, how many siblings they have, it's like it were more personal than what we've ever had before, which were nice – it made people be able to relate to him a little bit more than maybe what we would have with us old manager.'

Turner's day job was also at Oakwell, teaching in the Reds' Community department.

'I basically live here,' she joked. Success on the pitch meant that she was happy to go to work every day during the week – and return there at weekends to play.

'It is a good feeling, we're playing really well at the minute, and it's positive energy around the team and the girls. We're enjoying training and enjoying games at the weekend, which wasn't necessarily the case last year, so it is really nice, and it's a nice break, if you've had a tough week at work, to enjoy the games at the weekend – it's really positive.'

The problems of the previous season had weighed heavily on her at the time, but now she felt much less burdened.

'Compared to last year …' she mused. 'I was running round like an idiot trying to sort everyone out, everyone had issues that they needed to discuss before training. Trying to get that team atmosphere was nearly impossible last year, but this year everyone has just gelled, and I think that's why we're getting new players into the team from other teams – and they're noticing it is a really nice club to play for because they're your friends as well as your team-mates. There's no one that's got a hidden agenda or an ego or anything, they do it because they enjoy doing it, and they enjoy spending time with each other. That's the reason why I've stayed here for the amount of seasons that I have. It's definitely not because I work here, because I would like to see a different four walls, but I think that's a massive part of the success, the team ethic, everything like that.'

That team ethic continued to extend outside the first-team squad and included the younger age groups as well as local schools, and as the season had progressed Turner became more and more excited about the possibility that the Barnsley players might inspire girls to play football.

'We've been adding little mascots at all us games, from the age groups and things, which is really nice, because we've never had anything like that before,' she said, 'and it just creates that sense of community between the age groups and the different teams, and again we haven't had that relationship before.

'That's something that I'm really passionate about. When I were younger, I always had my sister to look up to, but other girls don't, so I think being a role model in a way like that, most of them can relate to them. When I were their age, women's football weren't really recognised as much as it is now, there's loads of opportunities for them to have a full-time job in it, to have a career, so I push that over anything, to make their experience at Barnsley positive in addition, on top of that. If they remember they walked out with us for a game and we won, and we signed a programme or whatever it is, if that makes their day or their weekend, that's the least we can do. We've been pushing people to get involved with other community projects, coming down to soccer camps at the club, and trying to get people on matchdays to promote different things.

'Obviously with work and other commitments it is hard, but most people have contributed in some way or another. It is a family-run club and I think that sense of community is important to everybody, and I've then pushed that as captain, but life does get in the way sometimes.'

Turner loved being a role model, even if it did eat into her free time.

'I think when you enjoy it, it don't really feel like work, chatting to little girls – compared to the job I do nine to five it is an absolute breeze,' she said. 'I'd love to do that all day every day and get paid for it. I think everyone sees it like that, and they appreciate the little ones. We've never had fans, we've never had people who look up to us, so it is quite a shock. I think people, especially the young girls on the team, don't really know how to deal with it, so like Mollie [Crump], being 16, and having girls ask for her autograph, she's just a bit taken aback by it. I think everyone loves it, and when we have little mascots coming out with us. Most of the teams in the league have done that this year, and it's positive to see that it's not just us who are doing it.'

How did Turner feel about signing autographs and taking selfies?

'I don't even have an autograph!' she laughed. 'I'm going to have to make something up! I remember my sister telling me, "Just do your signature with your number on it," so that's all I do now.'

* * *

Annie Heatherson had a long career in the top flight of women's football, but her time at Yeovil was the first chance she had had to be fully professional. She was 34 at the start of the 2018/19 season, and training every day had been a bit of a shock. Indeed, when new manager Lee Burch had taken over, she was prepared to be told there was no place for her in the squad.

'I thought, "If you don't select me, I'll retire, I can't … I'm not going to move again to play for another team, I'm 34, I'll just find a career in something else," she reflected. 'To be fair Lee said to me he wanted me to be part of the team, and I said, "Brilliant, that's fine."

'We've laughed and joked this year. I was like, "I've got to retire," and he's like, "No, no, no, you can do it." Yeah, but mentally I can't. Mentally, working with the youngsters is a lot harder. I'm at a crossroads. Last summer I was like, "Can I afford mentally to do this?" because you've got to adapt to the younger generation coming in, and they work a lot differently to the way I have in the past. I'm very much go and get it, fight for it, never give up for it, where the mentality nowadays isn't like that. People don't realise how much psychology actually works in football, and if you don't get that right then you're screwed, in a way. That was the one thing – I was sitting there last year and thinking, "Well, psychologically, can I do this? Can I work with youngsters and can I be a support for youngsters, and can I really play myself?" But as soon as he offered the contract and the fact that he wanted me, I was like, "I'll have a stab at it and see where I go." I didn't think I'd get this far.'

Playing football for a living was the culmination of Heatherson's lifelong dream, but the physical challenge was steep. Recovery from a match took longer, but more than that she was unsure she could focus for another year.

'The amount of conversations I have with Lee where I'm like, "This is my last season, let's retire now" – he won't let me, he genuinely won't let me,' she said. 'He's like, "You've got two or three years in you at least," and I'm, "OK, maybe my body might, maybe technically I might, but I don't think I've got it mentally."'

She praised Burch for bringing together a group of players who had fine team spirit. She thought that playing for a smaller team motivated her personally, and she enjoyed exploring the potential of a team that was striving against the odds.

'I've always played for the underdog,' she said. 'I've had the opportunity to go and play for the big guns and I've never gone to play there. In my Charlton days, I had the offer to go to Arsenal, and I didn't want to be a winner, I wanted to be the one who upset the winner. I went to Charlton, they were underdogs. I went to Fulham, they were underdogs. I went to Millwall, they were underdogs. I went to Bristol, who were underdogs, and all four teams were predicted relegation and they all went on to get promoted. So when you look at our budget and what we can offer, that's fine, but if you've got the right mentality and the right drive and the right go and the psychology is right, you can achieve anything, and 99.99 per cent of the game is won in the head.'

Heatherson put a lot of store in psychology and mentality. Though Yeovil were bottom of the WSL, she refused to believe there was any chance of her team being relegated. She did, however, admit that a season of close scorelines ending in repeated defeats had affected the squad's confidence.

'A team can't grow in confidence if they're not getting scorelines,' she said. 'The players we've got – if a striker doesn't score, she gets blamed, if a goalkeeper lets a goal in, she gets blamed, the defender lets a player go by, she gets blamed. Hang on a sec, if we can win a game, there's points where we're ...'

She paused, thinking back to occasions during the past year when an individual's error had changed the direction of an entire game, and when she had been called upon to speak to a young player brooding over their mistake. She was quick to say that she only approached a team-mate with advice if they asked her for it.

'I said, "Look, when you know better, you do better, but you have to learn that,"' she recalled. 'This is a learning curve. Sometimes when you get goals and games going your way, the mentality changes and you'll ooze more confidence, and that's the only thing that we're missing, confidence, because we've only won one game.'

Although she stepped in to speak to younger players when required and requested, she did find herself slightly concerned about the way some progressed through the game now, and about the wages they received – and then paid to agents.

'I've never had an agent in the whole time I've been playing, I still don't have an agent, and my philosophy is, "Why do I need an agent? Surely my football should speak for itself?"' she said. 'What happens if you have an agent, an agent will go hunting for money, hunting for the bigger teams because then they get really good commission, and I think that's a really sad way that the game has gone – but we never had that. You have to go through the agent to get to a player, and yes, OK, professionally that's really nice – but what a ball-ache. What does the kid want to do? Do they want to play for Yeovil or do they want to sit on someone else's bench? Why have you got to interfere? That really bugs me. It's one of my bugbears. I see so many players with agents, and I think, "Do you know what? It's good if they get you on a ladder, but don't go money-grabbing," and that's really what the agents do now.

'"Well, she wants this amount of money."

'I'm not sure what team you're coming to, but we're Yeovil, where do you think we have that money? The only way you're going to get that is if you go to Chelsea, Arsenal, Liverpool – and she's not even that good yet, so why don't you stick her in this club, let's give her a couple of quid, let her speak for herself, let her football talk, and what will happen is if she's good enough Man City, Arsenal, Chelsea will come to the agent and then you can make that deal.'

The increased money in the WSL meant plenty of top-class players had been attracted to England – but sheer simple mathematics meant that not all of them would be able to have a regular starting spot in a first team. Heatherson pointed to the number of internationals who were named as substitutes week in, week out for top clubs.

'What are you doing?' she asked rhetorically. 'I'm not being funny. Four of those players could be spread out between the whole of WSL, and Yeovil could actually have a really good player on our hands. We could even the league up so much more, but no, you want to be greedy and have four goalkeepers. What are you going to do with four goalkeepers?'

She thought a draft system, such as the one popular in American sports, might go some way towards ensuring a more even spread of talent, but accepted it was unlikely in English football. Either way, she thought the current structure would need some adjustment if it was to be competitive and sustainable in the years to come.

'Some things are going to have to change – there's too much of a gap between the top four and the bottom five or however many,' she said. 'You've got the big guns stealing all the players and everyone else has just got to survive, avoiding relegation. If you can figure that out, you'll probably make millions.'

12

On the whistle

IT WASN'T until the start of February that the bad weather truly hit all of the UK. The snow fell, and as always it limited travel, making the roads dangerous and causing chaos on public transport.

It would be difficult to imagine Joanna Stimpson irritated or even vaguely troubled by such obstacles. The FA women's refereeing manager had been in post for two years, and even on a grey overcast day at Wembley Stadium, she still had a sunny smile. It was clear that she was telling the entire truth when she explained how much she loved her job.

Having said that, she had also loved her previous job, leading on referee recruitment at her county FA, which she had imagined would be the post that she would hold until retirement.

Perhaps, then, it was just that she loved refereeing in a sport she had come to quite late on; she began playing only in her 20s when she was diagnosed with diabetes and realised she needed to improve her fitness.

Once she was involved with a club, she found her role expanding, doing everything from washing the kit to running the line.

'It was on the back of that I decided to do the referees' course,' she said. 'I thought I could have a little bit of knowledge to know what I was doing when I was refereeing, so to start with I qualified as a referee when I was about 27, then progressed quite quickly through the ranks of the men's game.'

Stimpson then encountered what she thought was one of the biggest barriers to women hoping to make a career as a match official – the fitness test, devised decades ago, and initially intended to gauge the physical condition of men. Still used today, it measures speed and stamina by setting each participant a target of running 2,600 metres in 12 minutes. That would be an excellent and achievable time for anyone taking their running seriously – but, of course, in general women have less muscle mass and thus less explosive power than their male counterparts. Running a kilometre in four minutes and 40 seconds is likely to be slightly less sustainable for a woman.

Stimpson highlighted a mass of potential problems with this status quo. First of all, is middle-distance running really a useful indicator of how well a referee is equipped to keep up with play? Second, female footballers were likely to be a touch slower than their male equivalents, which would thus not require so much speed from their match official. Third, plenty of excellent female referees were not being allowed to progress through the men's game because they were simply physically unable to meet this arbitrary standard of fitness that had been conjured up years previously.

Now they were able to take a different test – and if they passed it, they could progress to referee at the top level of the women's game.

'We've based it on a FIFA fitness test, which is what they use for international referees, and it's more of an interval test,' explained Stimpson. 'They run for 75 metres, walk for 25 metres, run for 75 metres, walk for 25 metres, and then they do a series of sprints. Not all the girls pass that, but the majority of the girls pass that. It's a much more appropriate test.'

She knew that still might not be perfect, but it was better, and mentioned lots of pieces of research she would like to see, to ensure that everyone involved was getting what they required. For example, there were already data that indicated that referees covered a similar distance whether they were in charge of a men's match or a women's match, but there was not yet any work that showed how much of that ground was covered at a sprint. Maintaining good levels of communication with referees, and with those working with them, was also key to finding out what additional support they might need to do their job to the best of their abilities, and then providing it; after all, working in a professional football league for the first time also brings with it added pressure, with bigger crowds, media scrutiny and players and managers whose jobs could depend on a single decision.

'It's no secret, we've never made it a secret, that we probably weren't where we should have been in terms of refereeing in the women's game, and then when the women's game went like that,' Stimpson gestured upwards with her arm, 'we certainly have not gone like that, so we are on catch-up and we know that.

'So, looking at the referees we currently have and what do we need to do to – ' she paused, 'not necessarily improve them because we have a really good standard of referees operating in the women's leagues, [and] the guys and girls have operated for ten to 15 years in the top end of the semi-professional men's leagues, but it's what considerations we need to give to the differences, and one of the key differences is the media pressure, the environment, the spectators they have, the amount of spectators. It's things like that that we need to make sure we're preparing them for. In the men's game it can vary a lot, the amount of spectators you get, but a lot would be less than what we're having – we're having 4,000 spectators at some of our women's games now, so [we are] making sure that we better prepare them for the whole environment, not just for the decisions that they're making on the field.'

All referees received regular training. When they were at training sessions and given exercises to work through, footage and examples were now taken from the women's game as well as the men's. Stimpson was also keen to encourage female officials to create a support network of their own, leading the way by organising events and symposiums across the country. She was delighted when female officials set up their own WhatsApp group chats or joined in a conversation on Twitter using the hashtag girlsthatref, arguing that a collective ethos was important – if occasionally difficult to foster.

'As you progress, your friends become your competitors,' she said. 'You're all competing, especially at the top end – you're all competing for those big fixtures, for those FIFA appointments and things, but ultimately they're your biggest companions as well, they're your strength.'

She praised the importance of everyone having a mentor to offer guidance, answer questions – or simply give a thumbs-up for finding the right ground in time for kick-off. That, she felt, was key to retaining referees, and avoiding the disappearance of officiating talent. Her own mentor, back in Somerset, had been supportive in exactly that way.

'You could ring him on the way home from a game, and you'd maybe missed a penalty, and you are not sure [about the decision],' she recalled. 'You'd ring him, drop him a text, and he'd come back, [with] a few words, bit of reassurance – never said you were right if you were wrong, but what would you consider next time, what would you do slightly differently? He was a great support.'

Refereeing in women's football had grabbed the spotlight earlier in the season, when David McNamara forgot his coin for the toss prior to the televised fixture between Reading and

Manchester City. Instead, he asked captains Kirsty Pearce and Steph Houghton to play a quick game of rock-paper-scissors to decide who would kick off the match. The laws of the game require a coin toss, and the vision of two professional footballers engaging in a playground game was unedifying, particularly as it was being broadcast. It elicited a great deal of comment, and McNamara was later suspended for three weeks on a charge of 'not acting in the best interests of the game'. Stimpson, as the FA's representative, was approached for her reaction – and she had not even been watching the match live. Some months afterwards, it was still an episode that caused her discomfort to consider.

'It's not nice, because I think, and this is generally the case in refereeing, you get judged on one decision, or one call, and people forget to look at the bigger picture,' she said. 'Even that weekend you had some big performances, big decisions being made, girls and boys having great refereeing performances, and it was focused on that poor decision – and it was a poor decision that he made.

'I think in hindsight now David knows it was a poor decision, and we learn from it, and definitely again it's raised awareness, it's poor publicity but it's raised awareness for everybody – this is now the profile of the women's game, you can't get away with anything, you have to be 100 per cent professional in everything that we do. If nothing else, then that strong message has been delivered to all our referees.'

It would be easy to make an argument that such an incident would never be seen in the men's game, and the fact that it happened at all just reinforced negative stereotypes about the amateurism of women's football and people's refusal to take it seriously or even just apply the standard laws of the game to it.

'It's so hard to change that mindset, change that culture about it – it's just going to take time, isn't it?' responded Stimpson. 'We just have to keep chipping away and doing what we can. When you go back to grassroots football, people relax a little bit, and this does portray the perception that we don't take it seriously enough. I think people can see now the big changes we're making: the referees we've got on these games, the comms kit, the way we're professionalising it, actually we are taking it really seriously now, and we are.

'We have a match observer at every game now. They do a full report, three, four pages long, a full report on the referee's performance, analysing every decision – well, not *every* decision, but all key decisions they've made, the teamwork, the professionalism around the game, and they're marked on that. That goes into a merit list and people can see how they are performing. We can identify trends – if there's certain things that as a group we're not getting right all the time, why are we not getting that right? Is that because it's very different to what we're doing in the men's game? And then we taper that in their training and development to make sure we identify persistent problems or challenges and that we're learning.'

Most of the observers were either current or retired officials, and their role would be to speak to the officiating team before the match and then discuss some of the key decisions afterwards.

'We're fortunate that we have the footage of the WSL,' said Stimpson, 'so if there's anything we're not really sure about, we don't use it for the observation, but in terms of training and development, we'll use the footage afterwards to go back and look at the instance and check referees' decisions. There was an incident of handball in the box at Birmingham and the referee didn't give the penalty. We went back and looked afterwards, and there was a good reason why she didn't give the penalty, but actually what we identified was her patrol path – her positioning as she moved in to make that decision wasn't good. We're not going to criticise you on whether or not that was or wasn't a handball because a lot of it comes down to opinion, but what we are going to give you development on is your positioning going in. If you'd have altered it slightly, you'd have been in a much better position to give that decision and ultimately sell it to people as well. In all refereeing it's not about giving the decision it's how you sell that decision. If you're not in a credible position to give it, you're not going to sell it.'

Communication between referees and managers as well as players was also increasing, with Stimpson leading plans to provide a mandatory briefing session with clubs; currently this kind of liaison was optional and not all clubs took up the offer.

'I think we should be going into there and seeing the players every summer and giving them an update on the laws, having a good conversation with the players,' she said. 'We've probably over the last two years seen most clubs, but not all of them, so we want to get that mandated. It's so important. Everything we do, I'd say it ties into education, and that doesn't matter whether that's managers [or] players, just education around what we're trying to do and what we're trying to achieve, and the players are key in that.

'We find, and I talk quite broadly here, women tend to be a little bit more ...' she paused. 'They want more clarification, they're a little bit more intrigued. When we make decisions they do want to know exactly why you've made that call, why you've done this that and the other. Guys will have a little bit of a throw their arms around and move on, but girls actually want that clarification, so I think that education is really, really important.'

Still, for the foreseeable future, it would be unsurprising that there would continue to be some glitches with the officiating at the top of the women's game. After all, these were amateur referees in charge of professional matches; and of course mistakes would be inevitable regardless.

'Our vision is to have a full-time group of professional referees operating in the Women's Super League,' explained

Stimpson. 'That's what we want as an organisation, that's what the league deserves, but at the moment do we have the right people to form that group? Probably not. Do we know exactly how that group looks at the moment? If you look at PGMOL [Professional Game Match Officials Limited], who support the Premier League, that's funded by the Premier League, by the EFL, and partly by ourselves. Are clubs in a position at the moment to be able to support this funding? Do they want to? That is our vision, that is what we're striving for.'

Would that group refereeing in the Women's Super League be an all-female group? Stimpson admitted that would be something she would like to see personally, but was quick to point out that it was not FA policy. Some of her recent research indicated that referees had once had to take on women's matches as an obligation; now they were enjoying the opportunity.

'If we've got guys who want to progress, girls who want to progress, the pathway is there for both,' she said.

* * *

If a teenager needs some extra pocket money, the first ports of call are usually local shops, entertainment complexes or hotels; or they might offer out their services for a spot of manual labour or babysitting. If that teenager is committed to keeping their Saturdays free so they can play football, though, their choices are much more constricted.

Jade Wardle was 14 when she first picked up her whistle. Her plan was to spend her Saturdays kicking a ball, and her Sundays officiating in other leagues, picking up some wages along the way. She did her training along with her mother – who decided to qualify at the same time rather than dropping her daughter off at the session and then going back later to pick her up – and they were the only two female students on the course.

When Wardle began taking charge of matches, they were youth games, and it was a shock to the system.

'I didn't really like doing youth football that much, and especially some of the academies I was doing, some of the parents were horrible,' Wardle recalled. 'I had so many sexist comments. I was quite young so I didn't know how to deal with it that much, but I always had my mum there – she'd always run my line, so she was kind of always helping me.

'I remember there was one, I was doing an academy game, and it was the first time they'd had all-female officials. We all turned up, and the parents were like, "Isn't it time for you to go home and cook the roast dinner?" I'm like 15. Why are you telling me that? I don't even know how to cook! I've got my mum with me! I had a few times where teams refused to play because I was female and so I'd just take the match fee and go home.'

It was no wonder that on reflection she admitted to 'pretty much hating' refereeing during those first months, and that it took her a long time to decide to apply for promotion. After she began to referee for senior men's matches, she started to enjoy it much more, and concentrate more seriously on her progression.

'When I first started doing men's football, they saw I was quite young and female, so especially when it came to language, they always watched themselves,' she said. 'Every time someone accidentally swore, they'd really apologise a lot. In the end I'd be like, "You know what, it's fine, I've heard worse."'

Two years into her refereeing career, Wardle decided this would be the pathway she would follow rather than playing. Refereeing was now her great love, and she really feared getting injured in a tackle or just a random incident that would put her out of the game in both capacities.

"My RDO [referee development officer] said, "Look, you need to think about whether you want to become a referee or whether you want to be a player," she said. 'I left it for a bit and thought, "I can do both, it's fine." Then I got my first promotions, [and] I was like, "Actually, if I want to go further …" I thought, "I just want to carry on refereeing."'

Even though the sexism on the pitch had abated somewhat since stepping up to senior football, Wardle and her female colleagues continued to butt up against examples of insidious, inherent gender prejudice – even when being appointed to officiate at matches.

'Match confirmations!' she exclaimed. 'It's always, "good morning, gentlemen" or "good evening, gentlemen". I've given up telling them now. On some of the screenshots [I have], they change my name – it's either Jack, or Jamie, or Jake, or Jordan. I'm like, "How do you get this?" It says literally on Full-Time [the FA's database site] and MOAS [the match officials appointment system], it's Jade Wardle. I literally don't understand how it goes from that to this sudden drastic change. I've even been called Jemma, which is a female name – but you've added a couple of letters and changed a few!'

She was waiting to hear back about her next promotion up the refereeing ladder, but she was not fretting before receiving the decision letter; she had plenty to occupy her time as she was in the middle of writing her dissertation for her undergraduate degree in sport and exercise science at the University of Gloucester, where she was on a referees' scholarship. She talked with enthusiasm about the psychological support and strength and conditioning training she had benefitted from, and how she had been able to learn from classmates and lecturers with expertise in other sports, from netball to boxing.

'It's weird how you can still learn from other sports and incorporate it in your game,' she said. 'I never thought of having a script for certain situations, but in rugby they have a lot … and I've worked with some of the rugby referees to come up with my own scripts for certain situations. It's been really good.'

She did not, however, officiate in university matches any more, learning from bitter experience it was best to steer clear.

'There was one time I was refereeing a university game and I sent off one of the players, and he was in my lecture the next day – it was horrible,' she said with a slight laugh. 'He still goes on about it – two years later.'

* * *

'It's a lady ref!' one mother observed to her little girl, clad in replica kit and sporting a muddied pair of boots.

'Is it?' The child's head jerked up from her phone, and her eyes scanned the pitch where the officials awaited the arrival of the teams. She focused on the referee, and, realising her mother was indeed correct, gave a little nod. 'Good.'

Natalie Jackson was running most of the behind-the-scenes activities at Barnsley as they took on Liverpool Feds on the Oakwell astroturf in the middle of February, with the chairman overseas and the press officer on holiday. She had put together the matchday programme (although using the content that had been left with her along with a template, she was quick to point out), and she was corralling the junior players who were acting as mascots – this week, it was the under-tens who were squealing with excitement.

'The older they get, the cooler they think they should be about it, but five minutes when we're stood outside the dressing room, they are all bouncing around like it's the most exciting day of their lives,' she grinned. 'My favourites so far have been the under-nines, who on the way up to the dressing room were falling out with each other about who they were going to stand with, and they knew all the players' names. That blew my mind. That was the point [of getting the junior teams familiar with the first-team players] – I think I expected it to take longer than it did, but the under-nines, yeah, they were just excited to be on the pitch. They came to me the following week and one of them had got a laminated version of the picture, the team picture, that she was going to get them to sign.'

One of her biggest aims for the next season was to encourage sponsors to get involved with the club more, and see exactly where their contribution was going – on kit and facilities, primarily, but there were also lots of sponsorships in kind, meaning that the printing did not carry any additional costs, and nor did coach travel for away games. Of course, she also wanted more fans to attend matches, but she had been impressed with the way that crowds had expanded in just six months.

'Ticket sales – it's improving, but only because we had very few at the start of the season, and now we have some,' she said, surveying the stand. Jackson had her baby daughter with her again, and was joined by her parents, visiting from the Isle of Man and interested to see what it was she actually did with the club. It had been her father who had introduced her to football in the first place, and both parents had watched her play when she took up the sport at university. She had spent months explaining to them that the standard of women's football had improved dramatically in the decade or so since her graduation.

The 2-1 win against Feds was a good example of it – a match full of drama and controversy. Drew Greene was quick off the mark to capitalise on a wayward pass and turn it home to give the hosts the lead, but Feds utilised the long ball game to good effect and equalised before half-time. The match looked to be petering out into a score draw until seven minutes from time, when substitutes Amy Woodruff and Shannon Durkin took advantage of their fresh legs to combine to put Barnsley ahead. Then in injury-time, Feds thought they had equalised, while Barnsley thought that the ball had been put in the back of the net courtesy of the use of a hand. It looked like the referee had initially awarded it, and the visitors began to celebrate, much to the Reds' disgust.

Then it turned out the goal had not been given at all; either the referee's signals had been confused, or she had changed her mind after consultation with her assistants.

The final whistle blew – Barnsley had secured their deserved victory and three points. The players chatted with their counterparts, still slightly aggrieved at what they thought had been a deliberate handball, but obviously much less aggrieved than they would have been had it stood.

'I thought the ref gave it!' said a surprised Chris Hamilton. 'I'm sure she did and then she's changed her mind last minute.'

He thought it was a clear handball, and had told his counterparts so.

'I said to them, "You don't want to win a game like that anyway," and they kind of backed down, but yes, it was – I thought she gave it, so I panicked for a second.'

He was adamant his side had deserved the win, thinking that Feds had not created enough chances. Barnsley, on the other hand, had created plenty of chances but struggled to convert all of them, and he was pensive about the reasons why.

'When we do it in training, we pass into the net, we're clinical,' he said. 'On a matchday we seem to panic and just smash it – it's something we need to work on.'

Though their unbeaten run had finished the week before, losing to West Brom in the quarter-final of the FA Women's National League Plate, Hamilton had not spent the last seven days too disheartened.

'It was one chance they had from a 35-yard free kick, straight over the keeper's head, so again it was frustrating,' he recalled, 'but we've just said we'll go on a different run now. We've done 12 [matches], so let's go the rest of the season unbeaten now. Today's a good start.'

He acknowledged that it was very unlikely that his team could get promoted, with Burnley enjoying a huge lead at the top of the table, but he was happy to send his team out to chase a second-place finish.

'We'll try and finish as high as we can, but compared to last season we've made brilliant strides, and it's just about keeping doing that now,' he said. 'If we started the season again tomorrow with this squad, the ones we've brought in, I think we'd go and win it.'

* * *

Hamilton had been liaising with Sheffield United manager Carla Ward since he had been in post. As near neighbours it made sense to have a good working relationship, meaning that players could potentially be loaned between the two, enabling youngsters to get first-team experience, and others to progress their careers.

Ward was short of players one Wednesday afternoon in February. It was hardly an ideal time for that to happen – her side had to play Manchester United at home that evening. She was confident that she would be able to put out a starting 11, but she knew her substitutes' bench would not be full. Two of her squad were not able to make the match, six were injured and one was suspended. Ward had even considered re-registering as a player herself.

She was a bundle of nervous energy, admitting that she felt pre-match nerves as a manager much more than she ever had as a player, with the added frustration of being unable to affect the result directly. She had spoken with various members of her squad in the days before, and they reported excitement more than butterflies, meaning she knew she had to dial down her own anxieties.

She had plenty more to concentrate on. Although she was unable to get into the ground itself until two hours before kick-off, she had the kits ready to lay out, packed into the back of her car. As soon as the clock struck five, she would be straight through the door of the complex and beginning her preparation.

'We had a really good training session yesterday followed by a team meeting, a really good night together,' she said.

'I said to the girls, "Go out there and enjoy it, actually go and show what you're about, because we've been brilliant the last few games."'

Ward knew the stands would be full; the away fans had only a short journey to make, and there had been plenty of requests for complimentary tickets, with some of the men's first-team squad asking if they could come to watch as well. She was delighted with the interest the men's side of the club had shown in the women's team, and was, of course, already thinking about next season, particularly as her new baby would have been born by then.

'Because I'm full-time at the club and I've got my own business, from 7am to about midday I go into my office, and from midday to ten o'clock at night [I work at the] academy, but when the baby comes that'll change,' she said. The baby was due in May – at the end of the season.

'I'm on my A licence that week as well,' she added wryly. 'We don't do things by halves. At least it's exciting.'

* * *

A rose-gold moon peeked out from behind puffs of cloud in a charcoal sky. The floodlights dazzled in the Sheffield Olympic Legacy Park, illuminating an artificial pitch which had markings for almost every single sport imaginable, with rugby posts positioned just behind the goal nets, trembling mightily in the strong cross breeze that blew across the bowl that was once part of the famous old Don Valley Athletics stadium.

As expected, the stands were full, with a sizeable contingent of Manchester United fans, who were thrilled to see their side go in at half-time 3-0 up, with Katie Zelem starting the scoring in the first minute, followed by a strike from Lauren James, then an Ella Toone penalty. The hosts tightened things up in the second half, with Mollie Green adding a goal just after the break to secure a 4-0 win.

The Leyton Orient squad in the Brisbane Road changing room before their match against Norwich. (Leyton Orient WFC)

Captain Danielle Griffiths and Sophie Le Marchand pose after Leyton Orient win the Isthmian Cup. (Leyton Orient WFC)

Leyton Orient celebrate after lifting the Isthmian Cup. (Leyton Orient WFC)

Sophie Bell scores the winning penalty to secure the County Cup for Barnsley. (Dean Bradford)

Barnsley captain Lucy Turner. (Dean Bradford)

Barnsley's Lissa Woodhouse in action. (Arron Newman, Reds in the Community)

Goaldiggers in action in Lisbon. (Edith Whitehead)

Goaldiggers take time out in their gold kits. (Edith Whitehead)

Goaldiggers lift the trophy. (Edith Whitehead)

France-bound Lost Lionesses. (UEFA Together #WePlayStrong)

The Lost Lionesses en route to St Pancras to head to Lyon for the 2019 Women's World Cup semi-final. (UEFA Together #WePlayStrong)

Beth Mead is in the mix as Ellen White celebrates against the USA.

Steph Houghton places the ball on the penalty spot.

Karen Carney applauds the crowd.

Ellen White is dejected after the final whistle during the FIFA Women's World Cup semi final match at the Stade de Lyon.

'We didn't compete first half – didn't compete at all first half – and I think when you allow them a goal like that in the first minute, you're on the back foot from the word go,' said Ward afterwards. 'I said to them at half-time, "You've got to go and compete, stop showing them so much respect," but we competed in the second half and made it difficult.'

Ward had no issues with the scoreline; she thought the visitors were an excellent side and deserved their resounding win. It was just her side's lack of engagement in the first half that concerned her, meaning that she had a few choice words to share with them at half-time.

'I think it's one of those things,' she reflected. 'The occasion was quite a big occasion, and I think some of them, to be honest, they didn't quite get going. It was strange because we'd had a good week, but it is what it is, and we were a lot better in the second half.'

With over 1,000 fans in the crowd, there had been plenty of noise, and Ward had also seen some first-time visitors, clad with hooded jumpers so as to be as inconspicuous as possible in the partisan crowd.

'I've noticed quite a few of the [men's] players here, dotted around,' she added. 'That's always nice.'

* * *

Ashleigh Goddard was enjoying rather better weather. She had finally achieved her ambition of playing professional football, but she had not returned to London, nor to England. Instead, she was part of Apollon Limassol's campaign for a Champions League spot, and revelling in the Cyprus sun. It had not been her first choice; after the end of her spell in Scandinavia, she had spent the winter trying to get a place at a WSL club, but again the stars had not aligned. Once more she had been looking for trials to prove herself.

'It was going OK,' she said. 'I got a lot of "you fit in but you need to stand out," because they could only sign two players during the winter. For me, if I'm fitting in that means I'm ready to step up; I train twice a week and everybody else is training twice a day. So for me I was happy to fit in, but I completely understand – if you're on a trial you've got to stand out.'

WSL coaches wanted to see a complete player during a trial, but Goddard, still not fully professional, could offer them only her potential. So she cast her eyes further afield again, asking friends and contacts whether they knew anywhere that might be interested in her. Three days after emailing Apollon with her highlights reel, they flew her out there for a trial. Watching the first training sessions, she thought the standard was so high that she would never get a contract offer; with the pressure off, she was free to play her own way, and it impressed the coaches.

'I ended up signing and I've been here almost a month now,' she said, 'and it's all going very well – definitely landed on my feet here which is a nice change.'

Her contract ran until the end of the season, with an option for both sides to extend Goddard's stay. In the meantime, she was working hard with the new routine, joining the squad in the gym every morning, then heading to a training session on the pitch in the evening. All the coaching was done in English – the shared language of a squad hailing from many countries worldwide.

'It's everything I want,' she smiled. 'It's very intense, there's a lot of training, which is exactly what I've been asking for and trying to chase. We have gym sessions, they have a thing called a token machine which is basically like a …'

She paused.

'You know in tennis where they have the machine that shoots the ball over the net for you to hit? It's that, with a football. So that's incorporated into our gym sessions as well, which is awesome – you get a normal gym session but also technical training as well.'

During the evening pitch sessions, the squad played a lot of friendlies against boys' teams. The standard of teams in Apollon's domestic league were very variable; taking on boys' teams meant they got to test themselves and maintain an appropriate level of fitness for Champions League competition. Goddard had found her physical condition and her technique improving massively very quickly.

'I finished in Denmark in mid-November, so the last month and a half, two months, really the only training I was getting was if I was training at a club or if I go to the park myself and do my own running,' she explained. 'I was able to maintain a base fitness, but it's completely different to match fitness. When I first got here, I explained to the coach, "I am fit but I'm not match fit." He just threw me in straight away and said, "OK, the only way you're going to get fit is if we put you straight into training and push you."

'I feel like it's taken a bit of time to adapt. Don't get me wrong, the first two weeks, my body hated me. We'd have weights in the morning and then I'd have training in the evening and then by the next morning we'd have weights again and I'd be like, "I can't even walk." Honestly, my body hated me for a while, but I adapted, I'm used to it, I feel like I'm up with everyone else. Now I'm trying to push on; now I'm not just happy to match everyone, I want to be a bit fitter, I want to be a bit stronger. Don't get me wrong, sometimes we have days where my legs are a bit like jelly, but I speak to the other girls and they're like, "No, we're sore too," and that makes me feel better.'

Goddard had said before moving to Norway that she was fitter than she had ever been. Now she was even fitter, and she was noticing that her sharpness on the ball was improving.

'The time it takes between my first touch and actually passing the ball – that's the kind of thing that I'm trying to work on while I'm here,' she said.

She was also trying her hand at coaching during the day. As a secondary school teacher, she was used to working with young people; now she was helping out Apollon's manager with his academy, teaching children aged between five and eight.

'It's very different for me,' she said. 'I was a secondary school teacher – I taught 11 to 18 year olds. Five to 8 year olds is a completely different challenge.'

Yet these were all challenges she was enjoying.

'I feel like I've taken the scenic route to get where I am,' she reflected. 'I think a lot of people coming up now get opportunities very young, and you see professional players now 17, 18, 19 years old. I'm 26. I like to think I've still got a few years left, but it's certainly older for someone to get their first professional contract. At the beginning of the year, where it was all a bit tough, I wrote down a list of things I wanted to achieve, and getting my first professional contract was one of them, so I'm very, very happy. I think now the target is to win two leagues in one season; if I can, that would be awesome. That's the aim at the moment, then come May, June, that's when a new decision has to be made. Do I stay here, do I go back to England, do I go somewhere in Europe? At the moment, I just know that I'm very much enjoying my time here, I think I'm progressing as a player, and just taking it week by week.'

SPRING

13

Belief

WITH THREE months to go until the Women's World Cup, the nations who had qualified were gearing up. England flew out to the USA for what had become an annual tournament – the SheBelieves Cup, a four-team round-robin invitational. In previous years it had featured the top-four teams in the world; in 2019, Brazil and Japan joined the hosts and the Lionesses in competition.

For the first time, England lifted the trophy. They beat Brazil 2-1, drew with the USA 2-2, and eased past Japan 3-0 in the final game to secure their place at the top of the table. Arsenal's Beth Mead caught the attention with her goalscoring prowess, capped off with a truly magnificent strike against Brazil in the opening game, lashing in almost from the wing. The goal became one of the social media viral moments of the year, popularising the neologism 'crot' as people wondered whether she had intended it as a cross or a shot – or perhaps both.

'I did mean it!' she insisted the week afterwards. 'A lot of people questioned whether it was a cross! I hit it with everything I had and luckily it went where it was meant to go – but another time it would probably fly over the net.'

Mead had settled in to the senior squad under Phil Neville's leadership, and was evidently thriving. It was not that long ago that she had been playing alongside the juniors during the previous regime, despite being the country's leading goalscorer.

'Patience, I guess, is key,' she thought. 'It was frustrating not being picked. I thought I was playing some good football at the time, and, yeah, I didn't get my chance, but I guess it was just a waiting game, and patience, and I've luckily been given my opportunity and I'm really taking that now.'

She had plenty of praise for her England coach.

'I really get on with Phil,' she said. 'We have good communication on what I need to do better, what I'm doing well at. He watches all our games, he always gives us feedback, so I know where I am and where I'm stood with him. It's been a long time waiting, but I'm really enjoying myself within the England squad now.'

Good communication between a coach and a player should be key if success is to follow, and Mead felt that Neville did a good job with that.

'As a player you always question what could I have done better, what could I be doing better? Phil actually lets you know – you need to be a bit fitter, you need to run at players more and get past them, you need to be scoring more,' she said. 'You've got to know that if you're doing well you're putting yourself back in his eyeline for the England squad, so I think he's very good at communicating what he wants and what he expects from his players.'

In Neville's first few months in post, he had spoken in the media about speaking to his players every day via WhatsApp, explaining that he had a chat set up for each member of his squad. Mead elaborated that each conversation also included the backroom team, including medical staff, meaning that any queries or feedback could be discussed instantly. She felt that the team spirit throughout the camp was setting the Lionesses up beautifully for the summer's World Cup.

'Obviously we've been playing football and getting better, so we're going there with the right attitude,' she said, before adding with caution, 'but we know there's a lot more hard work to be done and it's over a lot more games. We did three games in SheBelieves and managed, but the World Cup is a different stage, different competition – you never know what's going to happen. We really need to ready ourselves and prepare ourselves for that, but we're in a very good position right now.'

So were her club side Arsenal, jousting with Manchester City at the top of the Women's Super League table. They had been leading for weeks at the start of the season before a mini-slump brought City back into contention.

'It's been an exciting season,' reflected Mead. 'At the start, obviously, we were playing some very good football. People were enjoying watching us. Then unfortunately we got hit by a few injuries, and it's kind of killed our momentum. It's been a little bit frustrating, but it's shown the character and the strength in our team to know we're still getting the job done. We're still in with a chance to win the league. So, yeah, it's been an exciting season of ups and downs, but a good one.'

Arsenal and City were due to meet on the last day of the season – and thus it could also be the title decider. Mead acknowledged that might be fun for the neutral, but wanted the trophy wrapped up for Arsenal before then.

'We can't drop any points,' she declared. 'It'll be quite nice to win it before we play them, but you never know in football. Hopefully we can get it done before then.'

Mead had just completed her second year as a full-time professional footballer; while at Sunderland, she had also taken a degree in sports development at Teesside University. For someone with such strong roots in the north-east, uprooting to London for a new way of life presented a challenge, but after a brief spell of homesickness she was thriving. She was completely dedicated to Arsenal's title challenge – but admitted her thoughts occasionally drifted to the summer's upcoming tournament.

'It's hard not to think about it,' she confessed. 'We've got a camp coming up with England. I think it's getting it right between club and international mindset, you've just got to flick between them sometimes. Right now it's all club; we go to camp and it's all England international mindset. Then we come back and we've got a league to win, so it's quickly switching over, but it's something that, as a professional footballer, you've just got to do sometimes.'

* * *

Wales's Helen Ward had watched England's success at home in north-west London with a combination of interest and envy. She had enjoyed a very successful season so far with Watford, who were comfortably mid-table in the National League Southern Premier Division, and felt that even though she was playing at a lower level than she had been used to, she had ultimately made the right choice for her at the moment.

'I feel like I still can play at a higher level, but at the same time I feel like I haven't got that much to prove any more,' she said, 'and the way it works obviously with my family and Watford being so local, the demands on my time are a lot less in terms of having to be with the team, if that makes sense. Obviously I still have to go out and do my own training in between times, but I'd still have to do that if I was with a Championship club, I'd imagine – it's only an extra night that they train, so I'd still have to find the time to go to the gym anyway, so in that sense I kind of think, "Well, it's working for me."

'I'm still being called up to Wales, touch wood, and as long as that's happening and I'm scoring goals and I'm enjoying it … OK, I'm playing in a lower league, but the repetition of finding the net is something that even when I go into international football I'm still finding that I feel confident in front of goal, whereas if I'm sat on the bench or not scoring in the league above or two leagues above, all of a sudden it's like, "Oh my goodness, I haven't scored in this many games," and it weighs on your mind. Yeah, obviously, ideal world, Watford would be in the top league or the second league and I'd be happy there and everything would fit into place, but football doesn't work quite as easy as that so I have to weigh up the pros and cons and at the moment it's a happy balance.'

She had been intrigued to notice that her physical condition appeared to have improved since dropping down a level, and put that down to her increased experience of knowing how far to push her body. With one match and two squad training sessions a week, she organised her work-outs on the other days accordingly.

'At Watford we've got the GPS stuff I can use and that's a really good way of tracking what level I'm at,' she explained. 'It's funny, some sessions you feel like, "Oh, I really struggled," and then you look at your data and it's like, "Oh, actually I did OK," whereas if you don't have that information you might feel like you're not doing as well as you are, or vice versa – you might think, "I was flying there," but actually you didn't work as hard as you thought you had. So those sorts of things really help, which obviously I didn't have in the early days of my career – that sort of technology wasn't around. I've got myself a little routine where I train or play probably five days out of seven a week, generally speaking – there's other weeks where I do a bit more, or a bit less – but it seems to be working for me and I've managed to use all my experience of working with different fitness coaches and pulling little bits together that I know work for myself, and, touch wood, it seems to be going OK at the minute.'

Like other senior professionals, Ward acknowledged that recovery time now was a little more extended than it had been in her younger years.

'You do get to a certain age where it takes that little bit longer but again I've probably just learnt what you can carry on through and what you've got to keep an eye on,' she thought. 'I've got a bit of a problem with my back at the moment, but it tends to hurt more when I'm not doing anything than when I am, so in my head I think, "Well, it doesn't hurt at the moment, I might as well carry on," which is maybe not the most sensible idea, but you do have to adjust and adapt slightly as you get older. Youngsters come to me saying, "Oh, I've got sore hamstrings," and I think, "You wait till you wake up every day and there's never a day when something doesn't hurt!" Having kids probably doesn't help that either, because I think my core and my back are probably all in the wrong place at the minute.'

Ward's small son Charlie was playing on the living room floor in front of her, while her daughter was at school. Both had been to plenty of matches so far in the season ('How much of the game they actually watch I don't know, but I do hear Emily shouting from the sides'), but both stayed behind when Ward headed to international training camp, with her parents taking on caring responsibility.

'It's a bit of a nightmare, and I do spend a lot of my time away hoping that everybody isn't pulling their hair out, the children included,' she admitted. 'Matt, my husband, works over in Richmond, so he leaves the house just after six in the morning. When I'm away, obviously it's not fair to get them up at that time to take them over to my parents, and at the same time it's not fair for my parents to have to get up, so the kids actually stay with my mum and dad for most of the time I'm away. They love it there, they're very well looked after, no problem with that at all – but obviously it's hard work for my mum and dad. They've done their bit, bringing their kids up, so for them to have to do it again every so often, I do feel bad. Then my husband will go round there of an evening. He kind of loses his time with them on their own, it's not the same.

'At the same time, if I said to them, "OK, look, I'll give up, I'll stop playing," they wouldn't have it, so as much as I do feel guilty, I know that if they really wanted me to stop playing, they'd tell me. I know that if I do stop playing I'll miss it, and I have to go on as long as I'm able to. It can be a bit of a nightmare but we all get through it, and at the end of it everybody's happy to hand them back to me!'

With an impish grin she explained that international duty was a nice break in some ways – 'I don't have any responsibilities of cooking, cleaning, tidying, getting up, so for the first couple of days I'm like, "This is heaven." It's really nice, I don't have to worry about anything else apart from what colour t-shirt I've got to wear that day!' More seriously, although she missed her children when she was away, she hoped they would understand in years to come.

'I speak to them on FaceTime, especially Emily – not so much Charlie because he's still very young,' she said. 'Emily says, "Oh, when are you coming home? I miss you," and that gets to me because she's used to having me around a lot and picking her up from school and things. Yeah, it is hard, but I'm hoping it's something they look back on and feel proud of me for doing. It's not going to last forever, so I know that there's going to be plenty of times I'm going to be here for them and hopefully support them through their own careers, whether that's sport or otherwise.'

In the meantime, she tried her best to involve both children as much as possible in her international career, including airport runs and getting to meet the other players in the camp. Emily had even been on one of the camps as an infant – but that was not an experience Ward was too keen on repeating.

'I think it was actually more stressful than leaving her at home!' she said with a wry smile. 'I had people around who were there to look after her when I trained and stuff, but it was constantly making sure she wasn't annoying anyone. I know that they liked having her around but you don't want anyone to think, "OK, I've had enough of her now!" Everyone was very good. It wasn't something that I wanted to do all the time even if I could have done.'

Wales's next challenge on the pitch would be the qualifiers for the European Championships – but off the pitch they would have to cope with watching both England and Scotland compete in the summer's World Cup. Ward intended to watch it as a neutral, and had found her disappointment at missing out on the tournament was fading a little.

'Obviously it's still a little bit gut-wrenching that we didn't make it, but the longer time goes on the more you realise how well we did do,' she said. 'You look at the teams that are there, they're all very good teams, and it was always a difficult ask, especially in the group that we had. To do what we did then has massively helped our chances going into the Euro qualifiers. At the minute we're OK – once the World Cup starts and you think, "What if ...", that might be when it becomes a bit more emotional or whatever. We've had a lot of games in the time since, we've had to move on and we're very much focused on our next campaign. I think some of the girls are planning to go over to France and watch one or two games because they've got friends who play for Scotland or whatever, so I think everyone's like, "That's done now, let's crack on with the Euros and hopefully make our own history next time."'

* * *

Storm Freya was battering the country, with high winds and torrential rain, so it was perhaps not a big surprise that Doncaster Belles' home fixture against Fylde at the start of

March was postponed. It was a shame, though; Belles had battled hard through February to secure an unbeaten run in the league, which had resulted in coach Zoey Shaw picking up the manager of the month award. A pause in their momentum also meant that she could not get the immediate accolade from fans she deserved.

She had found out about the award on Friday, when she had a message from Edmunds to phone her as soon as possible.

'She said, "Phone me quick," and I phoned her and said, "Have we signed Fran Kirby?" She said, "No." I said, "OK, I'll have Nikita Parris then, if it's Nikita Parris."'

Shaw laughed.

'But yeah. No. It's good, it's a good achievement, personally and for the club. We're on a good run.'

Belles were second-bottom of the league, but nevertheless Shaw was pleased with her young squad. She had worked with many of them the season before when they had been the development side, and the financial problems during the previous summer had meant they were in the first team sooner than expected, with no experienced players to help them along.

'We'd literally done three weeks of pre-season, [and we got] the players in and explaining to them that you're the new first team,' she recalled. 'The look on some of the faces ... some looked scared to death, some looked like, "Is this a little bit of a joke?" And then you've got the others who'd been with me in the devs last season, they were ready – ready in their mind but probably not ready in their ability to play at that level. That was a tough discussion, and we lost a few players because of that transition. It just got too much for a couple of players throughout the season, and they've gone elsewhere to play maybe a standard which is more comfortable for them – they miss out on a massive learning curve, you come from an RTC [regional talent centre] at 16 and go straight into Belles and you're playing Blackburn first game of the season, you're up against Natasha Flint and Saffron Jordan, it's another level, it's ridiculous.'

It was also a big step up for Shaw. She had been coaching the development team for three seasons, but taking on the mantle of managing Belles was a burden and an honour of which she was very aware.

'The history with Doncaster Belles just speaks for itself,' she reflected. 'I think for a club to still be going after 50 years and to survive on pretty much the basics, every season, to try and get through another season but try and develop at the same time, to try and win titles and championships at the same time – it comes with a lot of stresses, and pressure, it comes with a lot of pressure, to be honest.'

Shaw knew very well that not many coaches would have wanted to take on the job in the situation that she did: a club without vast reserves of money, but a storied track record that meant there would always be some level of expectation to achieve great things.

'For me it's just a big challenge, a challenge that I was definitely ready for, because I knew some of the players, so I knew the culture that they've got,' she said. 'It was just getting them to play the right way and getting them to play in that environment, deal with the psychological side of them being 16, 17, [and] coming into a big set-up. It's been a challenge but I'm not regretting it.'

But Shaw also had another challenge to deal with off the pitch, caring for a baby daughter, born prematurely and needing additional medical attention because of that.

'There were lots of complications along the way – she was only born like three lbs she's only 10lbs 10 at the minute, she's eight months, so we're in and out of hospital appointments and other stuff going on with her,' she said. 'It's nice sometimes to go to football and just switch off from some of the stuff that might be happening at home, but on the flipside I have a partner at home who is dealing with a lot while I'm at football. It's swings and roundabouts.'

Meanwhile, Sheila Edmunds had found herself doing more on a Sunday with the match postponed than she would on a normal matchday. In 50 years of Belles, she had never had to call a game off due to weather previously, so it was all entirely new territory.

'We used to play on some horrendous pitches,' she recalled, 'but when I chatted with the ref – I met him this afternoon to get the paperwork signed – he said there was no way. There was standing water in both goalmouths and penalty boxes, a huge area in the centre and one down the sideline, he said; so the ball just wouldn't roll, it wouldn't be able to do anything. At Rossington, where we play, I can't think when they last called a game off, their pitch is superb. Anyway, hey ho, it was off.'

She had been on the phone to Shaw, to the opposition, to the match officials, to the club's media officer, to an FA representative who was intending to check on one of the Belles' players. She had already set up contingency arrangements with some fans who travelled to Rossington by bicycle.

'I've said to them, "Do you actually use social media? If not you have to give me your number, because if ever a game should get called off we've got no means of getting in touch with you,"' she said. 'Anyway, they did say they do check on social media, so hopefully that's covered all angles, and we've done the right thing.'

In their golden anniversary year, there had been significant media interest in the Belles, and Edmunds had taken to posting old photographs and memorabilia on social media. In the club's early days, all the trophies had been stored at Edmunds's parents' house as they had no home ground, and few cups were theirs to keep – they had to be returned after their season as holders. Personal mementoes were a different matter; Edmunds had plenty of those.

'My scrapbooks are all in a big container, and they keep going in the loft, out the loft, in the loft, out the loft,' she said. 'As far as medals and trophies, I've got a couple in my bedroom – which we call our library, we've got floor-to-ceiling bookshelves. My husband is an ex-pro footballer so he's got a few things on the wall from when he was playing at Leicester and Bournemouth, and I've got some photos from my playing days, and I've got a couple – the first cup we won, which was a little trophy, then one where we actually got a medal, like the men usually do, which for me meant a lot. Then a couple of trophies, I've got them on a bookcase – but all my other things are in storage with my scrapbooks really. They come out now and again when people ask about things, so I'm sure this year I'll be up and down those loft ladders.'

Edmunds also had plenty of old kits, having laundered them all for many years. Now she was intending to auction off some of them in a fundraising exercise. Financially, the club were doing reasonably well, and were comfortably going to make it through the season, with a good run of results reflected in Shaw's manager of the month award.

'If you're at the top of the league, [four consecutive draws] doesn't mean anything,' she pointed out. 'When you're down the bottom, scrapping for points, that's a massive milestone for a young team who are basically 16, 17, 18 year olds. It's gone really well in that respect. We're still looking to find a sponsor for next year, but financially we'll get through this season OK.'

She was still understandably wistful about the squad that had won WSL2 the previous year and scattered around the country when Belles moved down to the National League, and it was difficult for her not to think about how they might have done in the Championship had they stayed together with the necessary financial backing.

'All right, we lost all those players and the manager last year, but you look at where they are now, and I think, "Playing at Doncaster Belles put you on a platform, on a stage,"' said Edmunds. 'These clubs have come in for them – it was our responsibility to make sure they'd all got somewhere to go. I look at them now, people like Jess Sigsworth, Kirsty Hanson who scored for Man United today, and you look at the girls who are playing at Sheffield and you think, "Yeah, we must be doing something right, they've been picked up, they've been put on a contract with other clubs and they're still thriving."

'I do look at it and think I'm still really proud that on their CV somewhere it'll say they played for Doncaster Belles, and that's got to be a really good selling point for this club.'

14

Final countdowns

DANIELLE GRIFFITHS was preparing to lead her Leyton Orient side into two cup finals.

'They're both tough,' she said of the fixtures. 'I know our development team have had experience of Ashford in a different cup earlier this year and they got beat, so they're going to be difficult opposition. Actonians are an old foe, we've played them over the past couple of seasons and we've had some tough and tight games, but we go into both of them knowing that we have a chance, if we put in a good performance, we'll come away with both cups, which is positive.' Orient had picked up plenty of silverware under Griffiths's captaincy.

'I certainly didn't expect so many trophies in so short a succession – I hope that will continue this year,' she said. 'It's been brilliant. Obviously a lot of that is down to having good support at the club, a good solid group of players who have stuck with the team throughout and also some new additions each season which have only helped strengthen us.'

As the season went on, she felt more and more sure that the standard of play in their league had rocketed since the most recent restructure of the women's leagues.

'Look at Crawley and the results they're having – in our league and in cup runs against different opposition,' she pointed out. 'That's probably unheard of in our league – having success against other teams from different divisions. Billericay are another example, but you've also got other teams – Wimbledon beat Billericay this week so everyone's raising their game from week to week, and this league is a bit unpredictable. Anyone can beat anyone on any given week, it seems. This season we haven't got a team languishing at the bottom; Luton have beaten Wimbledon, Norwich have had a good run of results and everyone is in it each week for the three points, which is good and is the standard you want.'

One problem that remained was spells of fixture congestion, and some teams accumulating games in hand, dropping further and further behind in the chase for the title.

'Yeah, it's always the way,' said Griffiths. 'Everyone's county cups run at different times of the season – we've played most of our league games already with a couple of cup finals to come, whereas a lot of others have had their cup games and now have a lot of league games to come, so yeah, it's inconsistency.'

Orient were sitting fourth in the league table as Griffiths spoke, and she wondered now whether they should be a little higher. Her team had come fourth the previous season – their first season at that level – and she thought then they should probably have done better.

'We're ...' she paused. 'Not disappointed to be where we are – if we were two or three weeks into the season we probably would have expected to be there or thereabouts now. So it's not an unsuccessful season, we're pretty consistent with where we were last year but we know we're going to have to step up those few more levels if we want to be challenging for the title next season.'

Griffiths was also looking forward to another big stage – leading her side out at the Breyer Group Stadium, more commonly known as Brisbane Road, the home of Leyton Orient's men's side. The women had played there previously, but this would be their only appearance there for the 2018/19 season. The club announced it as part of their commemoration of International Women's Day in March, confirming that the women's fixture against Norwich City on 24 March would be held at the stadium.

* * *

The squad assembled at the entrance to the stadium's underground car park. It was a bright, sunny day, and walking into the dark was a sharp contrast; sunglasses were quickly pushed up on to foreheads and hairlines. They crossed the empty car park and through a big double door, walked up a small flight of stairs and were directly stepping on to the pitch.

Several of them had experienced games at this venue before, but nonetheless they took the opportunity to take a few selfies and upload a panoramic scan of the stadium to their social media. They were not allowed into the changing room yet.

Manager Chris Brayford was. He was already in there, setting out their customised kits at each peg, so that the first time they went in there, everything would be ready for them. In the meantime, some of the players took the chance to speak to the physiotherapist, or get some pre-game repairs in the medical room. When the squad were finally permitted, they took their places on the benches. The stereo was plugged in, the music was turned up, and everyone joined in with singing along to the power ballads of the 1980s. The players began their preparation by carefully removing the labels from their brand-new shirts and shorts; captain Griffiths took great pains to ask every woman to make sure she had the right size shorts, and to swap should they need to.

Each player had also been given a complimentary matchday programme. Some were flicking through it;

others were sitting and reading intently, waiting for their team talk, complete with presentation. Brayford was the butt of plenty of jokes due to his lack of computer skills, but when he started the briefing, the room was silent as the players listened intently. He began by talking about the players from the opposition and their qualities, but mostly he focused on Orient's strengths, illustrating his point with video clips.

'Make sure we take set pieces for what they are today – a great opportunity – because they're a weakness for Norwich,' he said. 'They're a young side, they do work very hard for each other, which is commendable, it's impressive, they've got talent.

'This is the type of occasion where a young player might start to let their head get down. For us, every single time one of our players gets their head up to pick a pass – we're playing the same shape today as we have the past few weeks, 4-4-1-1 – but we're looking to get that attacker forward every time we're in possession. You must be moving off, to get off the shoulder, can you get behind the player, get in between the lines, create those opportunities moving forward. Move the ball swiftly, we've got the opportunity with our shape. From a defensive perspective, very good in recent weeks, much more resilient, much more focused, been very good, need to keep that same attention today, readiness for their counter, because they've got quick players on the wing who can cause problems. When we win it, we've got to be attacking at pace on the break.'

Brayford revealed his starting 11, complete with head-shot photographs of each player.

'It's the same side that we played against Wimbledon [in the previous fixture] because I think we deserve that in terms of the performance, how we played, I think that was fantastic. Then on the bench we've got fantastic options.'

He concluded the talk with a gentle confidence boost.

'Final, final little thing. You guys have played here before, I know you won't get intimidated by the occasion because it's just another game, but make sure you don't let anything distract you – who's in the crowd, friends, whatever. Don't worry about mistakes. Just focus on your job, keep the intensity and the rest will fall into place. I can't emphasise enough – you all grace that pitch. We are so lucky to have you as part of the team, so today is when others get a chance to see that, because you are fantastic – so go out there and show that. You should be there.'

* * *

The Orient players took longer to complete their warm-up than the Norwich team did. Goalkeeper Naomi was stopped on her way back to the changing room as the referee expressed her concern that her bright yellow shirt was not different enough from the visitors' kit. Naomi asked whether her grey kit – not the new, customised shirt – would be acceptable. The official inspected it, and agreed.

'I think this suits you better!' she said, and Naomi laughed. 'Same, same!'

The two women shook hands and headed back into their respective dressing rooms. Kick-off was a few minutes away, and Griffiths reminded her players not to rush themselves.

'Make sure we're ready! No stress!' she called. These final preparations were not in Brayford's domain; this was all down to her as the squad took their last chance for a trip to the bathroom, to tie up their hair, and to remove any jewellery they might have forgotten. The assistant referee stood outside the door ready to inspect any adornments plus the studs on their boots.

Orient were dominant from the off. Although the deadlock was broken by an own goal, forwards Suaila Cardoso Queni and Hayley Barton added strikes before the interval, giving the hosts a comfortable cushion. At half-time, there were jugs of orange squash, Jaffa cakes and jelly sweets ready for the players to refuel. They took turns to stretch out their muscles and keep warm with a foam roller, and the physio was again on hand to provide taping to anyone who wanted it. The players chatted amongst themselves; one admitted that she had expected the own goal to be disallowed for a foul on the Norwich defender. Brayford jokingly asked if anyone wanted to claim the goal herself rather than attributing it to an own goal, and striker Sophie Le Marchand gladly put her hand up, arguing that she was the nearest Orient player to the incident.

Brayford congratulated his players on a half well done, but reminded them to stay alert, while Griffiths said she wanted to ensure that the clean sheet was maintained. All agreed they could add plenty more goals to their afternoon's tally. However, they managed just one more – another from Barton – and the visitors grabbed themselves a consolation, ruining Griffiths's plan of not conceding.

Brayford had not been impressed with some of the officiating, particularly some very late offside flags against his team. After the final whistle blew, though, he could be satisfied with a job well done from his team.

'Little lapse in the second half when they pushed and came at us, but good on them, I think they're a good team, I thought they played good football, a young, talented team,' he reflected. 'We're really pleased. We dominated the game, we've got to be pleased with that, and to be honest, we could have scored a lot more.'

Orient had certainly created plenty of chances, with a final touch just letting them down, but he was not too worried about that: 'There were two or three where I don't think anyone in the stadium could believe they didn't go in, but they don't change the result.'

With most of their league fixtures played, Orient would now be turning their attention to their two cup finals, and Brayford was expecting big things in both.

'One of the things is we need to make sure we prepare for them properly and stuff, but it would be amazing to win one, and really to win both.'

* * *

Hayley Barton's goal was surely one of the most spectacular that ground had ever seen. Cutting in from the right, she created herself the space she required, leaving her marker stranded in the box. She then delicately moved the ball onto her left foot, and curled it beautifully into the top corner on the far side of the net.

'When I cut in, I heard a "ooh!" and you can hear it on the video!' she chuckled a week later. 'It's a "ooh", and then a bit of a roar. It's quite nice, it's not something we get a lot of at Mile End!'

Barton was playing down just how good her goal had been – 'Definitely don't get many of them, that's for sure!' she joked – but it was clear that she was thrilled both with the meticulously planned strike and having a permanent record of it on film.

'I remember thinking that each time I'd gone down the line – and it's always been the case with Norwich – that they would slide in,' she recalled, 'and I think I had taken it down the line every time before that. I thought, "OK, I'll cut in, and maybe she'll go flying past me," and she did, and I think when you don't have much time to think about it, you just hit it.'

Coach Brayford had sent her the footage from behind the goal, which tracked the exquisite curve of the ball, and she had enjoyed watching it again, just to check her memory of what actually happened.

'It all happens so quick and you think maybe it wasn't as good as it felt,' she explained, 'and I thought, "Wow, it really curled!" – and I'm not left-footed! I was just shocked. Straight afterwards I felt shocked, and I'm not one to celebrate naturally, I didn't know what to do. I just thought, "Oh gosh, I shocked myself!" I've always been someone who would prefer to try and walk the ball into the net than try and shoot from far away or try and shoot on my first touch, it's a bit uncharacteristic.'

Barton had been with Orient for three years. Her playing career prior to that had been a little patchy. She had started playing seriously as a 16-year-old, but on going to university left it for a while, focusing on her studies. After graduation, the on-off relationship with the game continued, and she began to miss playing, and think about finding a new team. She had not played for around three years when she found Orient, in its previous incarnation Kikk.

'I think sometimes it's nice to go and have a break from things,' she reflected. 'The number-one thing for me was finding a team that was local – I don't have like loads and loads of time, and they were literally a stone's throw from where I work.'

Her day job was in a charity for disability sport, and though the office hours were regular, she still liked to make the most of her limited free time. Added to that, she also had a stomach condition that could be debilitating, meaning she had to use her energy wisely.

'For me, I like training once a week with football because it still means I can do other bits and pieces I want to do other than football,' she explained, 'whereas I feel that if I was to train twice a week with a team, I wouldn't be able to do other bits I enjoy doing, just because I can't overdo it.'

She liked that others in the squad shared her mindset – although they took competition seriously, they also had other interests and priorities, making it a friendly and welcoming club. The supportiveness in the club extended to players' families and partners. Barton was sponsored by captain Griffiths's partner, while her own partner sponsored veteran Fran Cagetti. She had also had bad experiences with other clubs, where coaches had personal relationships with players, leading to poor dynamics and bias in team selection.

'I've been involved with quite a few teams with a lot of internal politics, and they perhaps take themselves too seriously,' she said. 'A lot of people do work full-time, have got other things they enjoy doing in life – it doesn't all revolve around football. But at the same time we all share that passion, we all do want to win, we do want to get as far as we can, it's just a balance.

'I don't think I've ever had that with another team. It's always been too much about the results and looking ahead. Maybe things are changing, but I have friends who play for other teams, and the teams we play, you still see a lot of bickering on the pitch, and we don't have that at all. It really is the most supportive team I've ever played for. We play because we love it. Frankly we could all use that time – giving up our Sundays to go away to Norwich and stuff, it's not great on a Monday – but we do it because we love playing and we love playing together.'

* * *

The FA People's Cup, a five-a-side tournament intended for amateur footballers of all standards, was alluring to the women of Goal Diggers. They felt that five-a-side was their strongest format of the game, so they put together several squads to enter the 2019 edition. Though Goal Diggers picked players on availability and interest, and not on performance, they were hopeful of a good showing in the initial local stages. Hannah Wright captained one of the teams, leading a squad of six through three group games, quarter-finals, then semi-finals, then a final: all 12-minute games, with no half-time – and no goalkeeper.

They did not win their final, but they qualified for the next stage of the competition anyway.

'I think some of the other teams took it quite seriously,' Wright said afterwards. 'There was quite a competitive element to it compared to some of the other stuff we play in. So going through our group games there were a couple of teams we were playing where I was a bit surprised by the competitive nature. I'm definitely competitive, but I personally got absolutely clattered. I was hobbling around for three days after. However, having said that, the team we were playing in the final, they just had Canada on their shirts, and I joked at the beginning, "Are you actually Canada?" and they were really good so I wouldn't be surprised if they were. That was a really nice, friendly match, really good standard.'

Because they were through to the next phase, some long-standing Goal Diggers rules were being tweaked. The same squad were going to get the chance to continue their campaign, rather than offering each spot on the team on the usual first-come, first-served basis; and those six were also going to get a special training session before their next matches.

'It's the first time we've done anything like that,' she said. 'We don't want to get battered.'

Wright was a very involved member of the club, serving on the committee and helping to organise their special events. But she had only been playing football for two and a half years – since she had joined Goal Diggers in the first place.

'It's kind of taken over my life,' she said. She had played sport as a child, and had captained her university at hockey. She had looked for a hockey club after graduation, but could not find one whose atmosphere suited her. Her hockey stick went into a cupboard and she was playing no sport at all.

'I literally was just miserable,' she admitted. As an Arsenal fan, she had occasionally found herself wanting to try football, but all the clubs she contacted were serious teams, competing in leagues, and only looking to sign players who could raise their standard – not complete beginners. Then she met up with an old friend from hockey, who mentioned that she trained with Goal Diggers, and Wright thought that sounded like exactly the kind of thing she had been wishing for.

'I know 26 isn't old,' she said, 'but for me, sport has been such a big part of my life. I always had it. Then I got to this part of my life where work started, and I was like, "Oh God, I'm not going to be able to play any sport," and [football] is literally the easiest sport to like take a small kit bag, there's pitches everywhere, which is obviously difficult getting on [for formal matches], but you can just go to a park and play football, and I've never had that as a sport before.'

In March, the Diggers team got their chance in the next round, heading out to Romford. They had enjoyed their training sessions against a local five-a-side team, all the better to prepare them for competition.

Getting there at 10am was a tough start to the day, with every player trying to jump on the same Central Line train.

'You forget that it forks when you go eastways, so some of us were on the wrong train, some of us were getting off the train, others were getting on, it was quite comical,' reported Wright. 'We all managed to get there on time, not ending up in Epping or anything like that, which was good.'

Diggers lost their first match before winning their next two, progressing to the semi-finals – and meeting the team who beat them in the final of their previous round.

'They beat us again,' said Wright. 'We actually started quite well against them, and thought we were on to something here, and then in the second half of the match ... they've just got shots like actual bullets. I was playing in goal quite a lot but I am not an actual goalie, and I was quite proud of myself in the earlier games. Then when we played them I was like, "Wow, I'll literally just break an arm rather than save anything."'

With their rivals progressing to the final to then decide who would go through to the national competition, the Diggers squad stayed to cheer them on to victory.

'We weren't friends with them but felt that on the sidelines – cheering them on, it was massively intense. They were 3-1 down and levelled up to 3-3, and then it went to a penalty shoot-out, which ended up being sudden death for ages, because the goals are so short and wide, for a goalie to save, and the penalty scorer is really close ...' Wright stopped, before summarising, 'And eventually Canada won, which we were very pleased about.'

It had been a wonderful experience for Wright and her team-mates. Defeat meant nothing, because in a squad not picked on performance, enjoying football was the only important thing.

'When you play for Goal Diggers, you're not really expecting to get to those sort of competitions,' said Wright. 'Both me and [team-mate] Anna had never played before Goal Diggers, and we are playing with people who have played football their whole lives. Even when we were playing this Canada team, they are Canadian – obviously women's football in Canada and the way they are treated as youth players is completely different to how it is here. You can just tell they're a load of expats who have got together and decided to play football together, and they look like a flipping professional team who have been playing together for years.'

She laughed when she thought back to their last match against the Canadians.

'They said, "We wish we were playing you in the final," and I was like, "I'm not surprised, you thrashed us," but they said, "You had great sportsmanship as well." It's quite nice when you hear things like that.'

* * *

Sheffield United's Carla Ward was named the Championship manager of the month in March. Her side had gone four games unbeaten; in this final stretch of the season, they were really settling into such a high level of football, and their coach was thrilled, not least because it had been a tricky time. Ward had long been upfront about their budget limitations, but there were other issues to deal with, most notably a high-profile case where one of her players was charged with making racist comments to an opposition player. In her first full campaign in management, Ward had dealt with a huge range of challenges, and had been pleased with the way her squad had responded after the racism charge.

'I haven't had any talk in training – there was never any talk around the training ground,' she said. 'They were all very well aware it was not to be spoken about, and they were excellent. I almost felt like they went out there with a bit of a point to prove – they wanted to show that they wanted to let their football do the talking at the end of the day, and not let the focus be anything else, and they did exactly that.'

Sheffield United had recently announced that their ground in the Olympic Legacy Park was to be developed and made into a permanent home, on which the women's side would have sole claim. The building work was to start in the close season, with the intention of opening it up at the start of the 2020/21 campaign.

'That'll be ours and only ours,' enthused Ward. 'It'll be amazing. We'll be based down there, it'll be great.'

Ward was also in the midst of taking her UEFA A licence, a requirement of coaches at the Championship level. The syllabus, she thought, was much as she had expected, simply codifying what a coach at that level would be doing anyway, but she did find one part of it rather tougher – the physical aspect, despite being officially retired for only a matter of months.

'You have to join in all the sessions, and I am not joking, I thought I was rolling back the years as a player, and my word, I couldn't move [afterwards],' she laughed. 'I did the first day on Sunday and I couldn't move, [nor] on Monday, and I still can't move now. Your head and your heart is telling you to do one thing and your body to do the other, so don't worry about that – I well and truly know that I'm retired now.'

Her former Sheffield coach Helen Mitchell had once said that Ward would never hang up her boots, and Ward had agreed. Now, though, she had accepted it, and management had given her a new focus beyond playing – as had the imminent arrival of her baby with her long-term partner. When the season began again, she would also have some tough targets to meet; Sheffield United had big ambitions for the future. Should they finish in the promotion spots of the Championship in the future, they would apply to go up a tier without a doubt; professional football in the WSL would follow.

'I think the club will be wanting it within a couple of years, to be honest,' revealed Ward. 'There's been sit-down talks in the last few weeks of where the club wants to go. They'll back it, they want to know what's going on, they want to know what we need – so yeah, they're fully supportive and they're for sure helping us with everything that they can.'

She was already thinking about transfer targets during the summer; after finding herself limited with budget and numbers the previous year, as players in the area gravitated towards the professional opportunity offered by Manchester United, she was hopeful that Sheffield United's grand plans would prove attractive. Also, she admitted, she had learnt a lot about making signings, and working out who would be the most beneficial additions to the squad.

'We might have brought players in thinking one thing,' she said, 'but things change and you learn quickly, and all of a sudden we might be looking for a different type of player. I'd say this year has been massively a learning curve – and we'll be looking forward to next season already.'

SUMMER

15

Fortune

YEOVIL, STILL fixed to the bottom of the WSL, all but confirmed their relegation when they announced their financial problems, stopping short of insolvency but still incurring a ten-point deduction as a penalty. Administrative staff had already been made redundant as a cost-cutting measure; manager Lee Burch knew that further punishments were inevitable.

'When the club started to realise what we needed to do to get through to the end of the season, we spoke, and we were trying to battle away and problem solve, that was really when we knew,' he said.

It probably did not come as a huge surprise to many people. Without backing from a big associated men's club, and reliant on sponsorship deals and crowdfunding, Burch thought they had always been operating hand to mouth. The news broke just before they faced games against Brighton and Everton, also hovering towards the lower end of the league.

'Yeah, the timing of that wasn't ideal, but it is what it is,' he said. 'We still had a lot to do [to stay up before the points deduction]. The ten points is ten points. I think that's something the league needs to look at. Is a ten-point deduction in a ten-team, 11-team league fair when you've got problems? It's the same deduction that Premier League, Championship sides do, but they've got a 40-game season, so a ten-point deduction in a small league is big. We said the same about suspended players. A player gets suspended for three games in the Premier League, he misses three games whatever percentage of the league that is, compared to three games in a 20-game season – it's a double whammy. I think that probably needs to be looked at. If we'd only had a six-point deduction, it makes things a little bit different, but I think with regards to that there was a mountain to climb, and we just had to keep fighting. We haven't looked at the league table for a while. We're just going to take it game by game.'

He did not think the players would be affected by the news; he had been pleased by their attitude and application throughout the season, regardless of results. A win against Everton – completing the double over them – in their penultimate away fixture of the season was just reward.

'Since the turn of the year, the performances have been really good,' he said. 'It was just getting the result that those performances merited – that's what we've got in the last two games. I think this result against Everton would have happened anyway. I certainly don't think the girls gave any more because of the situation. They had to travel up on the day. They left at half five in the morning. I had to travel myself in the car, driving eight hours. The players weren't in the best place they could be, but because they've been playing well, and I think the performances have been getting better – I've seen it in behind closed doors friendlies and stuff, we know that the team is getting better – so I think the form would have come anyway. That's just going to continue in these next four games.'

The club were intending to apply for a licence to compete in the Championship from the start of the 2019/20 season. The WSL experiment for Yeovil had been an interesting one but ultimately was a failure. For all that, Burch still felt it had been worthwhile.

'We felt we had a plan and a budget in place, but unfortunately as with all these things sometimes things just don't come to fruition, and you end up in the situations where you have to make decisions,' he said. 'I do still believe that the club should be applauded for trying to stay in the league and giving full-time football a go. We were actually very close to pulling that off – on and off the field. I think as much as people have lost their jobs – and that's the human element, it's not nice, I've been through that myself and that's not nice – I do think it was certainly worth a go, and the players appreciate it – they've said that, the fact they've been given the opportunity to play football at the top level and be full-time footballers, even if it was only for a year.'

* * *

Kelly Simmons, the FA's director of the women's professional game, was sad about the way Yeovil's season had panned out. She and her colleagues had been in talks with the club for weeks, but in the end the rules of the game had allowed little leeway; although she acknowledged Burch's views on the impact of a ten-point deduction, there had been no other option.

'What I can say is our rules gave no wiggle room,' she said. 'It was automatic. It wasn't "you shall" or "you may", it was a ten-point deduction. That's what it was. We had to do that to them once they'd triggered insolvency, there was no grey area on it, so it is what it is.'

Once that insolvency event had been triggered, the FA were able to give them their grant for the next season in advance, and Simmons and her team had worked with the club staff to help them strengthen ties with the local community, aiming to encourage investment from corporate partners and thus increase their income stream.

'It's massively challenging to play professional football without a big partner investment,' she said. 'I hate this side of the game and the job, but Yeovil were brilliant, they understood, we talked every day. We could then really support them and make sure they could make it to the end of the season. I think they were pretty gracious about the help they've had from the FA when they put their statements out. We're really pleased that they remain [operational], which is the most important thing.'

Clubs and fans alike were also concerned about how amateur clubs stepping up to the Championship, or from Championship to Super League, would fare financially. The financial price of instilling standards at each level of the game was also a concern the governing body had discussed, said Simmons.

'I'm not complacent at all about the step up and how hard we've got to work to make sure that clubs can come through,' she said. 'You've seen what's happened in the women's game in the last few years with clubs who haven't had that support – the game has gone professional and those clubs haven't been able to compete.'

Simmons admitted that ideally she would want women's football to generate enough revenue by itself that clubs did not have to rely on men's teams digging into their own coffers.

'That's got to be our vision and our mission down the line – to be able to generate enough money that if you come up from the Championship it's there for you to be able to come up and play, regardless of whether the men's club can afford to or want to put their hand in their pocket,' she said, adding that the top two teams in the Championship, Manchester United and Tottenham Hotspur, looked like they would be able to make the transition to professional full-time WSL football.

Other clubs in that division, though, would struggle.

'There's a lot of work to do around supporting that second tier of clubs, and helping them grow as well,' she said. 'The

worst thing is if you win on the pitch and you can't come up
– I hate that. I do feel mindful that without setting standards
and being really ambitious, the game would still be amateur,
semi and professional in one league – really varying standards
– but it does come with its challenges.'

Earlier in the month, the FA had announced with much
fanfare a sponsorship deal for the WSL courtesy of Barclays,
meaning the bank brand's name would be added to the
league's name as from 2019/20. More tangibly, Barclays were
also investing a sum of money into the game; no figures
had been confirmed, but the official statements mentioned
'eight figures' and 'multimillion pounds'. Much of that
money would be used at grassroots level, with Barclays also
becoming the lead partner of the FA Girls' Football School
Partnerships, a nationwide scheme to help develop girls' access
to football at school. It would not, however, be used in any
other senior league.

'It won't filter down into the Championship or National
League, because they're not the title sponsor of those leagues,'
explained Simmons. 'We've got to go out and find title
sponsors for those leagues, and actually if we can do that
then obviously they will benefit from having a partner that
wants to activate in that area.'

She revealed that negotiations had begun with some
interested companies, but in the meantime she was happy
to have Barclays on board – both for immediate financial
reasons, but also for the strategic impact.

'It just shows you where the interest [in] women's sport is,
women's football, and the emerging commercial investment
in it – really pleased with that,' she said. 'So now we've nailed
the deal, it's about how do we use Barclays' investment and
Barclays' reach and their partnership with the Premier League
to really increase awareness and visibility, so that's great.
When I came in [to the job], the clubs were saying to me,
"There's a lot going on but we haven't got a clear strategy of

what we're trying to achieve together," so we're committed to quite good progress around building a vision and strategy for the professional game between now and 2024.'

That meant imminent work around several key targets – securing more commercial revenue, the league's governance structure and the clubs having more input into that, developing future England players, and improving the standard of refereeing. Simmons thought that the speed of much of this development would depend on how the Lionesses fared at the summer's Women's World Cup.

'We're doing a big piece of work around who's our audience,' she said. 'England women, cup final, big events – it's families and young kids, little girls in their football kits. Women's Super League, the opportunity for increasing audience is coming from [age] 18 to 34 crossover from men's football club fans – male and female, but a slight male skew. That's what the clubs have been telling me they've been seeing. It's the difference between children who have got so much to do and have so many choices coming to big games and coming occasionally versus those who are the building of the diehards who come week in week out; [they] tend to be more adults and coming over in increasing numbers, and I know the clubs are really looking at how they market the game, I know they're looking at opening up the men's stadium for big games, I think we're going to see a lot of effort in that area to build attendances, which we really need to do.'

* * *

The new Barclays sponsorship had excited much discussion. Most players had been incredibly enthusiastic, thrilled at the idea that finally big money was coming into the women's game. One who was willing to express her concerns publicly was Crystal Palace goalkeeper Megen Lynch. A chef by profession, she lived in south London with her fiancée and team-mate Nikita Whinnett, a Scouser by birth, and their dog AJ. Their current home was an 18th-century pub, where Whinnett was the manager covering for a colleague's maternity leave, and Lynch catered for functions. On a cloudy March morning before the pub opened, Lynch sipped at a cup of tea, and considered the financial advantages of the sponsorship deal.

'Yeah, it is a massive step for women's football,' she said, 'but it's only those clubs [in the WSL] that are going to benefit from it. How's it going to work when teams drop out of that league, with that much money that's been pumped into them? Are they going to be professional in a semi-professional league? Is it going to be fair? Are they going to walk the league? I don't know. There's a lot of questions they haven't answered.'

She looked across the room at Whinnett. 'She's a bit like, "It's absolutely amazing, and it will help, and it will help everyone down the ladder." Does that mean the FA are going to put more money down the lower leagues? Because they can afford to do it now. They can afford to say, "Do you know what, we can take a little bit more away from them and put it down the ladder."'

As a semi-professional player, Lynch was very aware of how additional money in their league could make a real difference – changing people's lives beyond recognition. She also thought that the gap between the divisions in terms of players' daily routines and the way that clubs operated was bigger than anyone had really acknowledged.

'How can you have a professional league, [then] a semi-professional league, and then a completely different league underneath that?' she asked rhetorically. 'I know it's a challenge for men's teams as well, stepping up in their leagues, but they're still full-time – they're full-time up until six or seven tiers under the Premier League – whereas in women's football it's not going to be easy to step up.'

Lynch thought back to the national newspapers attempting to manufacture a scandal from the fact that some Palace players had been encouraged to find sponsors to cover some of their club fees. She sighed.

'That's what happens in all football! Every season when I was playing junior football at Charlton, we paid £220 a season to register and get your kit, and that's exactly what we do as seniors. We have to pay a sign-on fee. That's exactly what it is. It's not a sponsorship. It's a sign-on fee. If you can get someone to sponsor you to pay your sign-on fee, it means you don't have to pay out anything, and that's how it should be.'

Lynch knew that she and Whinnett were fortunate because they had enough years behind them to attract some sponsors; she had recently signed with a glove sponsor, and was slightly taken aback at the range and quality of products she had already benefitted from, saying, 'I've never had this treatment before!'

Of course, living and working in a pub meant lots of conversations about football with patrons.

'When the SheBelieves Cup was on, the Champions League game was on as well – it was on after the Champions League game, and one of our customers was like, "Are you going to put the women's football on after?"' recalled Lynch. 'Me and Nikita, we knew it was on, but it was like, "He's actually asking!"'

'It was really nice,' confirmed Whinnett. 'I put it on and all my regulars were like, "Your girls are on. Which ones do you know?"'

Others were less complimentary; Lynch had put up with one customer who proudly declared himself uninterested in football, but still felt it necessary to tell her that he thought women's football was not worth watching. He added that even though he had not seen her play, she herself was not worth watching; it was unsurprising when Lynch went on to say that she had walked out of the bar rather than continue the conversation.

'He felt so bad that he'd upset me, but I was like, "You don't even like football so why are you talking to me about football?"' she said.

Whinnett had not heard the conversation; if she had, she suspected she would have had a few words to say. The couple had met while both playing for Charlton; it had been down to Whinnett to make the first move.

'I asked Megen out!' she beamed. 'I had to find out whether she was gay or straight. I asked the team. She'd been there 15 years. Megen is like a closed vault. I was really shocked to hear that nobody knew anything about her.'

This was clearly a conversation the two had had many times previously. Lynch stepped in to defend herself, saying, 'Well, no, because football is football and then outside of football you can be you. So the girls at football – this is going to sound horrible because I've known quite a few of the girls I play football with for quite a long time, but they think they know me and they don't. Football's football. You know what I've let you know, basically. It's football. I'm so serious at football. It's a job so you have to be serious. You can have a laugh and a joke, but I'm not going to have a laugh and joke with people – '

'So I asked her outright,' interrupted Whinnett, ready to continue the story. '"Are you gay, straight, bisexual, what?" She was like, "I'm bisexual," and I was like, "Yes!" And then about eight weeks later I actually manned up.'

'But,' asked Lynch, 'shall I tell the whole incident of actually introducing me to your friends?'

There was a pause.

'Oh yeah,' replied Whinnett.

'So,' said Lynch, pleased to take the floor, 'she introduced me. I had two nicknames at football, at Charlton, at this time. I've actually got one of them tattooed on me. It's really cool, because we won a cup, and I'd said if we won a cup, I'd get it tattooed on me – I got called the Tank, I was a lot bigger at that time. So she introduced me to one of her friends and she was like, "This is Tank."

'I was like, "That's not my name – quite clearly not my name."

'Because I've got big hair and blue eyes, they called me Ariel [from The Little Mermaid] as well, so she was like, "It's Ariel!"

'"No, that's not my name. I follow you on Twitter! Did you not read my name on Twitter when you tagged me in stuff on Twitter? It says MEGEN LYNCH on Twitter."'

Whinnett grinned. 'I didn't know her name.'

Lynch carried on. '"My name's Megen. Really?!"'

'I used to call her babe!' Whinnett laughed. '"You all right, babe?"'

'So she asked me out not knowing my name, then called me everything but my name!'

'And then next week we've been together four years,' concluded Whinnett. 'We're engaged. We're meant to be getting married in December.'

They had also recently been approved as foster parents, and were looking forward to that new stage in their life together. Lynch was currently on the sidelines recovering from a knee injury; her fiancée sympathised hugely having suffered something similar not too long ago. Like other players in the second tier and below, they wished they had better and quicker access to sports medicine.

'Some girl kicked my knee, chipped the cartilage, and I got a locked knee – they just had to take that out,' explained Lynch, who heard a popping sound as soon as the opposition player made contact with her. 'No pain, I was lucky, I was really super-lucky, whereas Nikita had a very similar injury – she had a chipped bit and a floating bit, it was still hanging on and making her feel like she had a dislocation.'

'Mine was pushing my patella and locking my knee out,' added Whinnett. 'It was sitting in the joint, so I had to have reconstruction surgery where they reattached it because I didn't want a weakness in my knee.'

Whinnett ended up out of the game for almost a year. The initial schedule was for her to return after six months, and two MRI scans came back clear, confirming she would be fit to play, but as soon as she got back on the pitch, she suffered another injury.

'I self-diagnosed me,' she recalled. 'The physio, the surgeons, didn't have a clue what was going on. I said, "I've got a bit of bone or something floating round my knee."'

Both had been playing football since they were children. Lynch had relied on her dad for lifts to training and matches, but he was also caring for her mum at the same time; Whinnett's parents did not drive so needed offers of transport from friends and extended family. Having been football-mad youngsters idolising the grown-up players – both male and female – they were very committed to their community outreach via Crystal Palace, making appearances at schools and signing autographs and posing for selfies on matchdays. Lynch was obviously very proud that her fiancée was the favourite player of so many Palace-supporting children.

'Every week we get a message from parents saying, "Can my girl be your mascot?" to Nikita, because they just love her,' she revealed. 'I sat in the stand one day – people don't realise we're together because we're quite professional outside – so I was sitting in the stand, and I think I got literally an under-ten Crystal Palace girls' squad [sitting by me] and they were all, "The number nine's awesome, she's my favourite!" All of them!'

Lynch felt that being a role model was an important part of their work – even if they were just semi-professionals.

'I was exactly the same,' she admitted. '"Oh my God, there's Pauline Cope!" "Oh my God, there's Karen Hills!" "Oh my God, there's Eartha [Pond], or Fara Williams!" That was me growing up, so I know exactly where they're coming from. We've got a girl in the under-12s, she's also sponsored by the same guy who's my sponsor, and she always comes and she always gets her photo with me, no matter what, she absolutely loves it, and it's really cool because now she's got something to aim for. "OK, that's how good Megen was, can I be better than her?"'

After spending some time at other clubs in the London area, both were very happy at Palace.

'I'm committed to Palace because I absolutely love the club,' said Whinnett.

'Tell what you say to me all the time. Palace is like what?'

'Like Liverpool,' she responded. 'The fans, it's everything. In Liverpool there's nothing but football, there's Liverpool or Everton, and that's what you've got and that's what Palace is like, it's so family-orientated, you play with heart and passion and it doesn't matter how well you play or how bad you play, the fans will love you.'

If Palace had been able to offer them professional contracts, everything in their footballing world would be perfect. They both felt that anybody playing in the Championship should ultimately have professional football as their ambition, and Lynch pointed out that the next generation of young players coming through were already just as good as their older squadmates because they had benefitted from specialist training for their entire lives.

'It's like me – I am only as good as I am because of Pauline Cope,' acknowledged Lynch, referring once again to the former England goalkeeper. 'Pauline Cope was so strict – and Keith [Boanas, her husband and the former Charlton manager], I had both of them, they're amazing, by the way. They put the fundamentals into me. I had another coach there [at training] yesterday and I was doing a bit of hand work and he said, "Everything sticks like glue to you – everything sticks!" And I was like, "Yeah that's cos when I was younger, I got taught no matter how crappy your gloves are, everything sticks, you've got glue on your hands, everything sticks." That's the fundamentals I've taken when I was eight years old and I'm 27 now and I still use the same things, and I pass that on to the kids I coach now. It's all about fundamentals and trusting yourself and believing in yourself.'

Lynch had previously coached in Charlton's centre of excellence, and believed strongly that the best coaches should be working with younger cohorts, to ensure that those fundamentals were properly taught. She was passionate about the importance of good coaching and good facilities from an early age, which was one of the biggest reasons why she was concerned that any investment in the women's game should be able to flow down the pyramid. She saw the sport's long-term future, and feared for it if cash injections reached only those who had already reached the top.

'It's not this generation that you need to concentrate on,' she said. 'Yeah, I know that this generation might win you a trophy at the World Cup – might – but it's the future generations. You want what the men have done now – become more successful over the years – and that's what you want. You don't want instant success and then flop. You want success, success and even more success, and sustain it, like the US national team have, and Japan. OK, we're in the top three of the world – sustain it. But how are you going to do that if you're not doing it from grassroots upwards?'

* * *

'Note to all female players playing at present … enjoy and cherish the matchday experience and don't take it for granted because when you retire you will miss it and wished you had taken full advantage of having the talent and pleasure to play the beautiful game #IHaveRegrets'

These were the words Pauline Cope-Boanas tweeted in April 2019, two months before England headed to the

Women's World Cup in France, 24 years after she and her pioneer team-mates represented the country for the first time in an official FIFA tournament. The goalkeeper had won 60 international caps, and at club level had spent 22 years representing London teams – Millwall, Arsenal and Croydon, who became Charlton Athletic – winning the league, the FA Cup and League Cup multiple times.

The idea of Cope-Boanas having regrets was a puzzling one. As well as her exploits between the sticks, she was also very well known for her personality – loud, funny, exuberant, feisty, aggressive, argumentative. Since becoming a coach, working in football development, and watching how others coached teams, though, she had reflected on her career and her behaviour.

'I don't mind being a bit firm, but when you're screaming and shouting and upsetting them – that's how I was as a player,' she confessed. 'That's where I have my regrets about my behaviour – the way I used to speak to people, my own players, the opposition and the manager and the fans. If I could have had a mentor back then, I think I would have been a lot different.'

It was difficult to imagine Cope-Boanas responding to even well-intended suggestions from an outsider, though, and she admitted that people around her had tried to talk to her about the way she acted on the pitch. Former team-mate and England coach Hope Powell was one of them; husband and her ex-manager Keith Boanas was another.

'Had I had someone to pull me in when I was getting out of control, maybe I'd have been different – maybe people were scared to do it because of my temper,' she said. 'I was proper horrible, I must have been horrible to play with and play against, do you know what I mean? It upsets me sometimes talking about it.'

As well as her behaviour, she also regretted some of the decisions she had made – including opting to retire at the age of 36. One of the reasons she decided it was time to hang up her gloves was that she had been booked for shouting at her team-mate Casey Stoney to take a better corner kick.

'When you get booked for swearing at your own team-mate at the other end of the pitch and the referee's come and booked me, I thought, "Do you know what, it's time to call it a day,"' she said. 'I wasn't enjoying it. I used to wear a watch at the end of my career and think, "Right, 45 minutes and this game's over," and that's another regret – I used to wish the games over before they'd even started, and I just regret that so, so much.'

These feelings had started to coalesce when Cope-Boanas watched one of Carshalton Athletic's matches, where her husband was the assistant manager, and realised how much she had actually missed playing.

'I was there on the matchday, thinking, "How much do I miss this? How much did I not take advantage of how good I was? How much better I could have been?" I just wished my career away,' she said.

But she had taken steps to help young goalkeepers forging their own paths, coaching at some clubs, and telling her charges that they should not be mimicking her behaviour, even if they wanted to imitate some of her keeping style. She spoke fondly of one of her former players, Megen Lynch – 'She's a good kid, Meg. Well, not a kid, she's a grown woman now' – and hoped she would be able to mentor other players so they did not make the same mistakes she had.

'I would have loved the opportunity to be a mentor, to go round clubs and speak to goalkeepers, let them know it's all right to make a mistake, let them know it's OK to concede goals, let them know my experiences and what I did I wish I hadn't done – if I hadn't done that, how far I could have gone,' she said.

In terms of her achievements, she regretted little, but she admitted that she yearned to be playing at the top level now.

'I think I was probably born 20 years too early,' she reflected. 'What they've got now, you could only dream of that when I was growing up. I retired at 36, I reckon probably about 40, and if I had the opportunities that the keepers got now, I would have been world class, and I'm not blowing my own trumpet, I got where I was from natural talent.'

Cope-Boanas got specialist coaching only when she was with the England squad, making her debut there at the age of 25, although when she moved to Charlton late in her career there was a goalkeeper coach there for their twice-weekly training sessions, who also worked with the men's first-team goalkeeper, Dean Kiely. She was also employed at the club, which meant she would get messages from coach Mickey Cole asking her to train with Kiely before a matchday if she had some free time.

'The fact that Deano would rather train with me speaks volumes to how good he thought I was,' she said. 'I remember training with Deano, it used to be on a Friday afternoon, we used to work with Coley, and at the end me and Deano used to kick balls from out of our hands, off the floor, up and down the pitch. One day I was with Deano and he said, "Copey, if you was a man, you'd earn millions." And I went, "Deano, don't say that."'

Cope-Boanas never meant to be a goalkeeper – she started out as a centre-half.

'Back in the day I used to keep getting sent off, or told off, or involved in fights and arguments, I kept getting booked, and then one day the goalkeeper didn't turn up,' she recounted. 'I must have been about 13.'

Her manager was Ted Waller, father of Lou, later Cope-Boanas's long-time Millwall and England team-mate and still her close friend.

'He thought I was the only nutty one who might go in goal, so he stuck me in goal to keep me out of trouble, and I've been there ever since. It was obviously something that he saw in me, that I never saw. I never dreamt of being a goalkeeper. I was flying all over the place.'

Even after that, she was still not sure whether she was a goalkeeper or not; when she was called up for England junior trials, even the coaches were not clear whether they wanted her to play in defence or between the posts. Of course, football was a hobby for Cope-Boanas; she was working office hours, spending three years as the women's and girls' development officer at Charlton, never dreaming that ten years later the Lionesses would be professional players.

'When I used to go into schools, I did talks in assembly about my career, and do a Q&A,' she said. 'We did girls only sessions, and I used to say, "What's your ambitions then?", thinking they'd want to be a doctor or a veterinary surgeon, and one young girl said, "I want to be a professional footballer," and I never had the heart to tell her that was never going to happen – and I'm glad I didn't tell her that.'

Cope-Boanas's line of work now was in police custody, requiring her to cover shifts, meaning that she could not commit regularly to coaching at a club. She also wondered whether her reputation preceded her, and managers and directors did not want her involved with their players.

'There's so much I've got to give, but a lot of people probably don't approach me because of what I was like as a player,' she thought. 'If I go to clubs and approach them, they might think, "Pauline Cope, she's gobby, mouthy, a good keeper but a bad role model."'

Despite her regrets, Cope-Boanas had only good memories of her clubs, although she admitted to some lingering bitterness about her international career as she felt her generation of England players were largely overlooked, although she was grateful that her half-century of international caps were commemorated on the honour roll at the FA's St George's Park training complex; she was sad that she had not even been invited to showpiece matches. She wondered whether, if she had been a more compliant type of person, she might have been offered the role of England goalkeeping coach by now.

'I gave ten years of my time – never caused no nuisance to physio or coach, I was never rude or disrespectful or abusive to any of them because to me it was a privilege and an honour to play for England and to get picked,' she said. 'I was lucky enough to play 60 times for England, and that was over the course of ten years – look how many caps they get now. I used to have to take annual leave. We only started getting paid [to cover expenses] towards the end of my career. I was only getting 100 quid a day if I was away, but we didn't play for the money, we played for the love of it.'

Although she had expressed the wish that she had been born 20 years later so as to take advantage of all the opportunities female footballers received now, she did acknowledge that there were some benefits to playing in a pre-social media age.

'If I played today, it's like Big Brother, isn't it?' she asked rhetorically. 'I don't know if I'd play 90 minutes. This is why I don't get asked to do any TV work, because of my reputation – they probably think I'm going to throw the f-bomb in.'

The professionalism of modern footballers impressed her to an extent, but she could not help but wonder if her generation of players loved the sport more. She was not interested in the debates about equal pay for male and female athletes at international level; she thought that anyone selected to represent their nation ought to play for the privilege rather than a salary or any financial bonus.

'I think the competitiveness has gone away from the game,' she reflected. 'You don't see no afters or little square-ups and you don't see anyone getting angry and winding the team up – I think that's completely gone from the game. I used to love my tussles with [former Arsenal defender] Jayne Ludlow – we used to be forehead to forehead. You don't see that in the game in any way, shape or form.'

Perhaps that passion that Cope-Boanas felt on the football field emanated from her exactly because it was not her job – but she devoted all her spare time as well as her money to it, buying her own boots and gloves rather than getting freebies from a sponsor.

'I don't get angry like that at work!' she concurred. 'When I was playing, people never used to see me, training in the pissing rain ten o'clock at night, or going away and getting home at one o'clock on a Monday morning and having to be up at five to go to work.'

She wished she could apologise to anyone she had upset during her playing days – and hoped those still revelling in their footballing careers understood just how lucky they were. She wanted to tell them to pass on their knowledge and experience, and enjoy the perks of their jobs, from signing autographs to giving away pairs of sponsored boots and gloves.

'When you get it, you're really appreciative, and you want to give it to someone else,' she advised. 'Pass it on, then that's good – them kids will remember that. They'll remember that.'

16

Trophy hunt

ORIENT WERE aiming to end their season with two trophies. Promotion was out of the question reasonably early on in the year, but their cup progress had been excellent.

'Whilst obviously we want to finish as high as possible, there's always that element of we're not playing for promotion now, we're not playing to stay up, you're just playing to stay as high as you can,' said Hayley Barton. 'It's quite nice to have a different focus, to keep you motivated until the end of the season. I guess it's just keeping that balance. We still want to win the league games, but you have to weigh up that now we just want to win the two cup games – finish as high as we can, but I'd take winning the two cup games over those final league games. It should be good. It will be nice to finish with some silverware.'

First up was the Isthmian Cup Final in mid-April, hosted by Aveley FC. In terms of distance, Aveley – just past Rainham in Essex – was not far from Leyton. In terms of accessibility, it was not ideal for anyone. Anyone travelling by train would need to catch a bus from the station, then, lacking signposting, use a map to navigate a treacherous walk down a new bypass where the footpath was only partly finished; or of course they could take a cab or an Uber, but that ran the risk of the driver being thoroughly confused by this new football stadium and its equally new surrounding infrastructure, including a housing estate still midway through construction. On arrival at the ground, one large egress gate was open, ready to welcome fans, with a single person seated at a trestle table taking the ticket toll.

Still, it was a warm, sunny spring day, and as the sun set, the floodlights flickered on, shedding their beams across the pitch – an artificial surface. Neither Orient nor their opponents Ashford Town (Middlesex), from two divisions below, were used to playing full matches on anything other than grass, so the warm-up, to grow accustomed to the conditions, was crucial.

However, a Wednesday night kick-off for two amateur teams, involving significant travel from both home grounds, is always likely to cause problems. Though Orient were out on the pitch going through their drills by 7pm, there was no sign of Ashford until ten minutes later. The O's were not distracted by the late arrival of the opposition, but they could have been forgiven if they had fretted at all about the success of their finishing practice; few of their efforts made it into the net as shots were skied, scuffed wide, and bobbling.

As the squads trekked back in to the dressing room, they walked past the trophy, positioned on a plinth by the tunnel. It was replaced swiftly by the match ball, gathered by the referee as he led out both sides, and the formalities began, with the dignitaries from the club and sponsors Reposs being introduced to the players by each captain.

In the opening minutes, both teams were struggling with the bounce of the ball on the artificial surface, and it was only a series of great saves from Orient goalkeeper Naomi Ogunde that kept the scoresheet blank. A few minutes before half-time, Hayley Barton put the O's ahead with a calm finish slotted into the net, but it also resulted in a serious injury to the Ashford player challenging her, Nadia Peters, who was stretchered off.

Mist began to descend during the second half, and those who came equipped for winter weather rather than spring began to feel the benefit of extra layers. Orient kept the ball confidently, creating plenty of chances, and adding one more goal to their advantage, courtesy of full-back Leyre Bastyr.

When the final whistle blew, the celebrations were respectful, with handshakes with the opposition and the officials taking precedence. Once that was completed, the Orient players bounded around the pitch, hugging their friends and families in the stands, and posing for photos next to the sponsored celebratory hoarding that had been provided, and with bottles of sparkling wine appearing for the traditional dousing. Coach Brayford tried to anoint goalkeeper Ogunde, but she scampered away, calling back to him, 'You'll have to catch me first!'

Medals were presented to the match officials first, then the losing finalists. Griffiths began to prepare her team to collect their prizes, organising them into a rough queue, and telling them where to assemble for a photo opportunity when she lifted the trophy. Obediently they assembled behind the hoarding, and after Griffiths shook hands with all the dignitaries and was given the cup, she took three paces to her left to join the rest of her squad. She lifted the cup above her head, and all the players burst into song, leaping up and down on the spot with sheer glee.

* * *

Brayford had tried to take a step back and allow the players to enjoy the ceremonials, but they insisted that he also collected a medal from the presentation party.

'Trying to get him to have a medal or a photo for any of our successes is difficult,' said Griffiths afterwards. 'He deserves it. We try to include him, and get him included as much as possible, but he'll leave those medals for the other people who helped us get to the final – Sophie and Kayleigh and people like that who missed the final, make sure they get their recognition, which is very kind of him but he also deserves recognition for all the hard work he does.

'He's very modest, he will never take any credit for anything, and he'll always say he hasn't done much work when in fact he's done everything, really. I'm louder, but he definitely does all the work behind the scenes. All the organising for the games, we don't see half of what he does. The occasions that I do see the work that goes in, I'm a bit in awe of how he fits it all in with a day job as well.'

Griffiths had thoroughly enjoyed that cup final. The stadium facilities had been excellent, the club staff had been welcoming, and though the 3G had taken time to get used to, the pitch had been good. The chill in the stands had not spread to the players; artificial turf retains heat. She had left work slightly early – catching a train just after 5pm and sharing a cab with her team-mates from the nearest station to get to the ground ('It's not glamorous, no, but that's quite often the case with a lot of our games,' she smiled). Others had been delayed by an accident on the M25, resulting in the delayed kick-off, but she was pleased that her team had not been distracted by that. They had gone in as favourites against a team two divisions below, but who were riding high on confidence having secured promotion. Though Orient's win had not been as decisive as perhaps she might have hoped, Griffiths was never concerned about anyone failing to convert chances.

'You look up front and you've got Sophie, Hayley, you've got Suaila, Lisa Hollback – you know all of them can score goals, but I'm not worried,' she said. 'We've become patient. We know our chances are going to come and we will score a goal. There's plenty of people on the pitch who can score them, and I'm a defender so I certainly won't be thinking I could do any better! I have a lot of respect for them – I'm sure I'd do worse if I was in their position! They do a good job. It's not easy because a defender's job is to put people off in whatever way, I know that better than anyone.

'I might sound like a crazy person when I'm on the pitch and shouting various different things, but it's all part of the game and no one gets frustrated with each other. We're all in it together. We've certainly learnt throughout this season that if we continue to play for the whole 90 minutes, we'll definitely get a result against any team really.'

Griffiths hoped it would bode well for the next big match – a Capital Cup Final clash against regular foes Old Actonians. It was another mid-week match, meaning players would have to arrange an earlier finish time from their day jobs and travel in rush hour to the venue, Hanwell in west London.

'Preparation for a game midweek is difficult, let alone [for] a cup final, but no, it's the same for both teams,' she said. 'Our games against Actonians are always close. I can't remember a game that hasn't been one goal either way or a draw. They're a difficult team. Their captain was my captain at university, so I know them well – their right-back used to play for us, one of their centre-backs as well I also know from university, so it's going to be a challenge. They've got the top goalscorer in the league. But on our day we can beat any team, we're confident we can beat any team, so we'll see what happens.'

In the meantime, Griffiths had wedding plans to finalise, with one month to go until the big day. Her team-mates had already arranged a football-themed hen party for her, with every squad member imitating her distinctive hairstyle, with fringe quiffed up at the front, and donning a captain's armband as an accessory to their finery.

'I don't think Chris wanted to hear about it on the Sunday!' she smiled.

* * *

One of Griffiths's greatest delights of the season had been Lisa Hollback's player of the match award in the Isthmian Cup Final.

'That was her first cup final ever!' she explained. 'Before the game, she was excited and super-nervous. We were saying, "Lisa, you'll be fine, don't worry, it's like any other game." And then after she didn't actually know what she'd won when she went to pick up the trophy – so we had to explain to her that it was player of the match once she'd come back into the group. She thought that everyone was getting called up one by one! She didn't know she'd got player of the match until she came back in. Thoroughly deserved. She's been brilliant for the past couple of seasons.'

'I've never played a cup final before, so I wasn't sure how it works,' admitted Hollback later. 'I thought they were just presenting every player's name – giving them the award. They were like, "No, no, you won," and I was like, "What?"'

Hollback's impressive display had been enjoyed by the crowd, which included some of her colleagues from a London firm where she worked as a quantity surveyor. She was very grateful that her workmates were so supportive – and understanding of the times when she needed to leave the office early for a match.

Born and raised in a small village in Sweden, Hollback started playing football in her late teens but stopped when she went to university. She took it up again seriously when she lived in Melbourne, Australia, as part of her time out travelling the world and visiting friends. She ended up in London after meeting her partner, an Englishman, in Australia, and they opted to head back to the United Kingdom rather than back to Sweden ('he's progressing but he's not really there yet with his Swedish,' she explained with a half-laugh).

It was he who encouraged her to go to the Orient trials; she had never played at such a high standard previously, and having learnt of the club's history, she was somewhat overawed.

'I didn't know anything about Leyton Orient,' she admitted. 'I found this team [online], and I came home and told my boyfriend – when he was younger he was like a Leyton Orient supporter. And he told me about the club and everything, and I was like, "No way, I'm not going there." He was like, "No, no, go and try out."

'It took me a few weeks before I even dared to show up, and when I was there, my first training, oh my God, you should have seen me. I was basically standing the whole training with my mouth open, just so shocked by how good everyone was.'

She returned home thinking she would never go there again, despite the squad making her very welcome; she simply thought she was not good enough to keep up with them. She was still evidently slightly surprised that she was part of the team and playing at such a high level, but at the age of 27 she was more concerned with enjoying her football than with chasing medals – although they were a very pleasant and welcome bonus.

'I'm basically more happy with the people who are around the team – my team-mates and stuff than winning cups and stuff,' she explained. 'Obviously that's very nice as well, especially when you've never done it before, but it's more the team spirit and the people in the team that makes it. What I'm trying to say is that maybe winning the league, that would be amazing, but I think going to training late when you're tired on a Wednesday and you still have a good time is a bit more the thing I get out of football these days.'

* * *

'I'm always happy!' beamed Chris Brayford. 'I hope they are too. It was a good season.'

He was, indeed, always happy when he was coaching his Orient team. Though the results had mostly been good, even when things were not going the O's way, a smile was never too far from his face.

'It's the whole cliché about you don't coach football, you coach people, and I think we're lucky with a great bunch,' he said, sipping at a cup of tea. 'That doesn't mean there aren't frustrations and stuff, but I enjoy the interactions. Are we getting better as a team? Are players getting better? And enjoyment isn't necessarily winning, again it's us and how we are. I enjoy that.

'Obviously I'm a football obsessive, but you're doing what you love. I wouldn't do it if I didn't enjoy it, but only in the same way that I think the players wouldn't play if they didn't enjoy it. I definitely think we're doing something right in that now, over the summer, quite a lot [of players from other teams] have contacted me independently [to enquire about joining], and I think that's a good sign. Win or lose, there's enthusiasm there, and love, and affection, and enjoyment – all those things, and they come off, and that's the most important thing in football.'

After the season had finished, the Orient manager had time to take stock. On a short break from his day job in the City of London, he could watch the world go by and assess his team's progress. They had lost the Capital Cup Final by a single goal – a result that Griffiths thought was probably a fair one. Her coach did not quite agree.

'I would say I don't think they were better than us,' he said. 'I think our frustration would be that we can play to a higher level and actually on the night we created more chances, we had more possession, we were the better team, but it's irrelevant because we got beat.

'One of the things that came through is they were geared up to play in the same way as if they were playing a team from a higher division. They were aggressive, they worked hard, and credit to them.'

He was a little disappointed in some of the officials' decisions, but accepted that ultimately they had no real impact on the overall result ('that's not the game, us not taking the chances beforehand is the game'). With one trophy in the cabinet, Brayford was hopeful that his team would once more be challenging for silverware in the next season, but that would bring with it its own problems. If Leyton Orient were promoted, they would be in the third tier of the pyramid, and they would have to consider whether or not they would be able to switch to a proper semi-professional set-up should they be presented with the chance to play in the Championship. Brayford thought that his team would be able to compete well in the National League Premier Division – but if they were to move up one step further, it would be much more of a challenge, requiring, of course, much more financial investment, but also administrative support behind the scenes. Brayford thought that Orient's men's club would continue their backing, and possibly extend it.

'Definitely it's a good relationship and we hope that it can build more,' he said. 'Clearly we couldn't be competitive in the Championship without some help – but you'd hope that if we can get up into the Championship, there'd be a motivation to give us that help.'

At the moment, he was happy with the way everything was running, and was managing his work-life balance well; he knew that some of his work colleagues were still surprised when they found out about his double life as a football coach.

'I'm lucky in my job – it's a good job and it gives you the ability to do other things,' he said. 'I often think the advantage might be to do it full-time, but you might be waking up in the morning and thinking, "It's half seven and I've got to go and coach in the rain and I'm not looking forward to it," but doing it part-time, it works well.'

Brayford claimed that he always looked forward to training – 'certainly more than some of the players!' he joked – and he was of course already planning for pre-season as well as the campaign ahead.

'We've got a really good squad,' he said. 'It's on the manager to do a better job and make sure we're put in the right position to win games. I genuinely think we can win that division next season. You can hold us to it.'

* * *

Arsenal might have missed out on lifting a cup on a showpiece occasion, but they secured the Women's Super League title with a game to go when they defeated Brighton at the Amex Community Stadium. That meant they would have the chance to celebrate their victory in front of their own fans, at Meadow Park, in the final match of the season – against second-placed Manchester City. It was no wonder there was a festive air around their London Colney training ground the week after the championship came home.

That celebratory atmosphere was added to by a peculiar sound – that of men's goalkeeper Petr Cech drumming on a full kit, set up in the centre of the indoor training hub, as part of a tribute to be filmed to mark the end of his career. Nonetheless, it was a rather unusual incident, and star striker Vivianne Miedema could well be forgiven for walking in, looking utterly bewildered and confused when her coach Joe Montemurro tried to persuade her to dance along to the drum beat. Equally, though, she could be forgiven for dancing all the time, celebrating an incredible season in which she won the league's Golden Boot for the top scorer as well as the PFA Players' Player of the Year award.

The 22-year-old had gone on the record plenty of times saying that she did not keep count of her goals, and that resolution held firm. She wondered if it was because she had not always played as an out and out striker, but as a number ten.

'I like to be part of the play, like to assist goals, and it's all not about just scoring for me, so yeah, obviously it is my job to score goals because I'm a number nine, but it's not like at the beginning of the season I target myself, "Oh, this is how many goals you need to score, and if you don't score that many goals you've had a shit season" – I don't think like that at all,' said the Dutchwoman.

Although Manchester City's Nikita Parris won the Football Writers' Association's Player of the Year award, Miedema was more than delighted with her honour from her peers – particularly as her compatriot Virgil van Dijk of Liverpool picked up the equivalent award on the men's side.

'Just amazing to get that recognition, I would say,' she reflected, describing the entire ceremony as a 'really special night'.

Beth Mead had been enjoying a special day. That morning, she had received the email confirming that she would be part of England's World Cup squad in the summer. She had been told to expect a notification either way at 8am, so she set her alarm to ensure she was awake and ready. In the end, the email arrived one minute early. She was already looking forward to the Lionesses' first match in France – against Scotland.

'What an amazing game to open a World Cup up with – us v Scotland is huge!' she said. 'Hopefully it's an amazing game to watch, obviously we want to be on the winning end of it, but yeah, I think it's going to be an exciting start to a World Cup.'

She joked that she had been practising her French with goalkeeper Pauline Peyraud-Magnin – 'I don't have that much. Hello, goodbye, how are you, my name is, je m'appelle Bethany, au revoir, bonjour, comme ci, comme ca.'

She hadn't allowed herself to think too much about the summer while there was still a WSL title to win. Now, seven years after the Gunners' last league championship, it was, as Mead said, 'job complete'.

'Honestly, it's a nice weight off our shoulders as a team, to be able to go to the Man City game and just be able to enjoy it and not worry about a league being on the line, and probably City would have felt the same [had they been in the same situation],' she said.

'It's definitely nice to have it wrapped up going into the last game,' confirmed club captain Kim Little. 'I think a big part of this season has been about winning all the games that we should win, and then the games against Chelsea and Manchester City … yes, we need to win the majority of them too, but if we win the games that we should win, then we will be in this position, and that's what we've done this year. We've lost obviously to Chelsea and City in the cups, Chelsea in the league, City in the league, which is disappointing, we want to be able to beat them too, but fundamentally we've won the rest of our games, and they haven't, so we've been more consistent. That's what's won us the league this season.'

28-year-old Little had returned to Arsenal in 2017 following a two-year spell with Seattle Reign and on loan at Melbourne Victory. Since then, she had suffered a cruciate ligament injury and then a broken leg, but a fit and on-form Little remained thrillingly dangerous. She said that those serious injuries did not linger on her mind – 'If I get injured, I get injured, it's part of what we do' – but she was pleased to be able to bring back the title to Meadow Park and excited at the prospect of Champions League football.

'As players we want to play in the biggest club competition in the world, and the club has not had Champions League for a little while,' she said. 'It's nice, definitely, to get that back firstly, and also to win the league. I for one am very excited about playing Champions League games again.'

Manager Joe Montemurro was too. An Arsenal fan from childhood, who named his favourite player as Liam Brady, the Australian was just as thoughtful as his captain when reflecting on the season just gone.

'If I were to summarise our direction, qualifying for Europe was the big thing – that was the most important thing,' he said. 'That for us solidified where we wanted to be, and also solidified where we want to be. That was the big thing for us, and it just brings its own challenges. Have we been building towards it? Yes. Obviously pulling the squad together, the way that we play, the way that we train, we are preparing ourselves for it, so it's exciting times.'

He talked about the way he wanted his team to play – 'the Arsenal way', focusing on ball possession – but was honest that he thought the core base had already been in place before his arrival; all the players needed was belief in themselves.

'We always knew we were on the right track, and to get the accolades and win the league in advance has been a real pleasure, but all credit to the girls and the staff, they've believed in what we wanted to do and have succeeded in doing it,' he said.

He smiled as he thought of the forthcoming fixture, where the Manchester City players were expected to form a guard of honour to welcome to the pitch the team that had bested them overall during the season.

'I don't know how it's going to sit with the City players!' he said. 'This is a special opportunity for the players to know that they're going into a game knowing that they're going to lift the trophy, it's fantastic and I just want them to really enjoy and cherish it, and have fun.'

* * *

West Ham reached the FA Cup Final in their first season as professionals. The marketing campaign trumpeted their hopes for the biggest crowd ever for a women's football match in England, but those ambitions were soon hamstrung. The Premier League refused to move West Ham's men's fixture against Southampton in an essentially meaningless encounter earlier in the day, meaning that fans who followed both sides – or indeed those who might have been tempted to a women's match for the first time considering it was a showpiece occasion – had to make a choice about which game to attend.

Despite the rain, it was a festive atmosphere on Wembley Way as usual, with the half-and-half scarves from unofficial vendors, along with other more formal indicators of what a big match this was, and what a big crowd was expected – masses of security, plus helpful guides with megaphones shouting out directions to guide newcomers around the stadium complex.

If you looked at the colours around the ground, it was obvious that one end was supposed to be for City fans and the other for West Ham, with giant banners indicating club allegiance on the top tier of seating. However, women's football in England has long prided itself on the lack of segregation needed at matches, and there were pockets of fans in club colours all over the place, along with huge groups of little girls, there in the tracksuits of their own clubs, and accompanied by their coaches and parents. It was no wonder that the stadium steps were congested as everyone tried to take a selfie, fitting in themselves, their friends, and as much of the pitch as possible. The waves, complete with high-pitched ululations, started ten minutes into the match; not a sign of the crowd being bored, as it sometimes is at men's matches, but a sign of the party atmosphere.

Manchester City were entirely dominant on the pitch, but began to look slightly disturbed as they reached half-time without scoring. Nikita Parris thumped the ground with anger as she thought she deserved a penalty; Georgia Stanway had a wry smile as she got the ball in the net despite knowing she was offside. At the other end, West Ham put on some pressure, with Karen Bardsley making a great fingertip save to bat away Jane Ross's effort.

But as soon as Keira Walsh put City ahead seven minutes into the second half, the result seemed inevitable. Late goals from Lauren Hemp and Stanway made the scoreline seem more decisive than perhaps it really was; and those who were there just for interest rather than commitment began to filter away from Wembley's crowd of 43,264 as Nick Cushing's side completed a domestic cup double. Of course, it was possible that some may have been endeavouring to negotiate transport issues, with engineering works causing chaos on the railway lines across the country, which made it even stranger that journalists could be overheard complaining about the relative lack of City fans at Wembley compared to the hordes of West Ham fans, who only had to deal with a short journey on the Jubilee line to take them across London.

As the supporters emptied out of the stands, and the media representatives packed up their kit, a handful of staff members sat in front of the big screens in the press lounge to watch the post-match interviews, beginning with Durham-born City and Lionesses captain Steph Houghton.

'Where's she from? She doesn't sound …' one trailed off.

'Up north … somewhere,' came the response.

* * *

Barnsley had a cup final to look forward to as well – the Sheffield and Hallamshire County Cup, at Rotherham's New York Stadium. They prepared for it with an end-of-season match at Bolton Wanderers' University of Bolton Stadium, and the entire experience was a new one for many of the players, used to the smaller pitches and more intense crowds.

'It's usually people stood on the sidelines, really, so to have a proper stadium, and obviously a crowd – I think we got about 250 people, which in a stadium like that looks a small amount of people – it was really good,' said striker Lissa Woodhouse afterwards. 'When you're on the pitch they seem so far away. Usually I can hear people shouting on the sidelines, and I couldn't hear anything, I could only hear my own players, I couldn't even hear the manager or anything. It was surreal.'

Woodhouse had enjoyed a spectacular season – her first at such a high level of competition. Previously she had been part of squads playing in local leagues, and she had played for a representative team at university, but had not considered stepping up until she heard about the pre-season trials at Barnsley.

'Just coming to Oakwell where the trials were and seeing the set-up at Oakwell, I was straight away a bit sceptical to be honest,' she confessed. 'Because I hadn't played for a team for a while, I didn't know how I'd fare up against people who'd played regularly at that high level. At the end of trials [Chris] said, "We're really interested in you," and I was a bit shocked.'

Hamilton's focus on fitness pre-season had been another shock for Woodhouse, who had been used to just playing five-a-side matches in training with her last team, but she felt it had really boosted their season.

'We didn't really even use a ball for the first few weeks,' she said. 'It was just pure fitness, trying to get us where we need to be, but the fitness we did at the start of this season has had such a positive effect. When it gets to important games this season, you can tell that our fitness compared to other teams has just been so good because of what we did in pre-season – but yeah, for me, it was a complete change, even in the changing room before the game, having our shirts put on pegs, and having protein shakes after games, just little things like that.'

Even so, Woodhouse still did not expect the season to be a great one, sharing the general hope that they would simply avoid relegation. The string of fine pre-season results took her aback.

'We did gel really well as a team,' she said. 'Considering we'd been put together as a mish-mash of people, because obviously Chris brought some people from his team from before and then there were a few newbies and a few people who'd been there a while, it was completely like from foundation level, so we didn't really expect too much, to be honest. Then pre-season happened, and we thought we might actually have something special here.'

The run of losses at the start of the season were quickly forgotten.

'From the Liverpool Feds game where we played away, from then on, we all worked so hard for each other,' she said. 'It's one of the most important things as well – we all get on so well. I've never been part of a team like this where we would literally do anything for each other, on the pitch and off the pitch, coaches included as well.'

Her own fitness had improved immeasurably over the year, picking up a few months in when she started a new job delivering post for the Royal Mail.

'I walk about 15k a day and then [go to] training at night,' she said. 'In games like the game at Bolton, because obviously it's a much bigger pitch, I noticed my fitness was so much better than it probably was at the start of the season, just because of this job, really.'

Because she started work so early in the day, she would usually finish by 3pm, meaning that sometimes she was able to fit in a gym session before going to training. The only downside was that working on Saturdays and then playing on Sundays meant that she did not get too many days off, but she was looking forward to being outside every morning when the weather improved.

Woodhouse was top scorer across the course of the season, but was delighted that the goals had been shared around the team, with even the defenders weighing in from set pieces. She thought it was a good sign for next season – and beyond.

'We didn't really realise how important them games would be at the start,' she admitted. 'If we just won even one of them at the start that we lost in that row, we could be on top now. Burnley, who have won the league already automatically – the two games we've played against them were such close games. To think they're the top side in the league, and when we've played them we matched them. In terms of where we're going as a club, I think next season is going to be very interesting considering where we've been this season – with our first season altogether with new managers. I think there is a lot of promise in this team.'

* * *

'The thing with Lissa,' said coach Chris Hamilton, 'she's never really played at this level before. You can get an eye for a player whenever you see them, and she has a raw ability we knew we could work on and we could help her along that road. This season has been a really good first season for her at this level as well, she's scored some great goals. We've been on her back quite a lot this season, she maybe thinks we've been hard on her, but it's the same with all the players, I wouldn't be having a go at them and trying to improve them and asking the questions if I didn't think they could do it.'

He had already been planning his signings for the close season, listening to his players about friends and opponents who were leaving clubs and might be interested in a move. He was proud that after a great season Barnsley would be a more attractive destination for quality players, enabling him to pick and choose the best additions to the squad, slotting into the system and philosophy he had developed with his team throughout the year.

'The girls know how hard to play, what I expect from them and how hard I want them to work, and what I expect on matchdays and through the week,' he explained, 'and they can help any new ones coming in, help them get to grips with that quickly because it'll probably be harder than last season for them. We already know the formations we want to play and our style of play, so we're already ahead of ourselves and where we were last season.

'The thing is only one team goes up from our league, so it is a very tough league. I'd say there are seven or eight teams that will go and try to win the league next year, so again it's going to be a really hard league – it's going to be only one that goes up, which is the challenging part of it.'

In the meantime, he was quietly confident his team would acquit themselves well in the cup final.

'It's another big challenge for us,' he said. 'Obviously they've done well in the league above us, so they're favourites going into it, but that might actually suit us. We'll go into Sunday confident in what we do, and we'll see what happens.'

His captain Lucy Turner agreed that they were underdogs, but she was adamant she would lead her side out ready to try to win.

'I don't think we go in to any game, whether we're playing Manchester City or anyone, we're not going to lay down and let them come at us,' she said. 'We're going to try and play the football that we know we can play, we don't really worry about the opposition too much. We play to the strengths that we have, breaking fast, where there's a space in behind, pressing high up the pitch.'

Turner had gone through the whole season comparing it to the year before, when the team had become so demoralised they expected to lose every time they took to the field. Hamilton's insistence on improving the team's fitness had paid dividends, but it was not always popular simply because of the physical demands on an amateur team.

'It was so unprofessional last year and now sometimes it's a bit too professional, the intensity, what we're required to do outside of football,' said Turner, 'but I think everyone appreciates the benefits and the hard work needs to be put in to reap the benefits on and off the pitch.'

She thought that Huddersfield, being in a higher division, would be the biggest test so far of the team's physical progress as well as their increased quality, but whatever happened, she knew her girls would work hard.

'At the weekend we were winning 1-0 and then went 2-1 down and then scored late on in the game,' she said, recalling their match against Bolton. 'I think that comes down to fitness and determination to never give up, which I think Chris has drilled into us quite well.'

Turner also took reassurance from her team's results in the cup competitions – rather than receiving a string of byes, they had actually had to put the wins together, and they had been rewarded with the final against Huddersfield.

'They're a good quality team, probably one of the best in Yorkshire,' she said. 'It will be a massive test for us. We have done well to get that far – it's a better chance to win it this year, more so than last year. We're going in confident to challenge them and give us best performance.'

* * *

Sophie Bell was excited. This was her first season with Barnsley, and she described herself as a 'reality check' for some of the less experienced players. Rather than someone who brought others back down to earth by reminding them of awkward facts, though, she boosted their confidence by reminding them of the year's achievements.

'I think it's got to the point now where we think we're not far off the top, really, at all,' she said, 'but at the start of the season we were like, "We just want to do as well as we can," so I think I've been getting everybody to look at the bigger picture of where we've come, and I think it feels like we're in the middle of it. Although we're in the end of the season, it doesn't feel like the end because I think next season we'll do even better than we've done this season.'

Bell had a fine football CV. She began her career just kicking a ball around on the beach in Devon, where she grew up, and played alongside the boys as a child after she and her family moved to Scunthorpe. When she needed to find a girls' team to play for, she was fortunate that it coincided with Scunthorpe United setting one up, and after that all her decisions were shaped by football – including a rather unusual choice for university study. Keen to go to Loughborough University, famous for its excellent sporting teams and brilliant facilities, she opted to combine subjects.

'I did the world's most random degree – I did English Literature, which was combined with sports science,' she revealed. 'It didn't make any sense whatsoever, but I was desperate to play then, so I played for them all my three years.'

Although her work on the English literature side of study was perhaps not the best ('my essays got slated, it was horrific'), in terms of football, it was perfect. Bell played for the university's first team, who had plenty of success during her time there. After graduation, Loughborough's links with a company which provided coaching for soccer camps in the USA proved invaluable.

'I thought, "Well, I don't know what I'm going to do after graduation,"' she recalled. 'I'm not the sort of person who stays in one place a long time, I quite liked the idea of going and doing something else, so I had an interview, did a bit of coaching, and ended up getting a five-month contract out there, literally as soon as my course finished. It finished one week and then the next week my mum was picking me up to take me to Heathrow – which she wasn't very happy about – to take me to America.'

Bell spent five years coaching in Philadelphia, returning to the UK every nine months to arrange a new visa, and joining the Scunthorpe United squad for training and matchday when she was in the area. Other than that, though, she had no opportunity for playing.

'I don't know if I regret now not playing for those five years,' she thought. 'I might have been in a different place now if I had played, but similarly the coaching experience over there has massively helped my game, and I think long term now, when I stop playing, I've got my UEFA B, that'll massively help.'

She had been offered a longer-term contract to stay in the States and coach, with the company sponsoring her visa permanently, but after five years in the job she had also met her partner, also British, and he wanted to return to the UK – more specifically Sheffield, where he was originally from. Bell had no job to go back to, although she had dreams of working in the football development sector, so began applying for any vacancies she could find – which was how she ended up in a call centre. It was not a job she enjoyed. When she heard about Teach First, a scheme to fast-track graduates into the teaching profession, she thought that might be something that could be a good fit.

'That was hardcore,' she said. 'I had to go to London for an interview for that, and you don't really get any choice in where you work, so I ended up working in a school in Sheffield. It's a very diverse school, and the Teach First schools, they all have to meet certain socioeconomic criteria, so it was quite a tough school, but to be fair I absolutely love it, it's been great. It was so hard the first year, I did my PGCE [postgraduate certificate in education, a qualification for teachers] while working as a teacher, so I was unqualified but I was doing the qualification at the same time, and that was really hard work, especially still training two nights a week for football and then travelling to games on a Sunday.'

Living and working in Sheffield meant that playing for Scunthorpe United was no longer a practical option. Bell messaged a friend who played for Sheffield United and ended up signing for them. They were a club in the process of massive changes; this was just before the licences for the Championship were announced, including United's imminent formal semi-professional status.

'When I look back now, the squad has evolved so much from where it was then,' she said. 'I think I was there four seasons, and from that season to the last one it snowballed massively in terms of where the club was going. I remember the first time we got invited to Bramall Lane, I think we were going to have a meal in the executive bit and then we were going on the pitch, and we were absolutely flapping that we didn't have anything to wear that matched, so our captain ended up buying us these four-pound tracksuit bottoms. We ended up walking out on the pitch in them and these horrible t-shirts, and you look at it now, just in four years, where it's come from, it's ridiculous.'

When United were about to begin their campaign in the Championship, it coincided with the news that nearby clubs Sheffield and Doncaster Rovers Belles were both dropping down to the National League, meaning there were an awful lot of players in the area with experience of playing in the second tier. Bell wondered at that point if her days at the club were numbered, even though she had been reassured that they wanted to keep her. She had been the team's vice-captain over the past few seasons, but knew that she would be overtaken in the pecking order by some of the new players coming in – and she had been told that she would probably not be in the first-team squad as a regular, although she would get a spot in the development team, plus a potential place on the subs' bench for Championship fixtures.

'I'm quite old now so I haven't got that many years left, and it just didn't feel right for me to stay there,' she said. 'I look back now and some of the girls are on the bench against Man City and I think, "Well, that would have been cool," but I honestly wouldn't have swapped this season for that. I've really enjoyed this season.'

Bell decided her best bet before she made a decision was to monitor what the other local players were choosing to do with the changing status of clubs in the area. Two of her former Scunthorpe team-mates had been playing for Nettleham and followed their manager when he was appointed at a new club – Chris Hamilton, the new Barnsley boss.

'They were like, "We've told him about you, he says you can come down," and I was like, "I've got a meeting tonight with United – if it goes badly, I'll come to training tonight with you," so I was turning up at Barnsley in my full Sheffield United kit, which really went down very well!' she laughed. Other teams found out that she was not intending to stay at Sheffield United and she did get further offers from elsewhere, but she had already made her mind up. 'To be fair, I really liked Barnsley from that very first training session. It was really good.'

Joining Barnsley involved a little bit of travel from her Sheffield workplace and home, but she was more than happy to do that. Now a fully fledged primary school teacher, her pupils, aged five and six, were intrigued to know that at the weekends Miss Bell was a footballer.

'This is the fourth year I've been teaching, and each year group has different levels of knowledge of football,' she explained. 'These ones I've got at the minute don't know a whole lot but they're quite enthusiastic – they love seeing pictures of it. If I've scored, I'll let them watch it in the morning – although my goals aren't really impressive, so they're generally not very impressed! They always ask to do it in PE, we've got these little tiny footballs they always want to get out. They're brilliant.'

Bell had not mentioned the forthcoming cup final to them, though. She was thinking about bringing the whole class to a match in the future.

'We were going to be playing at Legacy Park, just down the road, when we played Sheffield United in a friendly – the school is just down the road from there, they could have come to that one!' she said. 'They are desperate, they would absolutely love it. I should arrange that.'

* * *

Nervous laughter echoed round the Rotherham car park as the Barnsley squad descended from the team bus. They lined up to collect their kit bags from the luggage compartment, all looking smart in their black team tracksuits and red training tops. Chairman Steve Maddock was resplendent in suit and club-crested tie, looking more anxious than his players were.

Huddersfield Town were a strong side. This would be their fifth consecutive Sheffield and Hallamshire Challenge Cup final, and they were looking to retain it for the third season in a row. They were also a division above Barnsley – but the Reds also had a proud record in the competition, having reached the final for the last four years, winning only the 2016 trophy. Local MP Dan Jarvis had tweeted his support for them that morning, with the men's club urging fans to head to the stadium to cheer them on.

There was a small crowd gathering outside, waiting for the turnstiles to open. Little girls in their replica Huddersfield kits mingled with little girls in replica Barnsley kits, with no thought of rivalry or segregation. As they filed through the gates, they wandered happily around the stands, taking up their favourite vantage point. The most envied youngsters there were the mascots, some from junior teams but also from players' families, with Sophie Bell's small niece drawing the eye, with her hair tied up in bunches and decorated with red ribbons, wearing a shirt with her aunt's name and number on the back.

As soon as the match kicked off, Chris Hamilton was on the touchline, patrolling his technical area, clutching a bottle of water, keeping as composed as possible. It took only a few minutes for his team to impress him and crack that façade, going one-nil up and deservedly so after a good run from Drew Greene, tapped in smartly by her twin Darcie. The lead was doubled shortly after, thanks to a cheeky, nifty lob by Lissa Woodhouse, and that triggered plenty of hefty challenges flying in as the Terriers became more frustrated with their failure to make a breakthrough.

'Are we too deep?' the Huddersfield captain Kate Mallin asked her coach, evidently puzzled by her team's failure to deal with the side from a lower league.

But she was the one who got a goal back for them just before half-time after they had fistfuls of chances they failed to capitalise on, and some panic began to creep into the Barnsley back line. They were relieved when the half-time whistle blew and they could head off to the changing room to talk and to regroup. Striker Kath Smith limped off to join them, right sock rolled down to her ankle with an ice pack firmly attached, having been forced off early in the match.

Director Natalie Jackson was in the stands with baby Lexie. She had found out on arrival that there was no baby changing facility available on the lower levels of the stadium, and so she had to take a lift up to the higher floors, accompanied by a member of staff. At the start of the second half, rather than go through that complex procedure again, she just decided to change her on the floor of the concourse at the back of the stand.

On the pitch, Huddersfield notched an equaliser on the hour mark, setting up a frantic finale. Smith stood flamingo-like on the touchline as she urged her team-mates on with just a few minutes to go, and Woodhouse produced a touch of magic as she surged through on goal to set up substitute Amy Woodruff, who kept her head and slotted it home.

Just as the announcement came for the four minutes of additional time, the referee awarded a penalty to Huddersfield. Goalkeeper Skye Kirkham tried to make herself as big as possible, but to no avail – the spot kick was rifled home and another 30 minutes of play was imminent. All over the pitch there were tired legs and unsurprisingly increased levels of disgruntlement in the challenges.

'Come on, girls, let's keep going, come on,' shouted assistant manager Andy Glossop, accompanying his words with encouraging claps. There was little left to be given; Woodhouse was substituted, with no more miles left in her; two players tangled legs and both immediately went down with cramp, creating another delay in play. With no more energy available to anyone, a penalty shoot-out was inevitable.

Sophie Crosby slammed her kick home to start with, before goalkeeper Kirkham began an heroic display, saving the first two Huddersfield efforts as Danielle Whitham, Annie Ward and Sophie Bell all converted their penalties to give Barnsley a 4-1 victory in the shoot-out. It emerged later that Kirkham had played most of the match with broken fingers following a clash in the first half, making her penalty saves even more impressive. Although the Barnsley players were elated, the day did not end with the best displays of sportsmanship. Huddersfield goalkeeper Laura Carter complained vociferously that the referee had failed to blow her whistle to give the captain Mallin the signal to take the first Terriers penalty; that would have made no difference to the result, but it was understandable that in the despond of defeat she would be looking for a scapegoat. Plenty of her team-mates did not want to keep their runners-up medals, instead handing them over to young fans in the crowd; and some of the backroom staff were less than gracious in their handshakes with the opposition.

The Barnsley squad were aware of none of this. As soon as their formal trophy lift was over, they moved away from the main stand and began their celebrations proper, spraying the traditional champagne over everyone involved in the win, players and staff alike. Then it was time for an impromptu photo shoot, with lots of the little ball girls and young fans scampering up to take the opportunity to pose with the entire trophy-winning team.

CEO Steve Maddock could barely contain himself.

'It's unbelievable. That has to be the most topsy-turvy game I've ever been involved in. Unbelievable. Look at them! This is a year from finishing second to bottom. How good is that?'

He extended a hand to gesture at the stand, where two of the Barnsley FC owners were sitting, enjoying their first experience of a women's match, alongside directors of the women's club who had travelled thousands of miles for the special occasion.

'It's onwards and upwards,' he said. 'We've got a lot to do now, this is just the start.'

Captain Lucy Turner looked exhausted but delighted. In between posing for photos with small fans, she admitted that the prospect of a penalty shoot-out made her stomach turn with anxiety.

'We didn't make it easy, did we?' she laughed, before quickly noting how proud she was of her team.

'It's what all the girls deserve, really. We've worked so hard all year – to have a bit of silverware to put in us cabinet has made it worthwhile.'

* * *

The celebrations lasted long in to the night, with the entire squad enjoying a meal out in Barnsley. Sophie Bell – who scored the winning penalty – admitted she was one of the last party-goers standing, but made it into work the next day, much to the delight of her small pupils. The children were mesmerised by her medal, and all took turns wearing it, in carefully-counted slots of 15 minutes throughout the day. As a special treat, at the end of the afternoon they were allowed to watch some of the match highlights, including Miss Bell's winning goal.

'It's never happened to me, that, before!' she laughed. 'Chris said, "Who wants to take one?" and he knew I would take one. Then there was a lot of debate about who went first – lots of people didn't want to go first – and Sophie Crosby stood up and took the first one. I didn't really mind. I don't think we put a lot of thought into it to be honest, it was just what people were happy to do.

'Then obviously Skye saved those two. When their player took their [third penalty], it was like, "Oh God, if she misses this one then we've won," but I was thinking, "If she scores it then I just need to score!"'

Bell suspected she was one of the only players who had stayed calm enough to keep score and realise that their fourth penalty could be the winner – and watching the videos back confirmed it for her.

'The girls hadn't worked it out, I don't think!' she said. 'I think the girls thought I was going mad a bit too early!'

Bell had enjoyed being able to share the day with her small niece, who continued to grab the phone to tell her aunt that she too was Barnsley's number two – at least according to her shirt.

'She wanted to be like the big girls who were the mascots,' said Bell. 'She did really well, I was very impressed with her.'

Lissa Woodhouse's nephews had revelled in the opportunity to accompany her on to the pitch as well. Having them there had also helped her calm her usual pre-match nerves.

'I was nervous, like, all the night before and all in the morning, when we were at the [pre-match] meal and everything – I think I only had two pieces of chicken because I was really nervous!' she said. 'As soon as we got there and we started warming up, it all went away for some reason. That's really rare for me as well – I usually feel really nervous before most games. I think it was just the crowd and everything, and we had our mascots, our families, so that was a bit different – there was a lot going on and there wasn't any time to be nervous.'

The nerves may have been jangling, but it was not through fear; Woodhouse always had a sneaky feeling it would be a good day for Barnsley.

'I always felt like we were going to win,' she revealed. 'I felt that in the air, because there was no pressure on us at all to win. Obviously we were the underdogs, and we'd lost the last two years, so there was no pressure on us, and then when we went 2-0 up in about 11 minutes, I was thinking this cannot be how this is going to go for the whole game, and then obviously it didn't, and they came right back into it. I just don't think we ever gave up.'

Although the squad had practised penalties in training the week before, Woodhouse thought that perhaps they had not quite been ready for the physical toll of extra time; she was substituted because she simply could not run any more.

'Chris said he took me off because I looked like I was crippled, like I really couldn't do any more running,' she said, adding that she had only played half of the match the week before due to suffering from delayed onset muscle soreness (DOMS) in her legs. 'I said to him at half-time I didn't know if I was going to last 90 [minutes], and then obviously it went to extra-time so I was thinking, "I just need him to take me off," because it wasn't really fair that I couldn't run when there were other people on the bench who could run better.'

More practically – and fortunately – Woodhouse did not need to go into work on Monday and make her way round her lengthy postal route. She had booked the day off, thinking she might want to stay out late on the Sunday.

'I'm glad I did!' she grinned. 'I didn't want to go in! I could barely walk on Monday!'

Even a few days later, manager Hamilton still described himself as 'buzzing'.

'Obviously they pushed us all the way, they're a good side, they're a league above, so it was needed, I think,' he reflected. 'It was a brilliant day, a great day.'

He wondered whether Barnsley's commitment to passing, attacking football had surprised their opponents, and whether that had affected the Huddersfield attitude on the pitch.

'I don't think they expected us to come out the way we did, because we were underdogs, so I think that played into our hands a bit,' he said. 'We knew what we were about. We'd done our homework on them, I don't think they'd really done much homework on us. Obviously I don't know that, but the way we came out, I don't think they expected that.'

He revealed that the squad had practised penalties in training the session before the final, which calmed any potential nerves; and his quick team talk before the shoot-out began was also intended to stop any incipient panic.

'I took them in when it went to penalties and I said, "We've managed to draw the game, we probably should have won it in 90 minutes, they scored in the last minute, we were more than competitive in extra time, and extra time is a lot." I said, "Don't panic about it, just pick your corner and slot it. If you miss, you miss." We'd taken them to penalties and that was probably more than anyone expected anyway – except for us.'

With four penalties scored out of the four taken, Hamilton's pep talk clearly did its job; and the homework he and his players did on their opponents also helped. For a goalkeeper, a shoot-out is a no-lose situation; nobody expects you to save a single shot, and if you do you are the hero. That turned out to be the case for Skye Kirkham, who also benefitted from close attention to Huddersfield's previous cup matches.

'They played a cup game that went to penalties, and I said to Skye, "Look, I've watched the highlights, they might change it, but in this penalty shoot-out they always went to the goalkeeper's right." And the first two penalties went to the keeper's right, so the homework we're doing is definitely paying off.'

17

The end

YEOVIL'S DIFFICULT season ended in the inevitable relegation after their ten-point deduction for their financial issues. They had been assuming that they would drop down to the Championship, returning to semi-professional status, but when the FA announced the distribution of licences to compete from the 2019/20 season onwards, Yeovil were in neither of the top two tiers. Instead, they would drop down to the FA Women's National League Southern Premier Division, a two-division demotion.

Former AFC Bournemouth chairman Adam Murry had taken over the club from their previous owners and was hopeful for the future, saying in a statement, 'There has never been as much interest in the women's game and I am delighted to have been able to support the takeover. This great club has absolutely enormous potential.'

Annie Heatherson believed him. No longer a professional footballer, she had nevertheless committed her future to the club; no longer required full-time in the community department, she was going back to school, taking an access course in psychology with the intent of pursuing a career in family counselling.

'I knew before we went into WSL1 we weren't going to survive,' she reflected. The 35-year-old had been involved in initial meetings as the club pursued their licence for the top flight almost two years previously, and thought even then that some of their targets were unrealistic due to their lack of resources. That was particularly the case for the outreach work she was trying to do; full-time players did not have the time or ability to travel across the area to schools, especially when the training facilities and their home ground were some distance apart. She also feared that the well-publicised financial issues at the club had given them a certain stigma when she was reaching out to try and build community links.

Heatherson was hopeful, though, that new owner Murry would give Yeovil a renewed sense of purpose.

'His ambition and his passion,' she mused. 'We got a presentation last night, and when it's launched I think people are going to be absolutely blown away. His mission is to get us where we belong, which is top flight. He's got an idea, he's got a plan. I don't know how long it's going to take him to do that, but he's in for the long go, and he's really determined to make that dream happen for the club again – but next time it's done properly.'

Heatherson had once had a dream of her own – to be a professional footballer. The previous season had not been how she had imagined it.

'As much as it was a dream, I wasn't living the dream,' she said. 'It was really hard, it was heartbreaking, and it was probably the most difficult thing I've had to go through. The club is starting afresh, it's got a new identity, it's got a new owner, it's got a passion, it's got a drive, so it's a completely different club now. Going forward, there'll be a lot more positive stuff. It's just a shame this didn't happen two years ago.'

Lee Burch had departed the club, having spent a year there heading up what proved to be a failed experiment with professional football. Nevertheless, he was not too disappointed; what he had seen on the pitch had pleased him.

'It's been a good season at Yeovil as far as what we wanted to try to do there – and we got very close to doing that,' he said. 'Obviously the ultimate aim was to avoid relegation, and apart from the ten-point deduction we were very close to doing that, or certainly could have gone into the last few games with that still as an objective. Everything else was ticked off.'

After the points deduction, those aims changed, and Burch just wanted to get to the end of the season and enjoy the time on the pitch. He had been planning for next year's Championship campaign, and to learn that it would not be happening was a surprise.

'It obviously just changes the landscape of everything – as a club, as a staff, as players, and it really just threw a massive spanner in the works, with no time to plan, only time to react, and the club's been trying to do that ever since,' he said. 'It's just been really hard for everyone associated with the club because they worked so hard to get to that point, and then to have that taken away is not fair. What people forget, it's really the staff, the players and the fans who are the ones that lose out – especially the players. They're the ones who give things day in and day out, and worked really hard, and wanted to be there, and unfortunately they're the ones hit with things that they have no control over. Same for the fans – there's a core group of real hardcore fans down there.'

Burch was incredibly disappointed that he would not have the chance to lead his squad into a Championship campaign. He felt that financially the club would have been able to manage; he thought that they were 75 per cent of the way to being able to sustain a top-flight campaign with a full-time professional squad, so a second-tier campaign with a part-time squad would have been eminently achievable.

'I think the club is set up to be in the Championship,' he said. 'We'd have had a good side. The players were looking to stay, because they felt that they'd have had a really good go at it. You can't go toe to toe with teams like Man City week in and week out if you don't feel like you've got a good chance in the Championship. The staff that were retained there were excellent, and there was some good pull behind, but unfortunately they decided that's the way it should be, and they didn't want to risk the club falling foul of finances again. I'd be very surprised if that happened – and if it did, just put the same sanctions in again and let the club get naturally relegated because they've made the same mistake. Instead the Championship now has 11 teams, and someone gets a weekend off [with every round of fixtures] and Yeovil end up in the third tier.'

Burch thought that the problems Yeovil were facing were serious, but also indicative of wider problems in the women's game where teams were professional in only one division; clubs would have to consider whether they should stay professional after relegation, and if not their players would have to decide whether to take a chance that a relegated club could bounce straight back and be able to pay full-time wages again.

'What do they do?' he asked rhetorically. 'Do they keep quitting jobs to become professional, then lose their professionalism and drop back down to the Championship because they got relegated, go back to being semi-professional again, and then get promoted again?'

Burch had taken up the vacant head coach position at London Bees, meaning just evening training sessions, and much less travel time. With a wife and a family, he was intending to spend more time with them, and possibly run some coaching classes in the daytime.

'I'm looking forward to a season where I don't have to worry about licensing,' he admitted. 'I've lost points because of off-the-field stuff in the last two seasons. I've ended up with no money at two different clubs. I'm looking forward to having a season where I can go out there, get my head down, enjoy working, and try and get the best out of my players, and where we finish is where we deserve to finish.

'The missus works – she works every Saturday, I work every Sunday, so you've got to try and find the time to see each other. It's also about getting that balancing act right. Again, I like the fact I can just focus on the role. The more that I can do that, the better the team will be for it. I might do some other bits here and there but certainly not anything I feel will take away from what I want to do, which is give everything to Bees and have a good season there.'

He had no regrets about spending that year at Yeovil, despite the sad conclusion, and had particularly enjoyed being able to focus full-time on working with his players.

'The footballing side of things was brilliant,' he said. 'I knew when I went there, and so did the players, that we were going to be up against it, but it was a big challenge and the girls did really well. Losing eight games 2-1 shows how close we were to not just get away from relegation, but you switch half of those games into wins and you're in mid-table, that's how close we were, I genuinely believe that. I learnt a lot, playing against the top players, playing against the Man Cities and the Arsenals and the Chelseas competitively, not playing them in a one-off cup game, but playing them in the league, which is a bit different.

'When I was at Millwall I still had another job, I did it alongside – the same as the players, they had other jobs. When you're full-time, you can just focus everything on that. That was probably the [most] enjoyable thing, where you could just focus on the games week in, week out, worry about what was coming next, and when things do come up, the extra stuff that goes with football, you also have a lot more time to organise and sort them out. I just really enjoyed it. I've enjoyed it since I've been in the women's game the last few years. I've gone from a side that was winning a lot of games to a side that wasn't winning a lot of games, but I've enjoyed it both.'

Yeovil were not the only side undergoing massive changes. After working incredibly hard to secure proper medical treatment for her London Bees team-mates, captain Emma Beckett had left the club to cross north London. As part of the Tottenham Hotspur squad, she had won promotion to the Women's Super League. However, while her colleagues were preparing for life as professionals, she was considering her options. She did not want to be one of the players about whom Lee Burch had worried; she was not going to give up a good career for perhaps a solitary season as a professional footballer.

'I thought about five or six years ago I was born in the wrong generation to profit from football,' she said. 'I think it's great there's money coming into it now, but I was born ten years too early, so I went ahead and forged a career. Maybe a few years ago I could have been sold the dream.'

She was considering her options for the new season, and had received a few offers, but her heavy workload had meant she had not really had chance to think about any of it properly. She had been disappointed with her own performances for Tottenham, and wanted to hit the ground running in pre-season; having not long turned 32, she certainly had no plans to retire.

Although it would not apply to her directly, she hoped that there would be a safety net in place for players who had given up their job to turn professional, as she had concerns over what would happen to them if their team was then relegated the subsequent season; she worried for any of Yeovil's squad who were now scrabbling round to find new teams to enable them to keep their jobs as footballers. She did not, however, think that there was currently enough done to ensure players were financially secure, even though money was coming into the game; again, as Burch had said, promotion and relegation between a fully professional league and a semi-professional one was fraught with difficulty as the necessary budget ballooned in the top tier.

'You've seen it with Yeovil, you've seen it with other clubs, I can remember teams winning the NWSL in America and going bankrupt the next year – it's just not sustainable,' she said.

Elsewhere, Millwall Lionesses were in the middle of what seemed to be an identity crisis, with the existing team announcing its intention to break away from the men's club and be known as the London City Lionesses. The spokespeople for Millwall seemed rather bewildered by the entire episode, and simply stuck to the party line that they would maintain women's and girls' football provision via their community department, even if the current Lionesses would continue competing in the Championship but no longer bear their name.

Guiseley Vixens, in the National League, were folding altogether, explaining that they lacked the funding and infrastructure to continue operating as an independent club. The players had been informed of the decision at the end of the season, when they met at their training venue, and were told that liquidation was inevitable; funded by a single private investor, separate from the men's club who shared the Guiseley name, there was no more money, and no prospect of merging with another team. With the very specific licensing requirements set out by the Women's Super League and the Championship, running a women's team that would not be able to progress was judged to no longer be a viable option, and the entire project was cancelled.

One of their players, Bethan Davies, was well used to off-the-field manoeuvres affecting on-the-pitch matters. She was an experienced player, beginning her youth career with Cambridge United before debuting for London Bees, then moving to Leeds United when she relocated for university.

She signed for Doncaster Belles during her first year of study, when they were in what was then WSL2. After spending a short time out on loan at Guiseley Vixens, she returned to Belles, playing most of the matches in the second half of 2017/18, helping them to the WSL2 title.

'At the close of the season I was about to start my final year at university and a lot of Donny players were moving teams to sign for other clubs. I was aware a lot at the club was changing and was suspicious,' she said, reflecting with the benefit of a year's hindsight. When it became obvious that Belles' financial situation would mean demotion, Davies decided the best course of action would be to accept a permanent move to Vixens, which she saw as a fresh challenge; now, 12 months later, she was looking for yet another club. It was, she felt, inevitable as women's football went through such rapid changes.

'Notts County folded a few years ago, meaning that top international players had to move to other teams,' she pointed out. 'Donny Belles won WSL2 and then had to drop a league due to financial reasons – all the players including myself left to move to other clubs. Sheffield FC were forced to drop down a league last season too. Yeovil struggled to raise the money to stay in the Super League and are now forced to drop down two leagues.

'In comparison, Manchester United were able to jump straight into the Championship, and Sheffield United jumped up two leagues too. The best players move to these teams as they have the money to buy them and support them financially with travel etc. These teams then succeed – for example, look at Manchester United's success – and it leaves the other teams, who are without as much financial backing, struggling in the leagues they're in.'

She was not entirely critical of the game's progress, acknowledging the need for financial investment, and she was pleased that professional football was an option for the best female players, but she was concerned that performance on the pitch seemed to have so little bearing on whether a club should compete at the highest level. As one of Belles' WSL2-winning squad in 2018, she was incredibly disappointed that she and her team-mates had never had the chance to play in the top flight simply because of the club's behind-the-scenes issues.

'Women's football differs from men's in so many ways,' she said, 'but I fear that the way that money controls the men's game is happening to the women's game now too.'

After Guiseley's liquidation, Davies had plenty of offers from clubs in the National League and above – but in the end she opted to sign for Barnsley, liking what she heard from the management and ownership. They had recently announced plans to build their own 2,500-capacity stadium, allowing them a degree of independence, no longer in the literal and metaphorical shadow of the men's team. The finance for the project, they hoped, would come from grant funding and private investors.

* * *

'Whenever any money comes into the women's game, it always goes to the top tiers, where they've probably got enough,' said Doncaster Belles' Sheila Edmunds, echoing both Davies and Burch. 'I have had this conversation with the FA before. Some teams don't need what we all get, and some teams need more than what everybody gets. If you look at tier three and tier four, they get nothing.

'There's money to launch teams and get them started, but there's no money to keep them going. That's the area that's probably a little bit weak. Things have to be sustainable and keep going. We've gone through all the scenarios of teams buying a place in the league, and whether it's right or wrong, or whether it should just be on performance on the pitch, but we're beyond that now. Those rules and regs have all gone out the window. It's a whole different ball game, and I keep saying we can't live in the past and we can't, you have to move on – you have to find ways to try and survive.'

Belles had finished second from bottom in the FA Women's National League Northern Division with 18 points – three adrift from safety – and with a goal difference of minus 43. They had four wins on the books and six draws, and with such a set of results, relegation was inevitable, despite the bright spells during the season.

'We were fairly slow to start – it was a bit of a baptism of fire for these young players, coming from the centre of excellence and the development team,' recalled Edmunds. 'It was a really big step up for some of them, so it took them a while to get into it and buy into what we were trying to do.'

Manager Zoey Shaw had had recognition for steering her young side on the unbeaten run before Easter, but ultimately a string of end-of-season losses condemned them to relegation – to Division One Midlands. Edmunds was trying to stay positive.

'Looking at the situation as a whole, it was huge steps forward from what we started with in September, so I was pleased with that,' she said, 'but getting relegated is a bitter pill to swallow. Being in the fourth tier, it's not something I'm familiar with – I've never been in the third tier, never mind the fourth tier.'

Edmunds was stepping back from her full-time, overarching role in club operations. Belles had been taken in under the Club Doncaster umbrella at the end of March, once again aligning themselves with Doncaster Rovers men's team. Belles had a new chief executive as well as access to all the media and marketing support Club Doncaster could offer. Edmunds knew it was the right decision – for her as well as for the club – but she was finding it more difficult than she had expected.

'I thought it would be quite easy to hand it all over and let somebody else do it and give me a bit of time back, but I've found, as the weeks have gone on, I've been in a few meetings, and all of a sudden it's hit me – I haven't got that voice and control and know everything that's happening,' she admitted. 'It's all going well, it's all running smoothly, but I just don't have that involvement, and adjusting to that will take a bit of time. I suppose it's a bit like when I packed in playing – you find another angle, another approach to it.'

She had been assured she could have as much or as little involvement in the future as she liked, and she had also been offered the club's honorary presidency ('yes, I would love to have that!)'.

'I'm still here, I'm still around, I'm just not running around like an idiot like I was doing before,' she laughed. 'I might get to see a bit more football than I did last season!'

Edmunds's mantra was 'optimism', and she insisted she was optimistic for the future. Belles needed to regroup and rebuild, she knew, and she felt their biggest challenge would be retaining the young players they were working so hard to develop; but she was delighted that Club Doncaster had been so welcoming, and she was excited for the new season ahead.

'Hopefully there'll be plenty to cheer about,' she said, before adding, 'and a lot more goals!'

* * *

Ashleigh Goddard was back in England. It had been her first season as a professional footballer, and her most successful season ever. Apollon had finished as champions and had secured their place in the Champions League. FC Barcelona had led the league all year, and the destination of the title came down to the very last game.

'It was a home game, and amazing supporters of the men's Apollon team came to our game, and so it was probably one of the craziest experiences I've ever had,' she said. 'There were flares and fireworks and bangers, it was madness, it was awesome, it was so cool. They came with drums and everything as well. When it got to the game itself, we were losing 1-0 just before half-time, and bear in mind a draw was not good enough – we had to win. So we were 1-0 down and probably within the first five, ten minutes [of the second half] we scored again, it's 1-1, and we're pushing and pushing but it's not coming, and then honestly it was the last kick of the game. Our centre-back – her name is Ife, she was part of the Scottish international team, she was even in the Olympics for GB [Ifeoma Dieke] – she was up for a free kick, it went to a bit of a scramble, one of my team-mates crossed it in, and Ife had stayed up and she had a tap-in and everyone went crazy. It was epic, honestly it was so epic. We had like grown men climbing up the fence and bouncing on barbed wire. I was like, "What is going on?" But it was an amazing thing to be part of.'

Goddard admitted that the closest thing she had experienced to that in her career previously had been when London Bees knocked Chelsea out of the Continental Cup. Rather than just progressing in a competition, though, everything was on the line for Apollon, and the number and noise of the spectators simply heightened everything for her. Of course, the club officials were also delighted, and took the squad out for a celebration on the marina. When Goddard heard that the catering was 'finger food', however, she was expecting an English-style party buffet, and made sure she had dinner beforehand.

'I go in expecting sausage rolls, but the finger food was sushi and slices of fillet steak,' she laughed. 'It was ridiculous.'

Despite winning two league championships in one season, Goddard was cautious about her future. She had returned to England because playing professionally in the Women's Super League remained her ambition, and she was going to pursue it once more. She was picking the brains of friends who already played at that level, borrowing their fitness regimes where possible to ensure that she was physically up to the challenge should she get an opportunity. She did not have an agent and was reaching out to potential clubs to find out if they had need of a midfielder in her style – with two national league wins to her credit.

'The truth is, I'm kind of back where I started again,' she reflected. 'Obviously it was a real struggle when I first started because I left Bees, I left my job, I was just coming back from my shoulder surgery, and I was having no luck really with WSL1. I landed on my feet with Denmark and it was a good, competitive league, it was exactly what I needed at the time, we won the league, that was awesome, and then I was stuck again at Christmas, fell into Apollon, which was amazing, have been a part of one of the most epic games of my life, won a Champions League spot, but then for me the decision at the moment is to look at my options again because from the beginning WSL1 has always been my aim.

'Obviously now the massive thing I've got out of this year is I can say now I've been a professional footballer, and add two league titles to my CV, I've played abroad, I've been full-time, so I'm in a similar position to last summer – but a better one.'

* * *

Nikita Whinnett and Megen Lynch had both left Crystal Palace at the end of the season. Lynch had been released from the Palace squad after recovering from the injury that had kept her out of so much action, and Whinnett had not been able to agree terms with the club, despite having had no intention of leaving the club she loved. She was not shy about admitting that she had offers from other clubs to join them next season, and still had dreams of playing professionally.

The couple – and AJ the dog – had moved further out of town, and had a pub of their own to manage in Surrey, giving them both plenty of autonomy.

'I'm my own boss now!' exclaimed Whinnett. 'It's much easier because I can hire another manager. I didn't have that luxury [at the previous pub]. It's actually easier for me to get to football from here – we used to have to go into London to come out. It makes life loads easier.

'This place has already got a domestic kitchen downstairs and ready to go – we're going to give ourselves three or four weeks to figure out what we've got and who we're working with, and then [Megen is] going to open the kitchen up and she'll have her own kitchen again.'

* * *

'It shines in the sun!'

Fleur Cousens was beaming just like the rays warming the pleasant evening in a central London park. Goal Diggers had secured a deal to get 200 brand-new full kits courtesy of Nike and suppliers Kitbag, and their new primary colour was gold. In exchange, the club were to feature in a film over the summer, chronicling their progress alongside that of England's Lionesses.

'It's basically a film celebrating women's football, following a grassroots team, us, and the Lionesses, a professional team, and just looking at that – looking at how we love football and how it's a game for everyone,' she explained. The club had asked anyone interested in appearing in the film to write a short application about the impact football and Goal Diggers had had on their lives, and 30 responses had followed.

'Maybe I'm easily tearjerked, but the tears did flow – they were so nice,' said Cousens. 'Some people talked about how Goal Diggers helped them become comfortable in their body, comfortable in their sexuality, it's helped with their mental health – there is such a range of stuff. Some people talked about how they came from a really high level of football but didn't continue that – obviously you need to make the choice of if you want to go pro properly or not – and then talking about how Goal Diggers has helped them to still have a place in football.'

The narrative of the finished film followed Cousens, running her story parallel with that of England striker Toni Duggan. Yet despite their high profile and such big brands wanting to share in their success, they were still struggling to find appropriate pitch space with the capacity required for so many members wanting to train regularly, with local authorities remaining obstructive. Nevertheless, they did not let that put them off encouraging more people to take up football, with their most recent project aimed at over 40s playing the game for the first time.

'It's just so annoying when people like the FA are saying we want to double grassroots women's football by 2020, but how, when you're not giving us any space to play on?' said Cousens. 'Goal Diggers could be doubled by now if we had that pitch space – 100 per cent. Things are happening. Three years ago we were one of the only teams doing this – we were one of the only teams who existed in London that are non-ability-based, trying to open up the doors for beginners, trying to just break down all the barriers that prevented people from getting into the sport.

'But now the whole landscape has changed a lot in London because there are so many beginners' leagues now, which never existed before. There were only 11-a-side leagues, and that's not accessible if you've not played football before, so that's really exciting, because we're still getting four, five new members a week turning up to training, but there are so many options for people.

'Before, it was stressing me out – "we're the only people doing this, we're the only people who complete newbies can turn to" – but now we're not, so as much as we try to fight to get that space, it's a little bit heart-warming to know there are other people doing similar things.'

When Cousens set up Goal Diggers, she had no idea how much it would grow, nor how much it would be appreciated by its members.

'I never even really realised how much joy it would bring me,' she admitted. 'At the beginning I thought it would be a once a week, twice a week maximum thing, and that it would get people into the sport but it wouldn't grow. I can't believe so many people have been here for the whole four years and haven't left – our retention rate is so high, that's why we keep growing because we're not losing many members.

'It's so amazing, these people who have been here for four years – I just know them so well because I see them more than my family, I see them the whole time. I couldn't have imagined it to be this successful. Somehow we manage to create an atmosphere that's supportive enough that people do just want to make sure it continues.'

The latest volunteer-driven scheme was the Festival of Football, a series of events running across London during the Women's World Cup, including talks, screenings and exhibitions – all organised by Goal Diggers members, who were getting no reimbursement for their work.

'You don't get a single penny for your time – no perks,' said Cousens, adding that everyone bought into the club ethos, from coaches to absolute beginners. 'I never thought it would become this big, and I can't believe how much of my life it's taken over, but I wouldn't change it for the world.'

18

Four weeks in France

THE GLOSSY process of the Lionesses arriving in France for the Women's World Cup were a far cry from the way everything had run four years previously. The squad were shuttled around Nice for photo opportunities, mostly alongside adoring small children; even at their first open training session before facing Scotland in their first match, the small throng of media were permitted to stand pitchside, with red-and-white security tape marking out the zone they were to stay in, all the better for the photogenic youngsters, with stage-managed St George's flags clutched in their hands to sneak into the snaps. Training was at one venue; media briefings at another; the team were staying elsewhere; and the pre-match press conference was at the Stade de Nice itself. The taxi cabs of Nice were raking in plenty of business from the British media, endeavouring to keep up with the team's movements.

Players had evidently been listening to their media training, advised on how best to approach questions; their families too, out to support their girls, had been told to watch who they were speaking to and to take care in public. Head coach Phil Neville might have been better off listening to some of the guidance, snapping at a French journalist in the pre-match press conference as he did not like the way he characterised the domestic league.

But the opening weekend of the Women's World Cup also coincided with the finals of the men's Nations League. Had England's men managed to beat the Netherlands in the semi-final clash, they would have been playing the final at the same time as England's women took on Scotland. The Euro 2020 men's qualifiers were also going on over the weekend, and Real Madrid took the opportunity to announce the signing of Eden Hazard while Manchester United were being linked with a variety of big-name costly acquisitions, from Matthijs de Ligt to Harry Maguire. Even during the women's biggest tournament, the men's game continued to sidle its way back into the spotlight.

FIFA had had to fend off plenty of criticism before the tournament when fans noticed that if they had bought more than one ticket for a particular match – if, say, they were planning to attend with friends and family, including small children – they were not necessarily seated together.

On the day of the England v Scotland match, the preparations in the stadium began early, with the public address system carefully playing its recordings of 'God Save The Queen' and 'Flower of Scotland' on a loop. The throngs of fans began to make their way up to the ground, using taxis and lift-share apps in the absence of useful public transport on a Sunday; the Stade de Nice, right by a motorway, was not intended for easy pedestrian access. The Musee Nationale du Sport was in use as a media accreditation centre, and was the only place in the complex showing the day's early kick-offs on a big screen.

A small group of journalists clustered round one laptop to watch Brazil's Cristiane score a hat-trick against Jamaica in the second match of the day, over at Grenoble's Stade de Alpes. On hearing her name mentioned, one senior journalist in the Nice media tribune, carefully working his way through his paperwork to return to the office, perked up.

'Cristiano Ronaldo has scored a hat-trick?'

It had to be gently pointed out to him that it was a woman with a similar name who had achieved the feat in the tournament he was supposed to be covering.

There was plenty of noise as the gates opened, the stadium volunteers took their places, and the music began. There was plenty of noise too as the teams ran on to the pitch to begin their warm-ups, with the Scottish contingent of fans directing some boos towards the England squad.

The Lionesses' campaign started very well, with a 2-1 win courtesy of a Nikita Parris penalty followed by an Ellen White strike. Arsenal's Beth Mead had an impressive game as she did in the next match, against Argentina, setting up Jodie Taylor for the only goal. But she was rested for the final group encounter – against Japan, the country who had knocked England out of the 2015 tournament with that last-gasp Laura Bassett own goal. Toni Duggan, injured up until that point, slotted back into the side, with Mead on the bench alongside her Gunners' team-mate Leah Williamson.

England's round-of-16 match was the most controversial of the tournament, when they came up against a Cameroon side determined to employ physical tactics from the off, combined with a referee who failed to take control. There had been plenty of pre-match criticism of the liberal use of the video assistant referee in other games; here VAR clarified two marginal offside calls to confirm one goal and rule out another, but its usage frustrated Cameroon to such an extent that it looked at one point as if they would leave the pitch and refuse to return.

The match seared to its conclusion, with England pleased to win 3-0, but picking up a few knocks along the way, most notably captain Steph Houghton suffering a painful challenge at the end of the second half from a somewhat exuberant Alexandra Takounda.

Coach Phil Neville was livid afterwards.

'I sat through 90 minutes today and felt ashamed,' he fumed to the media. 'I'm completely and utterly ashamed of the opposition and their behaviour. I've never seen circumstances like that on a football pitch and I think that kind of behaviour is pretty sad. Think of all those young girls and boys watching.'

It seemed that neither Houghton nor central-defensive partner Millie Bright, suffering from sickness, would be fit enough to play in the quarter-final against Norway, who had proved a potent attacking threat so far. Both were named in the starting 11, however, and the skipper in particular excelled as the Lionesses finally put together a performance worthy of serious title contenders, logging another 3-0 victory, with goals from Jill Scott, Ellen White and Lucy Bronze – scoring a stunning long-range effort, similar to the one she notched against the same opponents four years previously. They were into the semi-finals – the third major tournament in a row in which they had reached the final four.

* * *

One group of travellers headed over to Lyon for the semi-final by train. A group of 11 ladies in their older years attracted little comment as they boarded the Eurostar at St Pancras International in London. These were women who had just stepped into the media spotlight thanks to a burst of interest in their achievements from almost half a century previously.

Some in the English media had dubbed them 'the lost Lionesses', but they were never really lost, just ignored. They were the women – teenage girls – who had represented the nation at the unofficial international tournaments before the FA formally lifted its ban on women's football, and when the Women's FA were attempting to organise the game into some kind of structure. Under the management of Harry Batt, a Luton man who managed Chiltern Valley, the squad were given the title 'British Independents' so as not to impinge on the auspices of the governing bodies – but were fundamentally an England side.

Batt and his squad headed to Italy in 1970 and to Mexico the year after to compete in invitational tournaments; though they were not sanctioned World Cups (because FIFA were not interested in organising such a thing) they still used the names. The teams played in the Azteca Stadium – venue of magical moments during the men's World Cup the year before – and attracted crowds of tens of thousands in the searing heat.

'We had a short while where we could walk on to the pitch and acclimatise ourselves,' recalled then-captain Carol Wilson, 'and the two first things I thought were, "Oh my God, we've got a flat pitch," because we used to play on sloping pitches in the UK, and the other thing was the heat. I looked up and they'd built a roof and there was an oval, just a very small gap, an oval, and I said to the girls, "I hope to God we're not playing any matches at lunchtime." Sure enough our match against Mexico was at lunchtime and the stadium was full, so you had the 40-odd degrees coming into the stadium with the sun, and then you had the body heat of 90-odd thousand people, so it was very hot.'

Some reports had suggested that Wilson and her team all had to take oxygen afterwards, but they sounded almost insulted at the very idea.

'I've spoken to all of the girls because I thought maybe it was just my memory gone,' said Wilson.

'We had to take salt tablets,' chimed in Jill Brader, nee Stockley.

'Yeah, we took salt tablets,' agreed Wilson. 'We trained extremely hard to get used to the altitude while we were out there, and make sure we were fit enough for the game.'

Brader was just 16 when she went to Mexico as one of the British Independents. She had grown up in Nuneaton and spent her childhood playing for a variety of representative sides, despite the ongoing formal ban, but that was not to say she received unwavering support.

'My father's brother came down to the house and said he wouldn't let his daughter play, and it wasn't right to let me play football,' she said, 'and my grandfather wanted to send me to boarding school to get this footballing issue out of my head. Looking back now, I'm so grateful that they let me go [to Mexico], being so young. It was amazing. They stuck up for me, my parents, said I should carry on playing.'

Wilson played in the back lanes near her home, using back doors as goal posts, necessitating good aim and accuracy to hit the target. She was usually the only girl amidst a cluster of boys, and never set foot in any kind of organised team, just relishing the opportunity to kick a ball. She became a physical training instructor in the Royal Air Force, continuing her kickabouts there; she thought their five-a-side matches were simply fun, but Harry Batt had been watching her when his team were on the pitch next door. He realised that she had not played in a proper 11-a-side match before, so invited her to Luton for some trials, and, after being impressed with what he saw, invited her to join his British Independents. This was in 1970, when he was about to take a squad out to Italy for the World Cup qualifying tournament there.

'He said he was putting a team together to go to Sicily to represent England – he said represent England, he didn't say it was the England team, and he was quite specific about that,' said Wilson. 'I thought I was in a dream world at that time. We went to Sicily, we played in the preliminary rounds, and we managed to get through.'

Even then, their presence at the finals was not guaranteed. After all, there was no funding for these women. Wilson thinks in retrospect that Batt worked 'tirelessly' to secure sponsorship that enabled them to pay for their flights and spend almost a month in Mexico, where they were quite shocked at their rapturous welcome.

'We did the country proud, I think,' said Wilson. 'We were kids, and we went out there. That [Azteca] stadium holds 107,000 and I didn't see many spare seats. I certainly know it was two and three times the size of crowds they're getting at the moment [at England matches]. It was just daunting. We had six men and his dog [watching us play] on a pitch in England, and at that we got hurled abuse half the time – and yet to go in front of all these people, screaming, and they thought you were gods. We weren't used to any of that, we really weren't, and it was exciting, daunting, terrifying, you had all these emotions at the same time.'

After the squad returned from Mexico, there were repercussions. Brader served a six-month ban handed down for representing an unauthorised team, then found the responsibilities of a young woman's life in the early 1970s catching up with her – but she refused to hang up her boots.

'My mum told me I had to go and get a career, so I went into nursing,' she said, 'but I still played for a while until I had children, and then I did a referee course, and coaching, [and I] managed to coach a team when my daughter was 14, 15. It's been amazing, really.'

Wilson was pleased to see the way the women's game had progressed, praising Batt as a visionary who had suffered painful and ridiculous sanctions for his efforts, and wondered what could have happened had he not been essentially half a century ahead of his time.

'Yes, the game has moved on and I'm so grateful, any move forward is a good thing – I just think it's not moved on as much as I would have liked,' she said. 'Maybe it's a personal thing, I'm sure it is – I'm sure there's lots of girls out there who think, "No, no, it's moved forward great, we're going in the right direction," and they are, but if I think 50 years have passed, maybe it's just not quick enough for me.'

UEFA had invited the team out to Lyon as part of their #weplaystrong promotion, highlighting the battles and achievements of women in football, and Wilson and Brader acknowledged that they would never have had the chance to attend such an occasion otherwise. Both were impressed with how the England team had played so far in the tournament and were incredibly excited to be heading to France themselves.

'They've done so well,' praised Wilson. 'They're getting stronger and stronger and stronger, and we're behind them 120 per cent.'

'They're such good ambassadors for the game,' interjected Brader, as Wilson murmured in agreement. 'Definitely. Phil Neville has done us proud as well. Amazing.'

* * *

There were mutterings of displeasure that the USA – the defending world champions – were arrogant. They had every reason to be, though; some observers thought it was distasteful for them to celebrate every one of their 13 goals against the amateurs of Thailand in their opening group fixture, but others pointed out that it was indicative of how seriously they took every match.

They would be England's opponents in the World Cup semi-final. The match earlier in 2019, during the SheBelieves Cup, would have no bearing on this encounter; World Cup tournament football would be entirely different. The USA would be expected to win, and win comfortably.

Inevitably, more controversy followed in the days before the match, with Lionesses coach Phil Neville bemused to hear that two members of his counterpart Jill Ellis's camp had been spotted at the England team hotel in Lyon – an option for the USA to move to should they reach the final, hosted in the same city. Headlines about 'spying' followed, with fans on social media baiting each other in the run-up to kick-off.

The USA fans dominated the stands at the Parc Olympique Lyonnais, and they were delighted when their team took an early lead courtesy of the head of Christen Press. England were rattled and losing composure, but Ellen White – continuing her goalscoring run – fired home an equaliser after 19 minutes following a fine ball from midfielder Keira Walsh to winger Beth Mead, who sent in an exquisite cross for the striker to lash home.

Alex Morgan, on her 30th birthday, scored what transpired to be the winning goal just after the half-hour. After nodding past Carly Telford, she embarked upon an odd mimed celebration, which was intended to be indicative of tea-drinking; whether it was a sly reference to the Boston Tea Party, a few days before Independence Day, or to clichés about the English, or to the slang expression 'sipping tea', with the meaning of subtly and quietly expressing scorn.

Just as with those exuberant celebrations against Thailand, it seemed out of place to take the trouble to gloat. It was obvious that England were underdogs and that the USA – with just one defeat in their previous 44 games – would be heavy favourites to make the World Cup Final yet again, even if the casual observer, steeped in men's football history rather than the alternative history of the women's game, might not have known.

Still, England had their chances to regroup. White got the ball in the net again midway through the second half, but it was disallowed for offside after the intervention of VAR. The technology offered England one more chance when Becky Sauerbrunn caught White in the area, and following a review referee Edina Alves Batista of Brazil pointed to the penalty spot.

Nikita Parris had taken all three of England's previous spot-kicks in the tournament, but scored only one – in the first match against Scotland. She had been typically bullish about the failures when questioned about her second miss, in the quarter-final victory against Norway, dismissing the suggestion that she might speak to one of the team's psychologists to deal with any stress or pressure she was feeling.

'I don't think I need to talk to a psychologist,' she told reporters. 'I'm confident in myself. It's not a case of I've missed a penalty and I'm down. I've just dominated the left-back for 80 or 90 minutes, I'm confident in myself and in my own ability.'

As far as Parris was concerned, she remained the team's penalty-taker – but it was captain Steph Houghton who stepped up in the 84th minute and saw her limp shot comfortably held by goalkeeper Alyssa Naeher, moving down to her right.

In the chaos and the emotion after the game, it was unclear whether the change of nominated penalty-taker was a call made on the pitch – whether the skipper had decided that she would take the responsibility herself in such a big moment – or whether it had been planned. Neville said afterwards that he had made the decision to shift Houghton into that role following Parris's misses and had spoken to both players individually as well as the squad.

'Steph was the best penalty-taker on the pitch,' the coach said to media. 'Nikita was our number-one penalty taker and then she missed two goals, and we spoke to Nikita, we spoke to the team, and we agreed that the next best penalty-taker on the pitch would take the penalty.'

Houghton, though, indicated that it had not been a discussion but an instruction – and one that she had received on matchday.

'I got told today that I was on the penalties,' she told reporters. 'I was confident because I had been scoring all week [in training] but I didn't connect with it properly and the goalkeeper guessed the right way.'

Ultimately England were beaten by a better team, but the failure to take those chances really stung. It might have been a third consecutive semi-final in a major tournament for the Lionesses, but it was also a third consecutive loss at that stage. Neville had made it clear that only a trophy win would constitute success – but after the semi-final he admitted he was happy with his side's achievement. Notably, it was also Neville's first experience of reaching that point of a major competition; and as a player he had never himself competed at a World Cup. His plans to rotate his squad throughout had served him well, with fresher players relishing their opportunities when given, but his inexperience as a coach had perhaps shown a little against the wily, professional USA.

* * *

England needed to regroup. Four days later, they had to face Sweden – beaten by the Netherlands in their own semi-final – in the play-off for the bronze medal. The 2015 squad had achieved third place, perhaps rather unexpectedly, beating their bogey team Germany with a Fara Williams penalty. It was catharsis after Laura Bassett's unfortunate late own-goal had given Japan the win in the semi-final. A bronze medal in 2019 would not have perhaps quite the same emotional release, but it would go some way to ameliorating the disappointments of Tuesday night's defeat.

But the group of Lionesses who took the field in Nice for the final time looked stunned. Defensive mistakes cost them dearly as Sweden raced to a 2-0 lead in the opening minutes; it was only a fabulous solo effort from Fran Kirby that forced them to gather themselves. Ellen White thought she had equalised – and marked the occasion with a 'tea-sipping' celebration of her own – but once again she was denied by the video assistant referee, who spotted a handball prior to her finish.

There were no more goals in the second half. Winger Karen Carney, who had announced her intention to retire from football, was given 16 minutes at the end to attempt to turn the match around, but even she could have no impact at that late point. Sweden were thrilled to have won the bronze medal; England coach Neville was less than magnanimous despite his apparent best efforts.

'We came here to win it and not finish fourth. Well done to Sweden but it is a nonsense game,' he said immediately afterwards.

Fans did not entirely agree; after England's failure to reach the final, they had hoped for another third-place finish for their team, and felt slightly disappointed that it had not happened.

'I feel England have had glimpses of being a world-class team, but they are still not quite there,' said supporter Chloe Goddard. 'Sloppy passing, a lack of clinical play and periods of low concentration cost us. If these issues can be fixed, then I think England could win a major trophy.'

She was proud of the players and their performances, but sad about the little mistakes that had proved the difference between a medal and empty hands. Fellow fan Shane Thomas wondered whether fighting for third place might be the best this England squad could have hoped for anyway, and had developed a theory to explain his thinking.

'Sometimes the most painful thing is being good at sport, because it means you're always close to your ultimate goal, yet the goal always remains out of reach,' he said. 'It's those who are great who tend to win the big prizes. Right now, England are banging their head on the ceiling of good. They're a good team, maybe a very good one, but not a great one, and they'll likely fail to win a major tournament until they can develop from good to great.'

He thought few of the players had performed to the best of their ability, but laid much of the blame for that with the coaching staff. He was puzzled by some of the tactics, some of the selections, and questioned the fitness of some of the players who had got match time.

'[It] would be unfair to say England have failed in France,' he said, 'although [I'm] not sure how much they've progressed, either.'

Former England goalkeeper Pauline Cope-Boanas had expected the Lionesses to win the World Cup.

'I'm not disappointed with England's performances – I'm disappointed we didn't win it,' she said.

'I'd like to think the squad that went out to '95 [Women's World Cup], if we'd had the training they've got now, I reckon we would have won it. I've spoken to a couple of ex-players who think the same as well. I don't know, it could be in the mind. I'm not saying that they have to be screaming and shouting and swearing at each other, but they didn't seem to have any passion when someone made a mistake, or we conceded a goal – no one looked upset about it. You look at the Americans, they're a completely different kettle of fish.'

Perhaps nerves had played a part, but she did not think fitness had been a problem; she admired the athleticism of the current squad and the focus they had on their football.

'They haven't got to get up at half past four in the morning and go to work, like I had to, and then come home after a 12-hour shift and then go to training,' she pointed out. 'They are full-time pros. They've got nutritionists available, they've got sports psychologists, they've got physios, they've got all the rehabilitation at St George's Park and at their clubs. There was no excuse for them not to go into that tournament as fit as their body can be.'

Although she had been sceptical about the process by which Phil Neville had been appointed to his job, she had almost been won over – until his description of the bronze medal match as a 'nonsense'.

'To not even get third, and to come out with that bloody comment ...' she exhaled. 'If I'd won bronze four years ago I'd have been straight on the radio, straight on the news this morning, I'd be up St George's Park, I'd be waiting for him to get off the plane.

'I couldn't believe that comment. Even if you think it, don't come out with it, mate!'

In 2009, an under-19 squad led by coach Mo Marley won the European Championships for their age group. That team that lifted the trophy in Belarus included Toni Duggan, Jade Moore and Lucy Bronze, all of whom were in the England squad for the 2019 World Cup. Jordan Nobbs and Izzy Christiansen had been there too, and would have been in France had it not been for injury. Cope-Boanas wondered why the rest of that squad had not progressed through to the senior team; some were still at WSL clubs, but others were out of the game altogether. She feared for the future of English domestic football and how it would impact on the national team; she knew that the FA would have invested plenty of money in the expectation of some kind of medal at the 2019 Women's World Cup, and she also knew that lots of players from overseas would be looking for moves to the WSL now that sponsorship deals were coming in.

'Where's that money going to go? It's not going to go to grassroots,' she said, pointing out that the WSL line-up increasingly resembled the men's Premier League. 'It all looks good on paper, but if they ain't producing any English players, if they ain't signing any English players, what good is that to England? We're never going to win a World Cup. This was our year, 100 per cent, this was our year. I'm sure the players thought that as well – 100 per cent.'

Cope-Boanas wondered why there were no former England players on the coaching staff, and thought that kind of link to history might go some way to creating a more competitive, more urgent mindset. She had seen the news coverage of 1971's Lost Lionesses, and their story had made her cry.

'What an unbelievable story,' she reflected. 'If it wasn't for them I wouldn't have achieved what I achieved. Psychologically that might have helped the players – someone like me going in. As gobby and as mouthy as I am, I loved my time with England and I never once took it for granted.

'I am so proud to be an ex-Lioness. That's what I am – I am a Lioness.'

EPILOGUE

19

Waking up

IN 1999, when the new Women's World Cup trophy was revealed, designer William Sawaya described his thought process for the way it looked: 'It starts with a simple movement at the bottom then rises upwards in a dancing crescendo of elegance, just like the level of interest that women's football is awakening in the world.'

And 20 years on, that interest was still just waking up – but 2019 could well have been a turning point. Domestic leagues were attracting huge attendances when given the opportunity, with Barcelona and Atletico Madrid bringing in 60,739 supporters to the Wanda Metropolitano in March; and across the world, television viewing figures for the Women's World Cup were massive. Of course the ratings in the USA were huge, and in England the Lionesses's semi-final loss to the USA drew in the highest live TV audience of 2019 up until that point with 11.7 million people watching.

A day after the Women's World Cup Final, newspapers reported that the future of the Women's Super League had some serious question-marks over it. There had been rumours for some time that the Premier League might take over its operations; with so many WSL and Championship teams attached to men's clubs in the Premier League, it made sense. The Premier League had picked up a popular product which needed investment in its infrastructure back in 1992, taking the old First Division and over the course of a quarter of a century making it a billion-dollar industry, with much-sought-after broadcast rights, a glamorous, aspirational product. Given the same time period, and the wave of popularity women's football was riding, surely they could do the same for the women's domestic game.

Yet the Premier League executives indicated that, even if the FA were keen to rid themselves of the responsibility of running the WSL, they were not keen to take it on. Sources suggested that it simply was not feasible to find the money immediately to pour into a league that was currently running at a loss. For all the talk of inspiring a generation, the powers-that-be were not inspired enough to put their hands any further into their pockets. Outcomes such as increased participation in football, and the intangibles such as national pride or women feeling connected with the sport, were not enough for the Premier League, interested only in profitability.

It was perhaps more incredible that the Women's FA Cup had no sponsor waiting in the wings after energy provider SSE's deal had ended after the 2019 final. The FA took the opportunity during the Women's World Cup to put out some subtle feelers, telling the media, 'With the audience figures at this summer's World Cup, it again just shows the interest is there. We want someone with our shared vision of growth for women's and girls' football.'

Certainly there was room for improvement in England. The USA's supremacy at world level had been proven on the pitch, and a few hours after the end of the final FIFA released figures that indicated that over a third of the female footballers in the world, registered players from amateur to professional and in all age groups, were based in the States.

With such impressive statistics, it was no wonder that they were invariably the best team in the world; they had their pick of 1.6 million girls and young women – the nation's premium sporting talent. England, meanwhile, had less than a tenth of that figure – 120,559.

The media, meanwhile, had decided women's football was worth a risk. The BBC were quick to announce that the Women's Euros, to be held in England in 2021, would be screened free-to-air, available for everyone to enjoy. The Lionesses had dropped three places in the global rankings after the Women's World Cup, and were now judged to be the fifth best team in the world. They did not have to qualify for a tournament they were hosting, and thus their next few years would be short of competitive action. However, because they had reached the semi-finals of the World Cup and because of the success of negotiations between the British football associations, they had also secured themselves the right to represent Team GB at the following summer's Tokyo Olympics. Phil Neville would coach that team, and although he could in theory select players from the other home nations, it seemed likely that the squad would be primarily English – just as Hope Powell's had been in London in 2012. In 12 months' time, then, they would be once more going for gold, chasing that dream.

20

Taking pride

A WEEK before I flew to Nice for the Women's World Cup, I was in a local café. I was not looking my best, I must admit, in the interests of accurate and honest chronicling; I had been gardening and cleaning the house, and was wearing jogging shorts and my polo shirt that I bought at Euro 2017 in the Netherlands.

The barista at the counter took my order, then did a double-take at my shirt. She beamed at me.

'You watch women's football? My two boys used to be coached by Rachel Yankey! She played for Arsenal and England – before women's football got noticed, when it wasn't like it is now.'

Women's football has certainly grabbed plenty of attention in the last three years since I wrote *The Roar of the Lionesses* – not all of it positive. Fans and journalists alike reported heavy-handed stewarding at England's warm-up matches for the World Cup, and lack of engagement from some players, who seemed as if they had received so much media training they could no longer hold a frank conversation. There were expressions of wondering if this was indicative of how things would progress in the future. Yet to those who had followed or reported on women's football for some years, this did not come as a surprise. Where men's clubs had swallowed up the women's team, there had often been occasions where over-the-top stewarding had scolded or pushed; I well-remembered a time a few years prior when, having been invited to a training session as part of a media day, intended to boost coverage of the domestic league, a steward promptly stuck posts in the ground and hooked a rope around, creating a makeshift 'media area' some dozens of metres away from the pitch where the squad were going through their drills. Colleagues in TV crews and photographers protested that they would not be able to get strong enough footage or images; those like me from the written press pointed out that they were unable to get a sense of the atmosphere or the detail without being able to hear what was being said.

'The women's team are just like the men's team now,' came the reply.

Fortunately the team's coach realised what was happening and asked the steward to lift the restrictions, and allowed us through. However, this incident is a microcosm of the way the top of the game is moving. Though the unique selling point of women's football has long been its accessibility, the elite game has now been encouraged to emulate the men's side of things. If players are fully professional, they will no longer have those 'nine-to-five jobs' that for so long made them seem 'just like us', playing for the love of the game. The specialist media, the writers and bloggers who covered women's football as a passion project will be ignored in favour of the national press, who may be able to offer more eyeballs on printed text or screens, but do not have the depth of historical knowledge that their predecessors did. Professional footballers will be warned of the dangers of the press – of having one's words taken out of context, or having one's personal life become public knowledge – and offered more media training, designed to present only the agreed party line at best and obfuscate at worst.

At an event prior to the 2019 Women's World Cup, I had been invited to speak about women's football. The audience were engaged, knowledgeable, passionate football fans. During the question-and-answer session, a comment came from the floor expressing her admiration for the Lionesses – but she quickly added that although she respected them, she could not love them any more. The squad in 2015 had won the love of the watching public because their success was unexpected, and their dealings with the media seemed natural and endearing. But this speaker said she thought this had been overtaken in the following four years – not just by their new-found professionalism, but also by their slick and perhaps ill-advised public appearances. She singled out their vocal support for former coach Mark Sampson when it seemed that their team-mate Eniola Aluko was being frozen out after she spoke about her treatment within the England set-up.

It is a bitter irony that at a time when access to the male England players has been increased – with every single squad member taking part in round-table conversations during their World Cup media day in the summer of 2018, roundly hailed as a breakthrough initiative, allowing them to be seen as real people and not just athletes – access to the women has decreased. One or two are selected for 'media duties' and presented at an agreed time at an agreed venue; easily set-up phone interviews with the Lionesses are very nearly a thing of the past. This was also the case in France; long-serving women's football journalists, serving their dedicated niche market, were prevented from gaining the access they wanted, quite often sidelined in favour of the big-name male journalists who had taken a break from covering the men's game for this tournament.

Of course, this is only at the very top level. The young professionals at teams in the lower half of the WSL are still happy to chat, hardly believing their luck that people are interested in them. The semi-professionals of the

Championship might be difficult to get hold of, because they spend all their time either at work or at training, but they too will talk. But if the long-term plan is indeed to make the women's game more like the men's, more clubs will turn professional, and more staff will step in to buffer players from fans and journalists.

Having said that, at important amateur fixtures, with strong FA involvement, hosted at big grounds, the lack of attention to detail remained palpable. A request for the press box this season was met with a blank stare and the response, 'We don't have a press box,' and a jokey question of whether I had meant to go to the nearby men's Premier League fixture. (I knew perfectly well that this ground had a press box, by the way; I had reported from there previously. Ironically, it had also hosted several Lionesses fixtures in the past.)

Will more teams turn professional soon? Perhaps, if there is a huge cash injection available from somewhere – probably a men's club. Will they be professional in the sense that most fans would understand it, training twice a day, with a salary that is enough to live on and enough to pay the rent or mortgage? And will they stay professional – is it a long-term plan, is it sustainable, is the money there and guaranteed for the next few seasons? The restructure of women's football in England was always intended to encourage greater competition on the pitch; the first years of the closed WSL was intended to share out talent and money and allow the professional women's game to put down roots. The quick expansion has meant that the talent pipeline has not yet developed, so overseas players have been drafted into top squads to strengthen the team; the clubs with the most money have attracted the biggest stars. It was also notable that as soon as Manchester United and Tottenham Hotspur secured promotion from the Championship, they announced new signings – established senior internationals, with the players who had got them to the WSL not offered a contract.

That may have been the choice of the players, of course; or it may have been indicative that in a relatively small league, no chances can be taken on those unproven at that level. Maintaining a place in the top tier is essential.

As I have found while writing this book, in a time when professionalisation is still relatively new, England has a generation of players with the footballing ability to play in the top-two tiers, but who have made the choice not to. For some, playing professionally is a dream, and they took the first opportunity they were offered; for some, they are still waiting for that chance and are poised to write their resignation letter to their employer as soon as they can; for others, it can never be an option. Perhaps they are already in their mid-30s and know they only have a few years of playing left; perhaps they have a well-paying vocation that will be their life's work after they have hung up their boots; perhaps they have a mortgage that requires a bigger salary than is offered in English professional football at the moment. Whatever their reasons, this drain away from the top two leagues means that the strength in depth is simply not there at the moment.

The day after England's semi-final loss to the USA, Southampton Saints announced that they would be closing down with immediate effect. They put it down to 'decreasing player numbers and lack of financial support'. In one way, that was almost understandable. Southampton as a place has a grand tradition of women's football, and in recent years has had three senior clubs (Saints, Southampton Women's, and Southampton) all in competition for the same local players and indeed local sponsorship.

But Southampton Saints had a glorious history, beginning their life as Red Star Southampton and gracing the top flight of the National Division as well as an FA Cup Final. The Southampton's men's club adopted them officially in 2001 after years of affiliation, but the women's team's funding ended when the men were relegated from the Premier League. When the men were promoted again, they later began their own women's side. Saints had also had a couple of legends as managers – Vanessa Raynbird, who had run the team until the men's club had folded them into their set-up, and Sue Lopez, one of the players who had kept the game going in England during the FA ban, and who had even spent some of her career in Italy when such a thing was rarely thought of.

To see Saints disband with immediate effect, during a summer in which women's football was dominating the English back pages, was sobering, if not exactly surprising. The long-term impact of the heavy focus on the Lionesses from authorities and media alike has been a concern since the WSL's expansion; indeed, Raynbird moved across the south coast to manage Portsmouth Ladies, and after great success on the pitch found her team outside the new two-division elite set-up, essentially relegating them due to their lack of financial support from a men's club.

It was also an odd coincidence for me, as my social media memories reminded me of a conversation I had had with a Southampton-born friend of mine a few years previously. He wanted to know why his club didn't have a women's team; of course, they did, they were just not in the WSL, so he had not seen any information about them or their games. I told him all about Red Star Southampton, and their descendants Southampton Saints, as well as Lopez and Raynbird and all their achievements. He had never heard about any of it before.

As for how women's football in England is perceived from the outside, this is still in flux. At the Isthmian Cup Final, one Ashford fan grew increasingly frustrated with the team, apparently ignoring the fact that they were amateurs playing against another amateur team ranked two divisions higher, and shouted obscenities at them throughout, supposedly in an effort to encourage them. Heads turned at every single one of his utterances, but nobody felt confident enough to challenge him – perhaps unsurprisingly, with him displaying such a degree of anger in such a small ground.

Afterwards, I wondered whether he was actually the father of one of the players, and that made me sadder than if he had just been a random spectator. Perhaps women's football is now taken seriously to such a degree that these aggressive parents with ludicrous and unfair high expectations have infiltrated it, just as they have done in junior boys' football, expecting their child to be a prodigious talent immediately.

On the same night as Orient lifted that cup, Manchester United secured promotion from the FA Women's Championship. That was no surprise. The fully professional team in a semi-professional league was always likely to grab one of the slots to go up to the WSL. So it was puzzling that the main Manchester United Twitter account failed to acknowledge it even happening on the night. The men didn't have a match that night, and it would hardly have been a stretch to create a graphic ready to use on social media as soon as Casey Stoney's team got the job done. For a club that had boasted a lot about its new commitment to women's football – following an embarrassing spell where they had ignored it to the degree that they had to get a model to show off their women's-fit replica kits – it seemed to be rather telling that they made no mention of it until 13 hours afterwards. If the FA's recommended pathway for women's clubs is for them to be fully integrated into men's clubs, then men's clubs need to do much more – and stop treating the women's game as an afterthought, there as a desperate effort to indicate belief in equality of opportunity.

* * *

I try to avoid Twitter spats if I can, but when TV presenter and England legend Gary Lineker suggested that if Manchester City were to win the FA Cup they would complete the first domestic treble in the history of English football, I couldn't help but point out that he had missed out a necessary word – 'men's'. Although the inconsistent scheduling of women's football means the number of domestic trebles completed is up for debate, it has certainly been achieved previously by Arsenal.

Lineker objected to the correction, and for days afterwards my mentions were lit up with tweets from men agreeing with him.

I did laugh when in his pre-match press conference City manager Pep Guardiola sided with me, pointing out to a journalist that it would be the first English domestic treble in men's football – 'The women have already done it.'

Language matters. To keep adding the qualifier 'women' but never bothering to point out when something applies to men – thinking that people will just automatically assume that if it's related to football, it's primarily about men – simply reinforces the idea that football is and will remain a male domain. Maybe players don't mind it – indeed, that's what I've been told plenty of times. But the casual use of these phrases in everyday conversation is also a casual reinforcement of stereotypical attitudes.

But women's football is not taken as seriously as the men's game, and even its major tournaments reflect that lackadaisical attitude towards it. The signage in Nice for England's first match of the Women's World Cup was less than ideal, and the city, pretty as it was, had inadequate infrastructure. My partner, not a football fan, said to me in the middle of the week that he was confused about the lack of build-up and presence in the city, adding, 'I know it's here, and I can't see it.' There was consternation prior to the tournament as it transpired that purchases of multiple tickets for some matches did not guarantee seats next to one another – or even near one another. FIFA issued a tweet in response: 'When you placed your order, a message indicating not all seats would be located next to each other did appear, before confirmation of your purchase. However, an exception could be made for parents whose seats are not next to the seats of their underage children (18 years old and younger).' Unsurprisingly, those affected were unimpressed with this kind of customer care.

Because of the authorities' failure to invest time, money and effort into the women's game, so much weight of expectation is put on female footballers. They are expected to inspire future generations and to set great examples for little girls in a way that their male counterparts aren't necessarily obliged to do, and they are continually reminded how fortunate they are to be playing football at all, and that they have a responsibility to behave well so as not to damage the fragile, precarious image of the game. When England coach Phil Neville gave an angry interview after his side's World Cup match against Cameroon, he reverted to that trope.

'My players kept their concentration fantastically, but those images are going out worldwide about how to act, the young girls playing all over the world that are seeing that behaviour,' he told the BBC. 'For me, it's not right. My daughter wants to be a footballer and if she watches that she will think: "No, I want to play netball."'

Later that same day came a much more inspirational piece of viewing – the legendary Marta speaking directly to camera in an impassioned plea to young women back at home after her Brazil side were knocked out of the competition by hosts France.

'This is what I ask of the girls,' she began. 'There won't be a Formiga forever. There won't be a Marta forever. There's not going to be a Cristiane. The women's game depends on you to survive. So think about that. Value it more. Cry in the beginning so you can smile in the end.'

* * *

'You've got to do more for girls. The world is changing. We've a massive responsibility to create a structure that maintains that. If that's my contribution to Barnsley, I'll be happy,' said Natalie Jackson.

When I wrote *The Roar of the Lionesses*, I wanted to document what was actually happening in women's football, alongside and beyond slick PR campaigns and profession-alisation. When one reader tweeted me to tell me he had started watching one of the teams I had covered in that book, it felt like an achievement – one I had never anticipated or expected, but one nonetheless. Women's football is certainly changing, as this book has shown; and however they perform on the pitch, whether they win a World Cup or not, the Lionesses will inevitably get most of the attention now. The England team who ultimately fell short in the summer of 2019 have been hailed as inspiring a generation and as a credit to their nation – but the amateurs and the volunteers and those who keep clubs running in the face of seemingly insurmountable obstacles and the fans are also those in whom we can take pride.